Chine

2022

Year of the Water Tiger

Donna Stellhorn

Published by
ETC Publishing
Carlsbad, California
WWW.ETCPUBLISHING.COM

First Edition, First Publication 2021

ISBN: 978-1-944622-34-3

Cover design by Gary Dunham and Donna Stellhorn

Acknowledgments

I want to thank Diane Ronngren-Dunham, who inspired me to write and helped me write many books. We all miss you so much. Thank you for being my astrology teacher, my editing angel, and my dear friend.

A big thank you to both Gary and Kelly at ETC Publishing for their support, patience, and hard work on these books each year. I couldn't have done it without their help. Their names should be on the cover too.

Contents

Introduction

2022 is the year of the Water Tiger. We have left the sedate and calm energy of the Metal Ox and 2021. Last year was represented by the mighty beast with the yoke strapped on his shoulders so he could plow the fields. There was a focus on planting new seeds, rebuilding, and keeping your nose to the grindstone. Many people changed jobs to find more financial rewards and stability. People cautiously reentered society or stayed on the sidelines. That was then. Now in 2022, the Water Tiger energy springs onto the scene.

While the Ox year was all work, now there's a desire for fun and adventure. Many people will be ready to cut loose and try new things. They're willing to break the rules for the sake of having experiences. While 2021 may have focused on reestablishing financial security, the Tiger year in 2022 means it's time to take risks and express yourself fully. Every one of you has been through a lot over the last few years. First, life changed dramatically, and then there was a need to work hard to rebuild. While the rebuilding is not yet done, there is a growing feeling that it's time to party.

Last year, you might have tested the waters, sticking your toe in to check the temperature. There's nothing like that during a Tiger year. The beginning of the year will be especially volatile. People will take bold, spontaneous action and move towards extremes. People will be cantankerous, argumentative, and make big changes without giving notice. But there will also be quiet periods during the year because the Tiger, like any cat, needs his naps. Then, towards the end of the year, things will calm down again as 2023 approaches with the energy of the peaceful Water Rabbit.

Last year, in the Ox year, there was an emphasis on teamwork, but now we move into the energy of the territorial Tiger. In 2022, borders will become even more important. This means countries may build walls, restrict immigration and travel, and there could be skirmishes or even war. There will likely be changes in governments, people changing parties, and some parties gaining power while others are losing power. There can be more secrets or countries spying on each other during the entire year. Sneak attacks could happen. There will be lots of roaring at each other, loud voices announcing dominance and giving warnings.

The deals and partnerships that formed in 2021 become quite fragile and could easily break apart. Instead of cooperation, there's more squabbling. Governments and corporations focus more on their own success rather than the common good. On the plus side, this energy can breathe new life into struggling businesses. There will be some amazing innovations in 2022, especially around power. This could mean better ways to store power, more effective ways of generating power, and more electricity for everyone.

On a more personal note, you may find yourself aware of your boundaries with others and boundaries in general, extending to many areas of your life. Protecting your data, passwords, and accounts becomes more crucial. Many people will move to find the space (territory) that really speaks to them. Many will host and attend parties, get-togethers, and celebrations. There may be more emphasis on hunting as a sport. And oddly enough, swimming could become very popular (Tiger is the cat that can swim.)

There will likely be more emphasis on parenting and parent's rights. More people will opt for homeschooling their kids. Others will fight the school system. College-age kids are more likely to take a gap year to go backpacking or try a creative business. The ones considering higher education may opt for an accelerated program to get them the knowledge or certificate that they need for the job in as little time as possible.

There's more emphasis on communication. Water Tiger years are talkative years. There will be more books, news reports, and courses on how to communicate with each other. There could be more scandals in this area, and people are more likely to offend with an offhanded remark. There also could be battles concerning free speech and political correctness.

Success will come to those who are confident and strong-willed. In 2022, it's good to pick a direction and move forward quickly. Some will find they're going in the wrong direction and promptly pivot to find a different path. In a Tiger year, being in motion is better than being still. You might try many new things this year just for the excitement of it. Even if you don't start the year feeling strong, you'll be more confident by the end of 2022 just because of the new things you've done.

There will be more emphasis on individual choices and creating a life that you are passionate about. More people may live an unconventional lifestyle, even choosing to be nomadic. There will be an emphasis on living off the land, building something from scratch, and homesteading. Roughing it is part of the adventure. Some people will take on the challenge of revitalizing city centers. There will be a desire to move to foreign lands, but there could be difficulties with tighter borders. The people who seem to compete, battle, and succeed will be the heroes in the Water Tiger year.

Colors will be brighter, and voices will be louder. You'll have periods of intense energy when you're quite active. But naps will also be quite popular. People will be more interested in sports, both playing and watching. Sports may become more violent (or hockey becomes more popular). But in the Water Tiger year, the individual player will be more important than the team.

There will be more spending and less saving. People will skip material objects and put their money into experiences. In the year of the Tiger, you can make money because you are taking more risks. Those who rise to leadership roles will gain the most success. Lots of job changes happen as people decide they need variety more than security. It's more likely many people will have faith in themselves during this time. And this is why they succeed.

World leaders will roar, exchanging sharp words back-and-forth, and even threats. Lines will be drawn, and people will be dared to cross them. Often people will vote for the most noticeable, flamboyant, passionate, in-your-face candidates this year.

Regarding relationships, people are more passionate but can be less romantic during the Tiger year. There are more one-night stands and "hooking up." Those who want a long-term relationship need to be patient. A lover may be here one day and vanish the next, only to return as though they had never left at all. It's easier to be in touch with your anger during a Tiger year. Expressing feelings can lead to problems in relationships or with other people in general. People will want to explore and experiences things rather than be bogged down in commitments or the tedium of marriage.

Because of this dynamic energy, there's often better health. There's more activity and exercise. This can work in your favor. There's less desire to sit on the sofa unless you're playing a fascinating video game. Overall, there's a focus on gaining better health by changing routines and diet. Tigers have sharp teeth and claws, so there can be an emphasis on dental and nail care.

The water Tiger year can bring you the courage and sense of adventure you need to make significant changes in your life. And you can come to the end of 2022 feeling proud of what you accomplished and with a renewed sense of confidence.

In This Book

In this installment of my annual Chinese Astrology series, you will find predictions for each month of the year. In addition, several Feng Shui cures are suggested for each Chinese Zodiac sign to help you focus and bring in positive energy. At the end of this book, you'll find sections on Feng Shui principles, the upcoming eclipses, Mercury retrograde, and the Flying Star. There is also an extensive section on compatibility.

In the predictions section, you'll find Your High-Energy Days. On these days, plan to take significant actions, make vital phone calls, and send emails. These are days when energy and luck come together for you, and you may find the most noteworthy happenings of the month will occur. The more positive action you take on these days, the better your overall results and satisfaction will be.

For more information on Chinese Astrology, check out my YouTube channel at https://www.youtube.com/c/DonnaStellhorn

If you would like a reading, please email me at DonnaStellhorn@gmail.com, and I'll send you the details.

I hope you enjoy this book and find it helpful. Please take a moment and review it so more people can find this book.

I wish you joy and prosperity in 2022.

Donna Stellhorn

Celebrating Chinese New Year

The biggest holiday of the year in China is Lunar New Year. Based on the lunar calendar, Lunar New Year falls on a different day each year—most often on the second New Moon after the Winter Solstice, which occurs in January or February. The 2022 Lunar New Year is on February 1, 2022.

Occasionally, the Lunar New Year will fall on the third New Moon after the Winter Solstice. We can next expect to experience this in the year 2033. In historical China, emperors were in charge of keeping time and told the people when significant dates would happen. Emperors marked these important dates with festivals. Lunar New Year is one such festival.

There's a Chinese legend—the tale of a "Nian," a fearsome creature with the head of a lion and the body of a bull. Every winter, the Nian would grow very hungry, and finding nothing to eat, he would come down into the villages to snack on the villagers. But over time, the villagers learned the Nian feared loud noises, fire, and the color red.

One night, the Nian was spotted coming down from the mountains, so the villagers lit fires, waved red flags, and made lots of noise by banging gongs and setting off firecrackers. Their village was spared, and to this day, New Year's is celebrated with lots of firecrackers and red banners.

Before New Year, there is much to do. The house undergoes a thorough cleaning to sweep away any of the remaining bad luck from last year. Lots of special foods to prepare. The night before New Year, it is considered "lucky" to stay up past midnight—to symbolize enjoying a long life. At midnight the firecrackers start popping.

On the first day of the New Year, everyone wears their best clothes, and everyone says only positive things to one another to secure good luck for everyone. Red envelopes are filled with money and given to children.

This begins a multi-day holiday. On Chinese New Year, there is the dance of the Golden Dragon (sometimes called the Lion Dance). This dragon is decorated with representations of the five elements, lights, silver, and fur. It can take as many as a hundred people to carry the Golden Dragon through the streets. At the end of the route, the dragon is met with firecrackers and cheers from the crowds.

On the second day of the New Year, there is a vegetarian feast, after which people visit relatives, bringing them oranges to wish them a prosperous new year. People eat long noodles—the longer, the better—to symbolize a long life. They indulge in Nian Gao—a cake made of rice flour, brown sugar, and oil—to bring prosperity.

I offer a series of videos on what to do before and during the New Year's Celebrations to bring luck.

Here's the link: *https://www.youtube.com/c/DonnaStellhorn*

Find Your Chinese Zodiac Sign

The annual Chinese Zodiac sign changes each year in January or February. If you were born in January or February of any year, check the date carefully to make sure you find your correct animal sign. Below you'll find listed the element and Yin or Yang quality for the year. If you have any difficulty determining your sign, element, and Yin or Yang quality, please email me at DONNASTELLHORN@GMAIL.COM with your birth date, and I will help you find your sign.

02/20/1920 to 02/07/1921 Yang Metal Monkey
02/08/1921 to 01/27/1922 Yin Metal Rooster (or Cock)
01/28/1922 to 2/15/1923 Yang Water Dog
02/16/1923 to 2/4/1924 Yin Water Pig (or Boar)
02/5/1924 to 1/24/1925 Yang Wood Rat
01/25/1925 to 2/12/1926 Yin Wood Ox
02/13/1926 to 2/1/1927 Yang Fire Tiger
02/2/1927 to 1/22/1928 Yin Fire Rabbit (or Hare)
01/23/1928 to 2/9/1929 Yang Earth Dragon
02/10/1929 to 1/29/1930 Yin Earth Snake
01/30/1930 to 2/16/1931 Yang Metal Horse
02/17/1931 to 2/5/1932 Yin Metal Sheep (or Goat or Ram)
02/6/1932 to 1/25/1933 Yang Water Monkey
01/26/1933 to 2/13/1934 Yin Water Rooster (or Cock)
02/14/1934 to 2/3/1935 Yang Wood Dog
02/4/1935 to 1/23/1936 Yin Wood Pig (or Boar)
01/24/1936 to 2/10/1937 Yang Fire Rat
02/11/1937 to 1/30/1938 Yin Fire Ox
01/31/1938 to 2/18/1939 Yang Earth Tiger
02/19/1939 to 2/7/1940 Yin Earth Rabbit (or Hare)
02/8/1940 to 1/26/1941 Yang Metal Dragon
01/27/1941 to 2/14/1942 Yin Metal Snake
02/15/1942 to 2/4/1943 Yang Water Horse
02/5/1943 to 1/24/1944 Yin Water Sheep (or Goat or Ram)
01/25/1944 to 2/12/1945 Yang Wood Monkey
02/13/1945 to 2/1/1946 Yin Wood Rooster (or Cock)
02/2/1946 to 1/21/1947 Yang Fire Dog
01/22/1947 to 2/9/1948 Yin Fire Pig (or Boar)

02/10/1948 to 1/28/1949 Yang Earth Rat
01/29/1949 to 2/16/1950 Yin Earth Ox
02/17/1950 to 2/5/1951 Yang Metal Tiger
02/6/1951 to 1/26/1952 Yin Metal Rabbit (or Hare)
01/27/1952 to 2/13/1953 Yang Water Dragon
02/14/1953 to 2/2/1954 Yin Water Snake
02/3/1954 to 1/23/1955 Yang Wood Horse
01/24/1955 to 2/11/1956 Yin Wood Sheep (or Goat or Ram)
02/12/1956 to 1/30/1957 Yang Fire Monkey
01/31/1957 to 2/17/1958 Yin Fire Rooster (or Cock)
02/18/1958 to 2/7/1959 Yang Earth Dog
02/8/1959 to 1/27/1960 Yin Earth Pig (or Boar)
01/28/1960 to 2/14/1961 Yang Metal Rat
02/15/1961 to 2/4/1962 Yin Metal Ox
02/5/1962 to 1/24/1963 Yang Water Tiger
01/25/1963 to 2/12/1964 Yin Water Rabbit (or Hare)
02/13/1964 to 2/1/1965 Yang Wood Dragon
02/2/1965 to 1/20/1966 Yin Wood Snake
01/21/1966 to 2/8/1967 Yang Fire Horse
02/9/1967 to 1/29/1968 Yin Fire Sheep (or Goat or Ram)
01/30/1968 to 2/16/1969 Yang Earth Monkey
02/17/1969 to 2/5/1970 Yin Earth Rooster (or Cock)
02/6/1970 to 1/26/1971 Yang Metal Dog
01/27/1971 to 2/14/1972 Yin Metal Pig (or Boar)
02/15/1972 to 2/2/1973 Yang Water Rat
02/3/1973 to 1/22/1974 Yin Water Ox
01/23/1974 to 2/10/1975 Yang Wood Tiger
02/11/1975 to 1/30/1976 Yin Wood Rabbit (or Hare)
01/31/1976 to 2/17/1977 Yang Fire Dragon
02/18/1977 to 2/6/1978 Yin Fire Snake
02/7/1978 to 1/27/1979 Yang Earth Horse
01/28/1979 to 2/15/1980 Yin Earth Sheep (or Goat or Ram)
02/16/1980 to 2/4/1981 Yang Metal Monkey
02/5/1981 to 1/24/1982 Yin Metal Rooster (or Cock)
01/25/1982 to 2/12/1983 Yang Water Dog
02/13/1983 to 2/1/1984 Yin Water Pig (or Boar)
02/2/1984 to 2/19/1985 Yang Wood Rat
02/20/1985 to 2/8/1986 Yin Wood Ox
02/9/1986 to 1/28/1987 Yang Fire Tiger

01/29/1987 to 2/16/1988 Yin Fire Rabbit (or Hare)
02/17/1988 to 2/5/1989 Yang Earth Dragon
02/6/1989 to 1/26/1990 Yang Earth Snake
01/27/1990 to 2/14/1991 Yang Metal Horse
02/15/1991 to 2/3/1992 Yin Metal Sheep (or Goat or Ram)
02/4/1992 to 1/22/1993 Yang Water Monkey
01/23/1993 to 2/9/1994 Yin Water Rooster (or Cock)
02/10/1994 to 1/30/1995 Yang Wood Dog
01/31/1995 to 2/18/1996 Yin Wood Pig (or Boar)
02/19/1996 to 2/6/1997 Yang Fire Rat
2/7/1997 to 1/27/1998 Yin Fire Ox
1/28/1998 to 2/15/1999 Yang Earth Tiger
2/16/1999 to 2/4/2000 Yin Earth Rabbit (or Hare)
2/5/2000 to 1/23/2001 Yang Metal Dragon
1/24/2001 to 2/11/2002 Yin Metal Snake
2/12/2002 to 1/31/2003 Yang Water Horse
2/1/2003 to 1/21/2004 Yin Water Sheep (or Goat or Ram)
1/22/2004 to 2/8/2005 Yang Wood Monkey
2/9/2005 to 1/28/2006 Yin Wood Rooster (or Cock)
1/29/2006 to 2/17/2007 Yang Fire Dog
2/18/2007 to 2/6/2008 Yin Fire Pig (or Boar)
2/7/2008 to 1/25/2009 Yang Earth Rat
1/26/2009 to 2/13/2010 Yin Earth Ox
2/14/2010 to 2/2/2011 Yang Metal Tiger
2/3/2011 to 1/22/2012 Yin Metal Rabbit (or Hare)
1/23/2012 to 2/09/2013 Yang Water Dragon
2/10/2013 to 1/30/2014 Yin Water Snake
1/31/2014 to 2/18/2015 Yang Wood Horse
2/19/2015 to 2/7/2016 Yin Wood Sheep (or Goat or Ram)
2/8/2016 to 1/27/2017 Yang Fire Monkey
1/28/2017 to 2/15/2018 Yin Fire Rooster (or Cock)
2/16/2018 to 2/4/2019 Yang Earth Dog
2/5/2019 to 1/24/2020 Yin Earth Pig (or Boar)
01/25/2020 to 2/11/2021 Yang Metal Rat
2/12/2021 to 1/31/2022 Yin Metal Ox
2/1/2022 to 1/21/2023 Yang Water Tiger
1/22/2023 to 2/9/2024 Yin Water Rabbit
2/10/2024 to 1/28/2025 Yang Wood Dragon
1/29/2025 to 2/16/2026 Yin Wood Snake

02/17/2026 to 02/05/2027 Yang Fire Horse
02/06/2027 to 01/25/2028 Yin Fire Sheep (or Goat or Ram)
01/26/2028 to 02/12/2029 Yang Earth Monkey
02/13/2029 to 02/02/2030 Yin Earth Rooster

Where Are You in the 12-year cycle?

In 2022, as the Year of the Water Tiger begins, we are in the third sign of the universal 12-year cycle of the Chinese Zodiac. However, your personal 12-year cycle is based on your individual Chinese zodiac sign. Here's where your sign falls in the 12-year cycle.

First, let's define the cycle itself. We can liken the 12-year cycle of the Chinese Zodiac to a single year on a farm in the following manner: three months of the year equals three years of the 12-year cycle.

Therefore, the first three years of the Chinese Zodiac represent the three months of spring, bringing the farmer the opportunity to plant seeds. The next three-year segment brings a similar energy. The three months of summer is when the farmer is busy tending the growing plants, weeding the garden, and protecting his fields.

This period is followed by the three-year segment representing the three months of autumn and harvest time. This period is marked by significant achievements but also hard work. The cycle ends with a three-year segment representing the three months of winter. The farmer finishes up tasks he didn't have time to complete during the other busy months of the year while he plans for the future. He eats from his storehouse of food and waits for the next spring planting season to begin.

If you are born in the Year of the Tiger, this year marks the beginning of your personal springtime, which will last for the coming three years. During this period you will want to plant lots of seeds by trying new things, meeting new people and going to new places. Anything new you do can sprout into real opportunities during these three years and the three following years.

For Rabbit, you are in your last year of winter. You have been through some busy years. It's time to think about what needs catching up, what to release or let go of. Think of what plans you need to put in place to make it easier for you to plant new seeds and start new things this year.

Dragon natives are in your second year of winter, and it's time to take stock of what you have accomplished over the past ten years. Where are the investments of your time and energy still paying off? Think of letting go of what isn't working and how you can accumulate more with less effort.

Snake natives are in the first year of winter. Your storehouse and pantry are as full as they will get. To gather more, you can use the skills you've developed over the last few years. Now you're clever in identifying and gathering opportunities others have missed. This is the year you begin your time of rest and recovery. You need to take care of yourself and your body.

Horse is in its last year of autumn, and the harvest is underway. Take everything you have learned so far and let the world know about your skills and what you have to offer. Demand to be paid what you are worth. This is when you can accumulate more.

Sheep (or Goat or Ram), you are in your second year of autumn, and the harvest is in full swing. Opportunities abound but require you to be out in the world to gather them up. Think big, connect with people who can help you gather even more.

Monkey, your autumn is beginning, and you must adjust to the new workload. That said, now is the period when you can gather what you want and need. Don't be shy. You can accumulate much with just a little effort.

Rooster, you are in the final year of your three-year summer. It's time to focus on the aspects of your life working the way you expect! Don't put effort into things in your life that are not bringing results. You also want to gather as many people around you as you can this year—people who will help you with your harvest in the coming three-year period.

Dog natives, you are in the middle of your summer. You see the results of the effort you've made over the past few years. There's still time to make decisions and point your life in a more fruitful direction. It's good to identify and implement ways to protect what's yours and weed out anything less desirable.

Pig natives, you are at the beginning of your summer. There are sprouts taking root everywhere. Many things you have tried now start yielding results. This is the year you need to be discerning and try not to be everything to everyone, nor should you attempt to take on every project alone. A good manager knows when to delegate.

Rat native, you are in your last year of spring. You have planted many new seeds over the past couple of years. Look at what is sprouting and determine if you're happy with it. You still have time to try new things, reinvent yourself, and make progress on your goals.

Ox natives, you are entering your second year of spring. You are creating new options for yourself but may not yet see impressive results. Now is an excellent time to study and improve your skills. Follow your heart and plant seeds for what you want to do with your life. The sprouts are coming soon.

Rat

January 31, 1900–February 18, 1901: Yang Metal Rat
February 18, 1912–February 5, 1913: Yang Water Rat
February 5, 1924–January 24, 1925: Yang Wood Rat
January 24, 1936–February 10, 1937: Yang Fire Rat
February 10, 1948–January 28, 1949: Yang Earth Rat
January 28, 1960–February 14, 1961: Yang Metal Rat
February 15, 1972–February 2, 1973: Yang Water Rat
February 2, 1984–February 19, 1985: Yang Wood Rat
February 19, 1996–February 6, 1997: Yang Fire Rat
February 7, 2008–January 25, 2009: Yang Earth Rat
January 25, 2020–February 11, 2021: Yang Metal Rat

Rat Personality

I am a Rat. It's hard to admit. I really wanted to be one of the cute animals. But after exploring so much about the 12 different Chinese Zodiac signs, I have come to love and appreciate being a Rat.

Rats are hardworking, ambitious, and thrifty. The Rat individual is very focused on getting ahead. Rats want to achieve success in life and aspire to reach the top first. They have a frugal reputation but are generous with loved ones. They are drawn to a bargain and are skilled at making and saving money.

In the traditional stories about the animals who make up the Chinese Zodiac, little Rat ran ahead of the other animals to be named the first of the Chinese Zodiac. This drive to move quickly shows that people born under this sign desire to arrive first and be noticed.

Rat natives want positive recognition for their work and to be awarded honors for their achievements. That said, they also love a challenge—but once the award is won, it's quickly tossed aside as Rat focuses on taking the next step up the ladder.

Even though Rat may not be the cutest of the Chinese Zodiac menagerie, they are well-liked. Initially reserved, they become more social as they get comfortable with their surroundings (it's perfectly understandable to be cautious when you're a little mouse!). You'll find Rat to be more talkative when topics relating to business and money are involved.

Rat makes a loyal friend. They may not have many close friends, but those who make it to Rat's inner circle will be looked out for and supported. Those born in Rat year will gravitate to other successful people. They have trouble tolerating lazy people and can't be bothered with anyone who wants a free ride.

Reading a Rat's feelings is easy. When upset (and they are easily irritated), they can be critical. They also compare and contrast everything. This helps them identify and locate the best of everything—from bargains to close friends. Rats are adept at writing and communication. They possess excellent memories and are always asking questions.

Rats like to accumulate, although it varies from Rat to Rat what they are collecting. Some Rats accumulate money, others material things and still others gather social or business contacts. Rat is adaptable and has acute intuition, so they can quickly determine the benefit in a situation.

Because Rat is the smallest of the animals of the Chinese Zodiac, safety and self-preservation are held paramount. They can sense danger, but Rat finds it hard to heed the warnings if they simultaneously smell opportunity and potential success. Rat needs only to follow their gut and finish what they start, to end up the wealthiest of all the signs.

Rat: Predictions for 2022

How to use your High-Energy Days: On these days, plan to take action for your most important goals, make vital phone calls, send important emails. Your high-energy days are when your energy and luck are the strongest for the month.

January 2022: *January 2 is the new moon. January 14 Mercury goes retrograde. January 17 is the full moon. On January 18, Uranus goes direct. On January 29, Venus goes direct. Your High-Energy Days are 2, 8, 14, 20, and 26.*

January brings the last month of the Metal Ox year, and Rat natives are in the flow. You're making many good connections, especially professional people who could open doors for you in your career in the future.

This month, Rat natives have a chance to be on stage. You might sing a solo with the choir or get asked to lead a company meeting in front of the CEO and other supervisors. If the idea of this brings you some anxiety, it's good to plan ahead and see who you can get to take your place.

January 2 brings the new moon and a career opportunity, something you have asked for. Soon you'll be entering the third of your seed planting years. New opportunities can be expected; however, this new chance may not increase your salary, merely more hours of work! So unless it's entirely in line with your goals, it might be something you want to pass on.

On January 14, Mercury goes retrograde, causing you to rethink some decisions you've made over the past two weeks. There's still time to renegotiate or to return to something you have done before. This retrograde energy could also slow down the progress you're making in your love life. Now your two schedules seem to be out of sync, and this could go on for a few weeks. You and your sweetheart may feel like two ships passing in the night.

January 17 has the full moon in your area of home and family. If you haven't moved in the last two years, moving energy is now very compelling, maybe because of some great opportunities in real estate. Or, there may be issues around neighbors; even changes in the neighborhood itself can cause you to rethink where you live.

While Rat natives tend to be quick on the draw, this is just the beginning of this energy, so a move doesn't have to happen immediately. It's good to avoid moving on Mercury retrograde—doing so can cause you to want to move again soon.

Now is the time to rejoice as the energy shifts into Water Tiger, a harmonious time for Rat natives. You can discover many opportunities in the months ahead.

February 2022: *February 1 is the new moon and begins the Year of the Water Tiger. February 3, Mercury goes direct. February 16 is the full moon. Your high-energy days are: 1, 7, 13, 19, and 25.*

The water Tiger year begins on February 1, and for Rat natives, the focus is on community and associations with interesting people. You start the year off by having opportunities to connect with like-minded others. This could lead to a new job, promotion, or collaboration opportunity.

The new moon is on February 1 and brings you a potential new friend. This person could become someone very influential in your life. This is an individual you look up to and admire, but they also have great admiration for you and your accomplishments. You're like two peas in a pod. You could meet this person when you're doing some work in the community or when doing activities with a professional organization.

February 3 brings the Water Tiger month, and also Mercury moves forward again. Rat native, now the energy really speeds up. You may find that your dance card is full. People want to see you, business contacts request meetings with you, and you have personal obligations as well. You may have to schedule in time for breaks and sleep. But this is a time to lean in and grab these opportunities.

The full moon is on February 16, and there's very potent romance energy for Rat native. But first, you must let go of someone from your past. This doesn't mean you're breaking up with someone but that you are letting go of an idealized version of a person you once knew. Make a clean start. Recognize that this past relationship was not meant to be. Moving forward now signals the Universe that you're ready for love.

March 2022: *March 2 is the new moon. The full moon is on March 18. Your high-energy days are: 3, 9, 15, 21, and 27.*

In March, you might need some downtime. Schedule a vacation or at least a long weekend. You're also more intuitive this month, which can mean you're picking up other people's energies. Consider doing a space clearing on the house. This can be done by burning sage or using a sage spray. Or dissolve some sea salt in water and spritz it around the house.

March 2 brings the new moon and Rat native; there's a lot of energy around reputation and your influence in the world. Something you post on social media could go viral. Past posts could be picked up and shared with many people. If you're doing some sort of business, this is a great time to market yourself. But be careful if you're posting something controversial, as it could take on a life of its own.

March 5 begins the Water Rabbit month, and Rat native, you may feel more competition around you. You and a coworker may go for the same job. Someone from another company could invade your sales territory. You may feel totally competitive now, even with siblings or other family members.

The full moon is on March 17. Rat native, this is an excellent time to look at your routines and habits. See if some bad habits have crept back in from your past. Focus on letting go of what you no longer want in your life. Create space for something new and better to come in. This could mean decluttering, dropping sugar from your diet, or even letting go of a person who is not a beneficial influence on you.

In some parts of the world, there will be a second new moon in March, and for other time zones, it will be April 1. This new moon brings love relationship opportunities for Rat native. Not only are you more noticeable now, but others are commenting on your confidence and poise. You're receiving compliments right and left. This is a great time to have a first date or allow your friends or family to fix you up on a blind date. If you're already in a love relationship, there's more harmony now happening between the two of you.

April 2022: *April 1 is the new moon. The full moon is on April 16. On April 29, Pluto goes retrograde. There is a partial solar eclipse on April 30. Your high-energy days are: 2, 8, 14, 20, and 26.*

April brings positive energy for focusing on bigger goals. Now you can take plans you've been working on for some time and begin implementing the steps. Once you begin, the Universe will step in to help supply you with the resources that you need. But it's up to you to start. Fortunately, Rat native, you're very good at starting things.

On April 4, the Wood Dragon month brings harmonious energy for Rat natives. You could have an enjoyable and adventurous time. This can translate into a whirlwind romance. You might fall head over heels and be ready to dance the night away. This positive energy is predicated on you taking a risk, such as saying "yes" when a stranger asks you to coffee.

The full moon is on April 16, and Rat native, you have a lot on your plate, and you may work behind the scenes. Do not hide. If you're hidden, you won't get the help you need. Make sure to speak up. This can result in coworkers pitching in, your supervisor hiring an assistant for you, or other help can come your way. Don't try to do it all yourself.

There is a solar eclipse on April 30, and Rat native, the spotlight is on your finances. Some great money opportunities come your way, but you need to put the structure in place to receive these. That is to pay attention to your investments, debt, and spending. Take some time over the next week or so to give yourself a written budget or review your investment portfolio. This way, when money starts to flow, you'll have the pitcher ready to catch the stream.

May 2022: *On May 10, Mercury goes retrograde. There is a total lunar eclipse on May 16. On May 30, there is a new moon. Your high-energy days are: 2, 8, 14, 20, and 26.*

During May, your focus on finances continues. You can remove financial blocks, especially around the concept of deserving. You also may release material objects, making space in your life for something better.

May 5 brings the Wood Snake month, and Rat native, you may feel a bit like you're chasing your tail. Work you thought finished may have to be redone. There could be computer issues or just a misunderstanding in what the assignment was. Instead of getting frustrated, try to look at ways you can improve systems, including using technology to streamline what you're doing, so it takes less time in the future.

On May 10, Mercury goes retrograde, and Rat native, you may have some issues around transportation or your vehicle in particular. If you need to get vehicle repairs, insist you get a warranty for the work, as it may not be correct the first time.

There is a lunar eclipse on May 15. Rat native, there are some strong possibilities for an intimate relationship. If you've been dating, you may take this relationship to the next level. If you're already in a love relationship, it's good to take extra time to care for each other now. If you're looking for love, you can find someone with whom you have great sexual chemistry, even if they're not your usual "type."

The new moon is on May 30, and Rat native, you could receive a contract for employment or something leading to financial gain. There is good energy around agreements, even handshake deals. If you would like to sell something of value, you can make a tidy profit. Mercury is still retrograde, so this may be a deal that had fallen through before but is now ready for your signature.

June 2022: *Mercury goes direct on June 3. On June 4, Saturn goes retrograde. On June 14, there is a full moon. Neptune goes retrograde on June 28. The new moon is on June 29. Your high-energy days are: 1, 7, 13, 19, and 25.*

In June, you can expect things to move forward again. Mercury turns direct on June 3, and something you have been waiting for now magically comes through. Communication of all kinds seems to flow more easily. And this month, a disagreement you had with a sibling or younger relative is now resolved.

June 5 brings the Fire Horse month, and Rat natives are not as readily seen. Therefore, you need to make sure you are counted. There could be simple, everyday issues like the server not taking your order, but it also can occur around critical situations such as the boss not seeing your contribution to the meeting or even thinking that you weren't there at all. Speak loudly and make sure your voice is counted during this month.

The full moon is on June 14, and Rat native, you might think of traveling or make travel plans. There is positive energy for taking a trip (and you can find a good deal). You may finish up school, or perhaps your kids are now out of school. You could plan a family vacation. Even if you have a hectic schedule, it's a good idea to give yourself at least a few days away from home.

June 28 is the new moon, and Rat native, now there's an emphasis on home and family. You may do some home renovations, decluttering, or welcome some guests. You might get a visit from siblings, cousins, or nieces and nephews. People could gather for a specific celebration such as the arrival of a baby or a wedding. There's happy energy at home during this time.

July 2022: *July 13 brings the full moon. There is a new moon on July 28. Also, on July 28, Jupiter goes retrograde. Your high-energy days are:1, 7, 13, 19, and 25.*

In July, some Rat natives could be packing to move. Others may be unpacking from a recent move. It's also possible you are redoing your home office or starting a business at home and using the garage to store inventory. You can get help if you need it. In addition, you can tap into some resources such as assistance from family and friends.

July 7 brings the Fire Sheep month, and somewhat easier energy begins for Rat native. But there are still some challenges as others ask you to make adjustments to your plans or changes in your schedule. However, no one can pivot as quickly and as easily as a Rat native. These requests could come from a close friend or your sweetheart, and so it's easy to comply with these changes in your plans.

The full moon is on July 13, and there are some significant changes connected to your career. It's possible the company is going through changes such as a merger or reworking its basic systems. This could bring openings if you want to move up in the company or change departments. There is also an opportunity to change locations if your company has remote offices. New job possibilities are also available to you.

The new moon is on July 28, and there is a lot of creativity and fertility energy around you. If you're looking to get pregnant, this could be the time when you have good luck and can find the help you need, such as a medical professional. If you have a creative project you're working on, now you can have a breakthrough. This could mean you're doing an art showing or your music debuts on a social media platform.

August 2022: *August 12 brings the full moon. Uranus goes retrograde on August 24. There is a new moon on August 27. Your high-energy days are: 6, 12, 18, 24, and 30.*

August brings an opportunity to get out of your comfort zone and do something truly memorable. This is where you want to take risks, whether in love, in business, or just following your dream goal. Focus your energy on doing something different. Look for adventure.

August 7 brings the Earth Monkey month and positive energy for Rat natives. You may connect with somebody who lives far away. This could be a job opportunity on the other side of the country. If you have a business, you may find help by outsourcing or importing goods and materials. For school, this could mean studying abroad or going to another country to teach English.

August 11 is the full moon, and Rat natives have a possibility to connect to a group or organization. This could be through some professional networking or a charitable function that you attend. You can start a Meetup group or take a board position in a group you belong to. Now you have the opportunity for some recognition within your community.

The new moon is on August 27, and Rat native, your attention turns to your health and well-being. You might take up meditation or restart a yoga program. You could do tai chi in the park or engage a personal trainer. This is also an excellent time to tweak your diet towards more healthful fare. You might eliminate sugar, processed food, or alcohol. You might cook more at home as well.

September 2022: *On September 10, there is a full moon, and Mercury goes retrograde. On September 25, there's the new moon. Your high-energy days are: 5, 11, 17, 23, and 29.*

September shines a spotlight on work and routines. You're likely busy at work, getting more paid hours and more engaging projects. Look at what aspects of your job you can streamline, automate, or delegate. If you own a business, you could do rather well. You have opportunities for hiring excellent help, as well as making financial gains through some well-crafted deals.

September 7 begins the Earth Rooster month, and Rat native, there's a lot of energy around authority figures. This includes parents or supervisors at work. But this is also good energy for you to rise to a position of authority. You might look at your skillset and know the value of what you've learned. Fill in the holes of what you need to know. This will strengthen your position. Authority figures around you could be helpful. It's also a time for you to step up and take your rightful place at the head of the table.

The full moon is on September 10, and the same day, Mercury goes retrograde. There could be issues around a relationship for Rat natives. There may be a miscommunication leading to a disagreement. If you're looking for love, you might find it hard to connect now. Your schedules may not sync up, or one of you ends up going to the wrong coffee shop and missing the date entirely.

The new moon is on September 25, now positive relationship energy returns. This is very beneficial for a love relationship, especially if you want to meet someone new. But, Rat native, this is also good energy for connecting with friends, mentors, or collaborating with an influencer. The energy is in your favor to make good connections, so it's wise now to reach out through direct messages or emails.

October 2022: *Mercury goes direct on October 2. On October 8, Pluto goes direct. There is a full moon on October 9. On October 23, Saturn goes direct. On October 25, there's a partial solar eclipse. On October 28, Jupiter goes retrograde. Mars goes retrograde on October 30. Your high-energy days are:5, 11, 17, 23, and 29.*

October can be a lucky month for Rat natives. Also, Mercury goes direct on October 2. Good energy continues around connecting with influential people. This is good for business partnerships as well as for finding people who support you as you actively pursue your dreams. If you own a business, you can find other companies to work with, either outsourcing some of your processes or doing collaborative advertising.

October 8 brings the Metal Dog month. Technology comes into focus. During this time, you might look at upgrading some equipment. This is also a great time to fill in some of your knowledge holes in technology. It's unnecessary to learn everything but to get more proficient at processes you use regularly. Find a teacher to guide you in using equipment or software.

The full moon is on October 9, and Rat native, you might receive some recognition or be put in the limelight. You might be on stage, leading a meeting, or tapped on the shoulder to receive some award. This is an excellent time to look for a job, as your resume will magically rise to the top of the pile. In addition, you might get publicity for your business through a podcast or magazine article.

The solar eclipse is on October 25. Rat native, this could bring some challenges connected to credit or loan applications. There could be some mistake in your banking that could leave you temporarily short of cash. It's also possible that somebody who owes you money has decided not to pay. And you may have to look at taking more direct action to get what you are owed.

November 2022: *November 8 brings the total lunar eclipse. On November 23, there is a new moon, and Jupiter goes direct. Your high-energy days are: 4, 10, 16, 23, and 28.*

November shows better energy around finances but still some challenges around dealing with people, especially friendships. You may find it necessary to step carefully and mindfully. It's pretty easy this month to overlook a birthday or, due to your busyness, forget to pick up a friend at the airport.

November 7 brings the Metal Pig month, and Rat native, it's a good idea to slow down and assess what's working and what's not working in your life. You might take on too much and need to let go of a project or an obligation. On the other hand, you may be procrastinating on what's necessary and using busy work to keep you from doing the things that are genuinely in line with your goals.

The lunar eclipse is on November 8, and Rat native, a new financial opportunity, is there for the taking, but it pulls you outside of your comfort zone. You may have to shift your schedule around or take on a project you're not sure you can get done within the deadline. It's also possible that you are lightening the load and letting go of some stuff. These could be aspirational objects like your guitar, surfboard, or sewing machine. These are things that you thought you were going to enjoy, but that you never ended up using.

The new moon is on November 23, and energy calms down considerably for Rat native. You might travel or welcome relatives who are visiting from out of town. There is more potent spiritual energy for you now. You might be attending religious services, reading sacred texts, or doing more prayer and meditation. There is a stronger connection with your guardian angel and guides now.

December 2022: *Neptune goes direct on December 3. The full moon is on December 8. There is a new moon on December 23.*

Mercury goes retrograde on December 29. Your high-energy days are: 4, 10, 16, 23, and 28.

In December, education is highlighted. It's possible you are in school and looking at final exams. Or you might take an accelerated course online. This is also when you could renew a professional license by doing continuing education or taking a state-mandated test. Look into study habits and techniques for reducing procrastination.

On December 7, it's the Water Rat month, your month. Additionally, it's also the full moon. Even though it's the last month of the calendar year, you may feel like it's time for a new beginning to happen. There is a possibility of a new job. A new friendship could turn romantic. You might take your existing love relationship to a more serious level by getting engaged or even getting married.

December 23 is the new moon, and Rat native, you look like you're the star of the show. You may be putting on a charity function and or leading religious services. You may get a promotion or a sizable bonus from your job. You may be newly married. People are celebrating your accomplishments. This is an excellent opportunity to look for a new job or promote your business through additional marketing.

On December 29, Mercury goes retrograde, which can delay a move or hold up changes at home you were planning. You might have trouble getting workers in or getting a work permit. If you're selling your house, the deal could fall through. Or, if you've had no nibbles on your house for sale, you might consider lowering the price. You might find it difficult to change apartments as you can't find a flat you like. You will need patience at this time.

January 2023: *January 6 brings the full moon. Mercury goes direct on January 18. The year of the water rabbit begins on January 22. Your high-energy days are. 3, 9, 15, 21, and 27.*

January has you making plans and poised for some genuine success. Your social media is getting more plays. Others are reaching out to you to share in your success. You could receive offers to collaborate or for sponsorship deals. You must be very visible now. If you hide, these deals and opportunities cannot find you.

January 5 begins the Water Ox month, and Rat native, your thoughts turn to finances. This can be a lucrative month for you. You might receive revenue from an additional source, or an investment starts to pay off. If you have a side business, you might see some profits from this (maybe for the first time), or your profit percentage rises. This is an excellent time to put extra revenue towards debt or long-term savings.

The full moon is on January 6, and you benefit significantly by letting go of something or finishing up a project. Take a look at things that have been unfinished for some time and allow yourself to release that which is just not going to get done. At the same time, you may end a connection or relationship with someone because you've grown apart.

On January 18, Mercury goes direct. Rat native, if you have been waiting for a job opportunity, now it finally comes through. If you expect some recognition at your current job—a promotion or salary increase—now the road is clear for this to happen.

The new moon is on January 22, and with that, the Year of the Water Rabbit begins. Rat native, you are now entering your seed-tending period. This will last for three years, and during this time, you can make great headway on projects and your most cherished goals. Focus your energy during these two weeks on making plans. For this next year, you'll be building a solid foundation, stabilizing finances, and strengthening your relationships.

Attract New Love

Rat native, the Year of the Water Tiger starts with lucky energy connecting intimately with someone special. You may feel somewhat reserved in principle, but in practice, you are ready to leap in. A first date can go from a casual coffee date to sexy fun pretty quickly. September could bring a lover back from your past. This will give you the opportunity for another go with this person. But October could see you running into the same issues you had with this individual before. It will be necessary to seek a different solution for this recurring issue. Overall, you could be lucky in love in 2022, primarily for short-term or passionate love relationships.

Traditionally and historically, jade was considered more valuable than diamonds throughout Asia. Jade is most commonly found in the shades of green and purple; green jade represents longevity. Jade can be carved into many things: from lucky charms to fine jewelry. Hang a jade charm in your bedroom to invite in the energy of love and beauty, or find a jade pendant to wear. Jade can be fragile, and if your Jade piece breaks, make sure to replace it.

Enhance Existing Love

2022 shows you, Rat native, working especially hard at your special love relationship. During the previous year, you may have had some challenges that were a little bit more public than you generally like. And now you're both on your best behavior. But more importantly, you are learning how to respect each other and empathize with your partner's situation. During the Year of the Water Tiger, you may feel like you were falling back into an old pattern, but this energy corrects itself pretty quickly. By the end of the year, you and your sweetheart could be seen by your friends and extended family as a model couple.

Cranes: If your relationship is worth keeping and you want to make it better and stronger than ever, choose the crane as your symbol for love this year. The crane is a symbol of fidelity and marital bliss in many cultures. To bring greater happiness to your relationship, find or make some paper cranes. This origami bird is simple to do and is said to bring fidelity and longevity. You can also hang a painting of actual cranes. Place the picture or the paper cranes in the bedroom where you can see them from the bed.

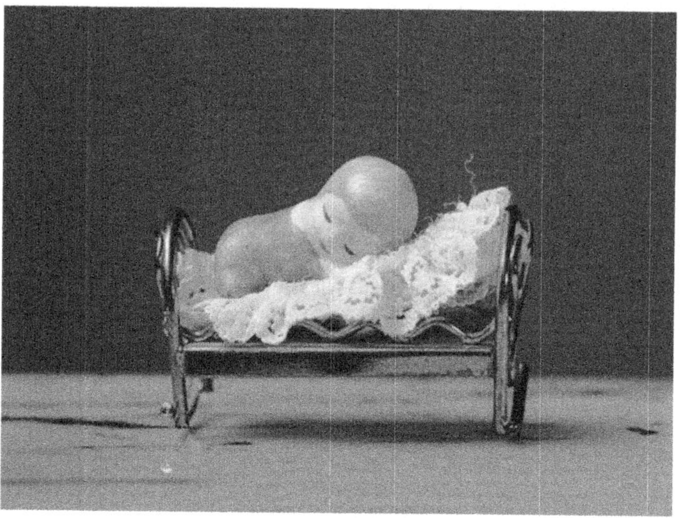

Looking to Conceive?

Child Figurine: When you're hoping to conceive, it's good Feng Shui to place a representation of what you want near where you sleep. This year, place a figurine of a sleeping child (or children) playing on your nightstand or dresser. Choose a figurine you like, one that brings joy to your heart. Or, ask a relative who has kids if they have a favorite figurine you could borrow. A borrowed figurine would have phenomenal fertility energy.

Place the figurine in your bedroom where you can easily see it from the bed. Picture the energy of the symbol entering your body and your life. Wash or dust the figurine regularly to increase the energy of this classic Feng Shui remedy.

(From Donna Stellhorn's book, Fertility Feng Shui)

Family and Kids

There are some potential changes for Rat natives in the area of home and children this year. It looks like something is coming to an end, and this could mean that you are changing residences or that older children are moving out, leaving you with an empty nest. There may now be a long distance between you and relatives that you used to see daily. There's also the possibility that you are bringing a renovation project to completion. You can get the final permits or local building inspections finished. Your home is likely the place for parties and celebrations in 2022. There will be times when your house is filled with life and laughter.

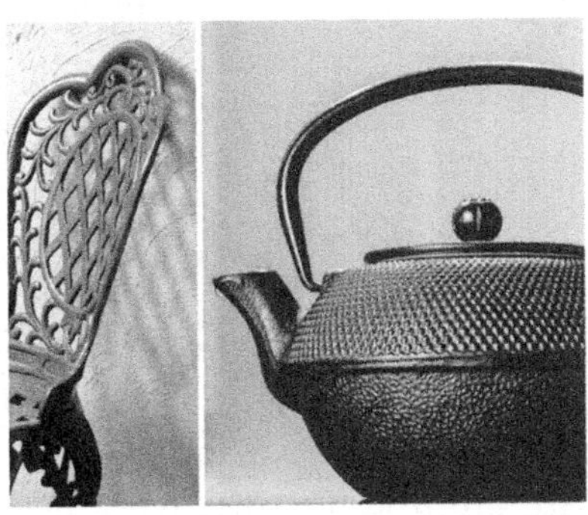

Iron: For added protection energy in your life, add things made of iron to the home. This can be in the form of furniture or decorative art on the walls. If you live in a less than safe area of town, consider adding an iron fence or an iron security door. Adding just a bit of iron will help bring in more protection energy. If the area where you live is already secure, then just a single piece of decorative iron art is all you need. If you start to feel uneasy, just add another piece. However, be careful about adding too much iron. It can keep you so secure opportunities have trouble getting to you.

Money

You are more aware of the power of money this year, Rat native. There are likely several opportunities to bring in more money in 2022. You might be able to stick to a stricter budget this year. You may be involved in investing or finding passive income sources. In the Year of the Water Tiger, you show opportunities to make money through your own business and investments. It's possible to make more per hour at your job or secure a raise, but this will take some effort. Your boss is likely to point to issues with the company itself and delay salary increases until the end of the year. So overall, this could be the year you transition to earning more income from your own business or investments than you do your job.

Bamboo: You are probably familiar with lucky bamboo, i.e., bamboo sticks growing in water or small pots with bamboo growing in stones and water. There are about ten species of bamboo grown in China. Some can measure a diameter of 3 feet and a height of 40 feet. Bamboo has many uses. It's been used for food, in the manufacture of paper, for making buckets and furniture. The leaves have been used to thatch roofs; the seeds and sap are used for medicinal purposes.

So this versatile plant is a perfect Feng Shui cure, a symbol of attracting money and benefit of all kinds this year. Place a lucky bamboo plant in your living room—in sight of your front door—to attract easy money opportunities.

Job or Career

For Rat native, some things are changing this year at your job. There may be transformations you've noticed in the whole industry or your particular company. Monitor the firm you work for's financial health. All these changes could cause you to move to a different company. However, it's more likely you would move to a different division or transfer within the company. Most of these changes could occur in May or December. It's also a possibility that a supervisor you like is moving on. Rat native, this could cause you to feel differently about the job itself. Overall, 2022 shows changes in your career.

Elephant: For those born in the year of the Rat, you can increase positive career energy by placing an elephant figurine (or a set of them) in your living room, home office, or dining room. Choose an elephant whose trunk is up triumphantly and point him or them towards the door. The elephant doesn't have to be large, but it should be prominently displayed so you can see it when you enter the room. Dust him regularly to re-energize the positive vibes.

Education

There's a great deal of focus on education in the Year of the Water Tiger. This year, you are taking your education seriously. For Rat native, you can build your skill set in areas that directly help your job situation or are vital in your business. Classes like video editing, estate planning, scriptwriting, and how to do an import/export business are the types of subjects you could be studying. These are likely to be accelerated courses, or they are geared toward practical application. This year preparing for tests, especially professional exams, is a good idea. This is not a year you can skate through.

Legal Matters

Legal matters go well as long as you're careful. For Rat native, this is not a year to casually get into a lawsuit. Avoid mentioning lawsuits (even in anger) as the other person may take the initiative, and you could find yourself in legal hot water. If you're already in a lawsuit, you have the opportunity to complete the process, such as finishing up a divorce or custody hearing. When it comes to contracts, review them carefully. Some negotiation will be possible. Overall, in 2022, there is success when you put in the sweat and hard work regarding legal matters.

Health and Well-Being

Rat native, your health is highlighted in the Year of the Water Tiger, and this could indicate that you're making a major change in your diet or how you exercise. This could also mean this is the year you conquer sleep issues, delve into alternative medicine, or get some cosmetic/elective surgery done. There are significant shifts in energy for you in May and November. During these times, you may go back to a health regimen that had been working for you before. In the Year of the Water Tiger, some of the best exercises for you will be out in nature, climbing rocks, or hiking, especially in groups or with a friend.

Salt Lamp: Consider adding a salt lamp to the home to bring in good health energy. Salt lamps are made from solid pieces of Himalayan rock salt. A hole is carved into the bottom of the salt block, and a small light bulb is placed inside. When lit, the lamp glows with a soft peach-colored light. Also, the heated salt emits negative ions into the air, like a miniature version of ocean air.

Combining the heavy object (the rock salt) and the negative ions it produces will bring stability and peace to an environment. Place the salt lamp in the living room or bedroom and keep the light on for long periods during the evening hours. You can also display several salt lamps since they come in many interesting shapes and sizes.

Ox

February 19, 1901–February 7, 1902: Yin Metal Ox
February 6, 1913–January 25, 1914: Yin Water Ox
January 25, 1925–February 12, 1926: Yin Wood Ox
February 11, 1937–January 30, 1938: Yin Fire Ox
January 29, 1949–February 16, 1950: Yin Earth Ox
February 15, 1961–February 4, 1962: Yin Metal Ox
February 3, 1973–January 22, 1974: Yin Water Ox
February 20, 1985–February 8, 1986: Yin Wood Ox
February 7, 1997–January 27, 1998: Yin Fire Ox
January 26, 2009–February 13, 2010: Yin Earth Ox
February 12, 2021–January 31, 2022: Yin Metal Ox

Ox Personality

Slow and steady, the Ox is continually making progress towards success and prosperity. Ox is the hardest working of all the signs of the Chinese Zodiac. Once they accept a task, they toil and toil until it's done. They like to finish one thing before starting another. Often, new projects will sit and gather dust while Ox completes any previous obligations—no matter how exciting or how profitable the new project may be.

Those born in the year of the Ox are intelligent and resourceful, although these qualities may not be apparent. Ox native is often introverted and shy. The truth is, they're shy until the need arises—then they will stand up in front of a group and take on a leadership role. As one of the largest and strongest animals of the Chinese Zodiac, Ox is never intimidated and rarely at a loss for words.

Ox individuals like a routine. They will stick to a particular way of doing things and may find it extremely difficult to change. In some ways, this is the key to Ox's success. They use tried-and-true methods and hard work to create the outcomes they want to manifest.

Ox never jumps in or relies on "luck" to succeed in their endeavors (or worse, "wings it"). Tenacity and dedication to a specific outcome bring Ox the most satisfaction and the most success.

Those born in Ox year have patience and understanding with others. They take pride in being a good and loyal friend. However, they are not particularly good at being a romantic partner. It wouldn't occur to them to fly you off to Paris at a moment's notice to enjoy a weekend vacation. However, once Ox does fall in love and marries, they are in it for the long haul. They are faithful and prove to be agreeable partners.

Ox, like buffalo, cannot be stopped once they begin moving. If an Ox person gets angry, expect to be run over. However, the Ox native can get stuck; they can walk the same path, doing the same things for so long they wear a rut so deep they can't climb out of it.

This can occur in the course of their career or daily work, but the same pattern can also show up in their intimate relationships. An Ox can hold on to grievances far longer than any other sign. You can quickly identify an unhappy Ox: they work all the time.

Because Ox is so self-disciplined, they expect similar behavior from other people in their lives. Ox will patiently instruct others, but should someone refuse to listen or pay attention to their excellent advice, Ox will turn away, head out, and never look back.

Ox doesn't believe in shortcuts, not for others, and not for themselves. They build things that last, designs copied around the world. Everything Ox receives, they have earned, and no one can say otherwise.

Ox natives dislike to be in debt. They want to settle accounts as soon as possible, preferably never get into debt in the first place! When they receive something as a gift, their gratitude overflows. That being said, Ox is also likely to remember an injustice for a very, very long, long, long time.

Ox: Predictions for 2022

How to use your High-Energy Days: On these days, plan to take action for your most important goals, make vital phone calls, send important emails. Your high-energy days are when your energy and luck are the strongest for the month.

January 2022: *January 2 is the new moon. January 14 has Mercury going retrograde. January 17 is the full moon. On January 18, Uranus goes direct. On January 29, Venus goes direct. Your High-Energy Days are 3, 9, 15, 21, and 27.*

January arrives, bringing the last month of the Metal Ox year. There's been quite a few ups and downs and some challenges for Ox natives. But when you look back, you see many new things are happening in your life. That's a good thing!

On January 2, the new moon comes in, and sometime over the next week or so, you receive some good news. There is an opportunity to gain a professional license or to pass a certification exam. Ox natives who are in school can get some good grades or get through a challenging project. It's now easy to get recognition.

On January 14, that pesky Mercury goes retrograde again, and some plans get put on hold. You may have been thinking of speaking to your supervisor about a new position, but you now may want to wait for a few weeks until the energy clears. There is also the possibility of traveling to a wedding or special event, but this trip could encounter many delays or interruptions. You may want to arrange travel insurance or allow a considerable amount of extra time to get to where you're going.

On January 17, there is a full moon, and Ox natives experience an emphasis on spirituality. You may attend church services more regularly or practice some spiritual work at home. This could include adding yoga to your daily routine, meditation, chanting, or other spiritual practices. If you haven't done so in a while, dust off your altar or do a space clearing.

February 2022: *February 1 is the new moon and begins the Year of the Water Tiger. February 3, Mercury goes direct. February 16 is the full moon. Your high-energy days are: 2, 8, 14, 20, and 26.*

The Water Tiger year begins on February 1, and you are pretty noticeable now. You might be singled out for a promotion at work (or at least some added responsibility). If you're looking for a job, you'll likely get more than one interview. You may negotiate a better salary or a more flexible work schedule.

The new moon is on February 1. There may be some added responsibility at home. Someone could move in, or you might get a new pet. There's also the possibility that you will gain rental property and so deal with tenants and contracts. Some Ox natives may build a house or do major renovations, and you could act as the manager of this process.

February 3 brings the Water Tiger month, and Mercury comes out of retrograde. A document or set of documents you have been waiting for now arrives. Now you can get to work on reviewing this agreement and getting it ready to sign. A postponed trip might be back on now. And some difficulties you are having related to travel seem to clear up magically.

The full moon is on February 16, and there's a lot of energy around ancestors and family heritage. You may receive a family heirloom or purchase an antique that reminds you of your upbringing. You may get together with family members to discuss a property owned by the whole family. In the year of the Water Tiger, there is the opportunity to determine shares and boundaries regarding land.

March 2022: *March 2 is the new moon. The full moon is on March 18. Your high-energy days are: 4, 10, 16, 23, and 28.*

March has you quite involved in the community. You may gain a board position in an organization you belong to. Or you may start your own group, gathering together with like-minded people for a hobby or professional activity. This is also an excellent time to get together with friends to socialize.

March 2 brings the new moon, and you may purchase some new technology. For example, you might replace an old computer or upgrade your camera. This is a good time to look into deals or to get something custom-built for you. If you're expanding your business into videos or doing a podcast, you may want special equipment, and now is the time to secure what you need.

March 5 brings the Water Rabbit month, and your mind turns to finances. You could be more mindful of what you're spending and what the whole family is doing with money and budgeting. You may receive some information about an excellent investment. It will need more research, but this could put you on the right track towards gaining some passive income.

The full moon is on March 17, and Ox native, there are some romantic opportunities for you and your sweetheart. It looks like you could have some fun over the next two weeks. Get a babysitter for the kids, so you have some time for yourselves. If you're looking for love, there's outstanding energy for using an online service or a professional matchmaker. You could meet someone with whom you have great chemistry.

In some parts of the world, there will be a second new moon on March 31, and for other time zones, it will be on April 1. This new moon brings a need for some downtime. You might look at meditation techniques either through private tutoring or by using an app. You might try journaling to bring your thoughts and feelings to the surface. You might also consider hypnosis or some self-hypnosis modality to clear away old energy.

April 2022: *April 1 is the new moon. The full moon is on April 16. On April 29, Pluto goes retrograde. There is a partial solar eclipse on April 30. Your high-energy days are: 3, 9, 15, 21, and 27.*

April brings a desire to work behind the scenes, finish up projects, and get some rest. You may endeavor to remove yourself from the society of others for a little while so you can regroup. Catching up on paperwork or your favorite television show is on the agenda now.

On April 4, the Wood Dragon month begins, and for the next four weeks, there's a lot of emphasis on home and family. During this time, your family may increase in number through marriage, adoption of a pet, it's or the birth of a child. Someone you know might get engaged. You could have a house filled with people are celebrating.

The full moon is on April 16, and Ox native, your work heats up again. You might be in charge of a large team or be the lead on a new product. At this time, you're getting along well with your coworkers and supervisor. But you also may recognize that your company or the industry you work in may not be a solid place to be in the future. Consider the long-term viability of your job so that you can plant seeds for your next position.

There is a solar eclipse on April 30, which could be a significant change in your life. This might be something you had planned a while back, and now those changes are happening. But what's more likely is you're deciding now, and several changes will unfold over the next few weeks or months. A new direction in your life is possible. You might go back to school or move to a faraway place. If you've made a significant change in the last year or so, this is just a shadow of that energy, and the shifts in your life will be minor.

May 2022: *On May 10, Mercury goes retrograde. There is a total lunar eclipse on May 16. On May 30, there is a new moon. Your high-energy days are: 3, 9, 15, 21, and 27.*

During May, you're in the spotlight. It's effortless for you to meet new friends and connect with someone special. If you're looking for love, you may find someone who's quite a a suitable match. This is positive energy for expanding your circle of friends. You can meet the friends of your friends. You may attend social gatherings and meet new people with like-minded interests.

May 5 brings the Wood Snake month and for the next four weeks, there's much emphasis on fertility, creativity, and children. Your kids may get out of school, and so you're getting ready for summer vacation. If you're looking to get pregnant, there are more opportunities over the next four weeks than usual. You can find helpful people, including medical professionals. Additionally, you might be inspired to do more art projects or activities related to music.

On May 10, Mercury goes retrograde, and Ox native, be careful about making large purchases over the next few weeks. You may end up with something that doesn't work, or you are disappointed with the quality. If you need to purchase, make sure it's returnable.

There is a lunar eclipse on May 15, and Ox native, this could be some of the most intense love energy for you all year. You may need to state your wishes to the person you're dating. Or perhaps you're bringing this person home to meet friends and family. If you're looking for love, engage a matchmaker or let your friends know they can fix you up on dates.

The new moon is on May 30, and over the next two weeks, there's a great deal of focus on finances. You may receive a windfall. You're naturally frugal, so you are likely to socket away any unexpected gains in a long-term savings account. However, Ox native, set a little aside so that you and your family can have some fun.

June 2022: *Mercury goes direct on June 3. On June 4, Saturn goes retrograde. On June 14, there is a full moon. Neptune goes retrograde on June 28. The new moon is on June 29. Your high-energy days are: 1, 7, 13, 19, and 25.*

June brings you, Ox native, a desire to pay off debts. You may look for investment opportunities to see if you can get a source of passive income going. Over the next four weeks, you have lots of extra energy for moneymaking activities.

Mercury goes direct on June 3, and over the next week or so, a document or a set of keys that you thought was lost now magically appears.

June 5 brings the Fire Horse month, and Ox native, there's an emphasis on health and well-being. Over the next four weeks, you might take care of annual medical appointments, change your diet, or look into getting a personal trainer. There is very favorable energy for engaging a friend as an accountability partner. You can help each other make sure you do walking, stretching, or get to yoga class.

The full moon is on June 14, and there is positive relationship energy, especially for an intimate relationship. If you're already in a committed relationship, you and your sweetheart might chase each other around the sofa more than usual. We might read romantic novels or watch rom-com movies. There's love on your mind, and there are opportunities for romance nearby.

June 28 is the new moon, and Ox native, there's a lot of emphasis on travel, transportation, and your vehicle. You may go on a trip. This could involve driving or at least parking at the airport. If you're looking for a new car or truck, you have good energy for making a solid deal.

July 2022: *July 13 brings the full moon. There is a new moon on July 28. Also, on July 28, Jupiter goes retrograde. Your high-energy days are:1, 7, 13, 19, and 25.*

July brings a lot of interaction with siblings or younger relatives. You might visit family members who live far away. During this month, you might work on the family tree or genealogy and discover your ancestors and the history of your family line.

July 7 brings the Fire Sheep month and an Ox native, over the next four weeks might find you are overlooked when you should receive acknowledgment or recognition. During this time, your energy is a bit hidden, and so it will be essential for you to stand up and take credit for the things you're doing. This could happen at work. But also at home, where you are toiling away, few people acknowledge how hard you're working.

The full moon is on July 13, and you might finish a legal matter or gain a professional license. You could take an online continuing education course for your job, take a government test for your real estate license, or become a notary public. If you have been involved in an ongoing legal case, it may conclude over the next week or two.

The new moon is on July 28, and you may host family or friends at home. This would include some young children or pets. The entire house is turned upside down with joy and laughter. This is a good time for outdoor barbecues, swim parties, or packing a picnic lunch and taking it to the beach.

August 2022: *August 12 brings the full moon. Uranus goes retrograde on August 24. There is a new moon on August 27. Your high-energy days are: 6, 12, 18, 24, and 30.*

August brings you more luck than usual. Ox native, your guardian angel is quite active over the next few weeks. This could mean you are taking some risks possibly, doing some sports or other physical activities. Take some risks socially as well. Reach out to people you want to meet, even influencers or people of high social standing. You could make a connection.

August 7 brings the Earth Monkey month, and over the next four weeks, you have access to additional resources. For example, if you want to build a website, you might realize that your daughter's boyfriend knows precisely how to do it. If you need a loan, you might find someone through your networking group or book club to help you. Ox native, you're already very good at manifesting opportunities and resources, but if you focus your energy now, you can get so much more.

August 11 is the full moon, and, Ox native, there's a lot of emphasis on your career now. A supervisor may be out on vacation or leave. Now, the power (and the responsibilities) is falling on your shoulders. As you prove to others that you can handle more, you put yourself in the line for future success. During this period, you could build your confidence.

The new moon is on August 27, and there's romance in the air. You and your sweetheart might do some fun (and sexy) things together. This could include dinners out or ballroom dancing. Perhaps you are doing a hobby together, such as golfing, water skiing, or gambling at the local casino. There's fun to be had over the next two weeks.

September 2022: *On September 10, there is a full moon, and Mercury goes retrograde. On September 25, there's the new moon. Your high-energy days are: 5, 11, 17, 23, and 29.*

September brings a focus on your money and potential investments. A friend may come to you and ask you to invest in their business. You might find an unusual investment quite intriguing. Consider doing currency trading, buying land, or selling off your beanie baby collection or other collectibles for profit.

September 7 begins the Earth Rooster month, and there is an emphasis on education. Ox native, you might send the kids off to school or attend school yourself. Over the next four weeks, you could prepare for a professional test or renew your professional license. There will be quite a few nights where you are focused on homework of some kind (either your children's homework or your own.)

The full moon is on September 10, and the same day, Mercury goes retrograde. Ox native, an old flame may come back into your life. This person may reach out to you on social media, or perhaps you run into them when you're shopping in town. There's still a smoldering flame of passion, but you (or this other person) may not be available for a relationship. This is just a walk down memory lane.

The new moon is on September 25, and Ox native, you're pretty busy at work. You may have a new position or project, and therefore you are dealing with the learning curve. There may be new management, and they are instituting new rules for the company and your department. It's a good idea to look at the processes you use to complete tasks. Don't get stuck in your ways. Look at what activities you can automate or perhaps delegate.

October 2022: *Mercury goes direct on October 2. On October 8, Pluto goes direct. There is a full moon on October 9. On October 23, Saturn goes direct. On October 25, there's a partial solar eclipse. On October 28, Jupiter goes retrograde. Mars goes retrograde on October 30. Your high-energy days are: 5, 11, 17, 23, and 29.*

October can be quite a lucky month for Ox natives. Mercury goes direct on October 2. The emphasis on work and career continues. You might hire an assistant. If you own a business, you may look for several new people to work for you. If you're hunting for a job, you might hire an interview coach or someone to help you spiff up your resume. Several opportunities are coming your way, and you could field offers soon.

October 8 brings the Metal Dog month, and over the next four weeks, others are noticing you. This means you can attract knowledgeable and helpful people to you. If needed, you can find medical professionals, a lawyer to help you with contracts, and some help at home for housekeeping or care for a family member. You're now considerably lucky at attracting quality help.

The full moon is on October 9, and there's an emphasis on routines and the processes you use to get through the day. You might be ready to drop a an unhealthy habit and embrace a new lifestyle. You could be inspired by a friend's success or a video you saw. Soon you may find you're reading everything you can get your hands on about health and well-being. You may take up meditation, learn to care for yourself through herbs or explore alternative medicine practices such as acupuncture.

The solar eclipse is on October 25, and a person close to you has a significant life change. This energy will ripple through your life. This could mean that your partner gets a job offer requiring a move to the other side of the country. Or you may decide to move from the city to a rural area and work remotely. Or one of your older children may have a big announcement to make that affects you and the rest of the family.

November 2022: *November 8 brings the total lunar eclipse. On November 23, there is a new moon, and Jupiter goes direct. Your high-energy days are: 4, 10, 16, 23, and 28.*

November shows you are meeting new people and making good connections. A former colleague or supervisor may reach out to you with a job opportunity. Or you may be tempted to go back into a business you've done before. You may feel entirely drawn to step back into the familiar, but you're still in a seed planting time, and so you do best when you do something new.

November 7 brings the Metal Pig month, and Ox native, you may recognize that it's time to upgrade your technology. You might get a new phone, laptop, or some peripheral equipment.

Some Ox natives will install solar power for the home. Also, you could teach others how to use a specific piece of technology or take a class yourself.

The lunar eclipse is on November 8, and there is some intense energy for Ox natives. Changes that begun last month are now very much affecting your life. You might consider a job change, a move, or altering some aspect in a meaningful relationship. While this could feel stressful at the moment, a few months from now, you will know that you made the right decisions. This is the time to go with your gut.

The new moon is on November 23, and the energy settles down considerably. Ox native, now you see you have many more helpful people around you. People seem to line up to ask you what they can do for you. Enlist others to help you with cherished goals, especially business, financial planning, or investments.

December 2022: *Neptune goes direct on December 3. The full moon is on December 8. There is a new moon on December 23. Mercury goes retrograde on December 29. Your high-energy days are: 4, 10, 16, 23, and 28.*

December brings an opportunity to feel more spiritually connected. Slow down and take more time off, maybe doing yoga or some form of meditation. This is an excellent time to refresh feng shui cures and to put the house in order.

On December 7, it's the Water Rat month, and also the full moon. A change of activities and a better diet gives you a lot of energy. You may find you are sleeping better and waking up ready to take on the day. There is a financial opportunity on the horizon, and it's time to consider getting outside your comfort zone to take on this challenge. A person comes along to play the role of mentor or advisor, giving you all the information you need.

December 23 is the new moon, and you're likely feeling more spiritually connected. You might attend religious services or do spiritual rituals at home. The home may be decorated for the holidays, and you might be in the kitchen, making traditional foods to serve your family. This is a great time to meditate on the year ahead and look at what you want to be doing a year from now. Trust in your ability to manifest this vision.

On December 29, Mercury goes retrograde. Over the next few weeks, you may find that any New Year's resolutions you have, get off to a very rough start. Ox native, don't be too hard on yourself, as the energy during this time is focused on looking backward, not in the future. Instead, review the past year to see what you learned and get clear about how you want to do better in the future.

January 2023: *January 6 brings the full moon. Mercury goes direct on January 18. The year of the water rabbit begins on January 22. Your high-energy days are. 3, 9, 15, 21, and 27.*

In January, you may be traveling. You might be off for a business trip or see relatives living in the next county or an adjacent state. You might travel to get out of the cold weather. Ox native, you could go some6place you have never been to before. Mercury is still retrograde, so your luggage may or may not arrive at the same place you do.

January 5 begins the Water Ox month, your month, which brings you the best time for doing new activities. Consider doing as many new things as you can think of—change toothpaste, try an ethnic cuisine for the first time, or take an alternative route to work. Even these minor changes can bring new opportunities. Of course, the greater the change, the better results you're going to get. And this could mean planning a career change, a move across the country, or a radical change in your diet.

The full moon is on January 6. Ox native, education comes back into focus. If you're in school, you might get back into the swing of things, remembering how to study and take tests. Or you help your kids with these activities. It's possible that over the last few months, studying has not been as interesting as you would've hoped, and now you (or one of your kids) is behind schedule. Now you can get caught up.

On January 18, Mercury goes direct, and now you're working on a lot of paperwork. You could do your taxes or shred old records. You can clear out past energies through accounting and boost future energy by keeping track of your finances.

The new moon is on January 22, bringing the beginning of the Year of the Water Rabbit. You are now entering your third seed planting period. During this time, many of the changes you've made over the last year or two are starting to solidify. There will be less disruption this year. You will enjoy the peaceful Rabbit energy. At the same time, you need to continue to ask for what you want as you flex your manifesting muscles.

Attract New Love

When attracting new love into your life, Ox native, it's good to take a philosophical approach in the Year of the Water Tiger. Examine your personal beliefs about how people connect and why you will find a great love match. Love and attraction boil down to chart connections (also known as soul connections). As you meet someone, you recognize whether or not there is a connection. In 2022, opportunities come when you put yourself in different places such as classes, conferences, spiritual get-togethers, and certainly when you're traveling. Recognize that this could be the year where a random seat assignment puts you seated next to your future sweetheart.

Potpourri: To attract new love this year, take a silver-toned bowl and place it on your bedside table. Place dried rose petals and other sweet-smelling herbs in the bowl. Write your wish for a new love relationship on a tiny piece of paper and put it in the bowl among the rose petals. About once a month, stir up rose petals and other herbs or replace them with fresh potpourri. This will re-energize the cure and bring new opportunities to you.

Enhance Existing Love

For Ox natives already in a love relationship, everything is aligning in your favor. If you're dating, you might take your relationship to the next level by proposing or actually having the wedding ceremony. You may celebrate a special anniversary by taking a 2nd honeymoon or perhaps 2nd renewing your vows. You seem more committed to each other and more determined to have peace, comfort, and harmony in your love relationships during the Year the Water Tiger. In fact, your friends are lifting you up as a role model for a happy love life in 2022.

Orchid: For those of you born in the Year of the Ox, promote love energy in your home by adding orchids. Orchids have gained tremendous popularity in recent years. You can find orchids in garden shops as well as the local grocery store. Orchids have long symbolized love, luxury, and beauty.

Choose an orchid with beautiful blooms and place the plant in your bedroom or family room. When the orchid loses its blooms and goes into its resting phase, continue to water and care for the plant.

When temperatures drop, a cared-for orchid will develop a bloom spike. They will continue to grow in cold weather, then produce blooms as temperatures turn warmer. Most orchids bloom once per year. If you can't wait for the new blooms to appear, just buy another orchid to display.

Looking to Conceive?

Rice Under Bed: In many parts of China, women who want to conceive place a bowl of uncooked rice under their bed. If you would like to test this traditional approach to becoming pregnant, take a decorative bowl made of porcelain or china and fill it about two-thirds full with uncooked rice (white rice is traditional). Place the bowl in the center, underneath the bed. Do not disturb the bowl until the baby is born.

(From Donna Stellhorn's book, Fertility Feng Shui)

Family and Kids

There are some changes at home. Older kids may move out or go off to college this year. 2022 and the Year of the Water Tiger may have you all out of the home more than you have been in a couple of years. Traveling together is possible, and you might consider camping, getting an RV to travel to national parks, or trying out an Airbnb. There's also the opportunity to welcome some distant relatives who are traveling to your area. These might be people you don't know well, but the more, the merrier.

Turtle Stack: To help you feel more safe and secure wherever you land, use the representation of the turtle to bring protection energy to you. In fact, three turtles would be even better. Find a figurine of three turtles stacked one on top of another. This represents protection, friendships, and security through community. Each turtle has everything they need with them to protect them no matter what comes. Place the figurine on your nightstand or in your family room.

Money

Money opportunities open up. You may receive more credentials or finished a college degree in the last year. This could lead to a promotion and a salary increase. There are also quite a few opportunities for making money through passive income sources. You may have been studying these for the last few years, and now you're ready to pull the trigger. Your ability to receive money centers on a shift in your philosophy regarding money. You have been frugal in the past, but now, you may be categorized as super frugal in the Year of the Water Tiger. And you're putting that extra money to good use, sending it out to make you more money through interest and dividends.

Ocean Wave: To stimulate monetary flow this year, add a picture of moving water to your home office or entryway. Position the picture, so the water seems to flow into the house.

The picture can be large or small, it can be a photo or a painting, and it can be of the ocean, a river, or a waterfall.

Job or Career

There's a strong possibility of some career shifts this year for Ox natives. You may have been thinking about making a career change last year, but the opportunity you wanted did not manifest. Now everything is lining up to help you get a new job or even a new vocation. If you're thinking about staying at your current company, the Universe may have other plans. It's wise to check to see if your company is financially solid before committing yourself to stay. Additionally, shifts in management may make the current job less enjoyable. Allow yourself to dream about changes in your career, and the Universe will make the doors quite obvious.

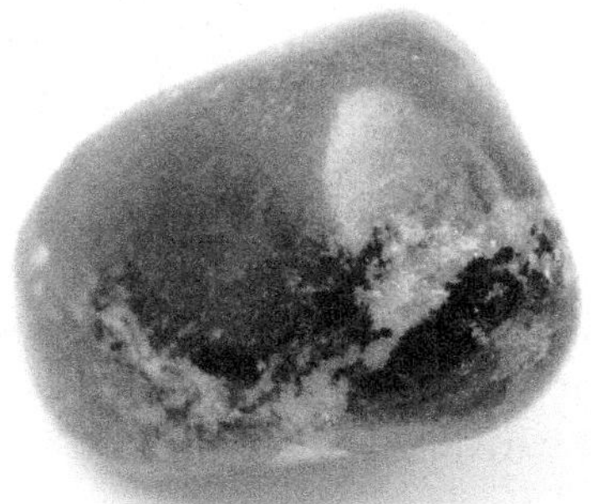

Lapis: Lapis has been called the gemstone of kings. It's a blue, opaque stone with flecks of pyrite that sparkle like gold. It's often made into jewelry, but you can also find small, tumbled pieces to carry your pocket or purse. Wear or carry the stone to remind yourself of your value and worth. Wash the stone with soap and water about once a week to clear it. This will help re-energize the stone. You can also carry this stone with you when you're going on job interviews to give you a boost in that area. If you prefer not to carry the stone with you, place it on your desk at work or at home or put it where you do financial matters in the home.

Education

Education is one of the most substantial areas for you in the Year of the Water Tiger. However, it will take concentration and focus to find the best institution or course of study that is aligned with your goals. You usually prefer to take a traditional route, which often means through a university and pursuing a four-year degree. In 2022, accelerated programs could offer a quick certificate of achievement and be a financially savvy way to go forward. However, consider carefully before investing in an extended program, as once you get in, you may find it's not as practical or as engaging as you'd hoped. On the other hand, video programs or vocational studies could hold the key to what you're looking for this year.

Legal Matters

There are some challenges around legal matters in 2022. The Year of the Water Tiger is naturally contentious. Ox native, you can be a little stubborn and could end up locking horns with an estranged partner, lousy boss, or a problematic neighbor. There are opportunities to settle out of court, but you would well to avoid legal entanglements entirely, as luck is not on your side with lawsuits in 2022. On the other hand, dealing with government agencies, gaining professional licenses, or building permits will all go smoothly.

Health and Well-Being

Your overall health improves during the Year of the Water Tiger. You may do more physical activities with your kids or get involved in a sport. You also may do more gardening and be in nature, which always gives you an emotional and physical boost. Ox native, the best thing you can do for your health this year is shift your thinking to the positive. You're very pragmatic, and sometimes this can lead you to a pessimistic outlook. But for the Water Tiger year, you'll see many opportunities open up for you. Yes, there are changes you need to make. As you look for the silver lining and recognize your talents and abilities, your general well-being increases, and so does your overall happiness.

Mirror Bagua: One Feng Shui cure I recommend for Ox Natives this year is the mirror; mirrors have many uses in Feng Shui. A particular mirror is recognized as a powerful symbol of protection, stronger than an ordinary mirror. It's known as the "Bagua mirror." This cure most commonly comprises an octagon-shaped wood frame with a small circular mirror in the center.

Symbols designed to attract the energy of protection and harmony are carved into or painted on the wooden frame. This type of mirror is never used facing into the house; it is always used pointing out of the house. Place or hang the mirror in a window facing outward. Specifically, to help protect your health, hang it in your bedroom or bathroom window. This will keep negative energy at bay.

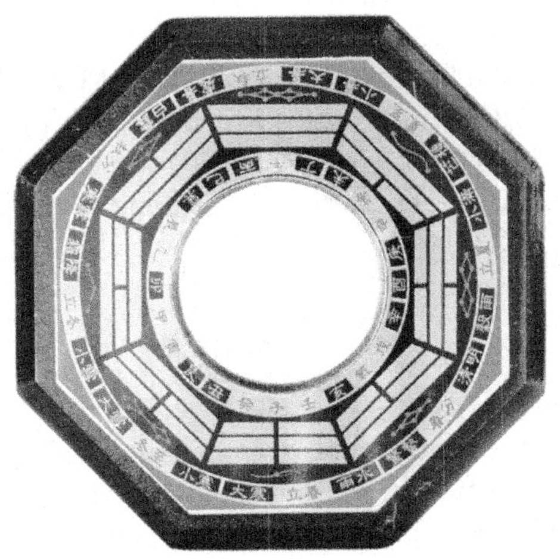

Tiger

February 8, 1902–January 28, 1903: Yang Water Tiger
January 26, 1914–February 13, 1915: Yang Wood Tiger
February 13, 1926–February 1, 1927: Yang Fire Tiger
January 31, 1938–February 18, 1939: Yang Earth Tiger
February 17, 1950–February 5, 1951: Yang Metal Tiger
February 5, 1962–January 24, 1963: Yang Water Tiger
January 23, 1974–February 10, 1975: Yang Wood Tiger
February 9, 1986–January 28, 1987: Yang Fire Tiger
January 28, 1998–February 15, 1999: Yang Earth Tiger
February 14, 2010–February 2, 2011: Yang Metal Tiger
February 1, 2022–January 21, 2023: Yang Water Tiger

Tiger Personality

There are two ways to think about Tiger. First and most apparent, consider the beautiful beast in its jungle habitat, hiding in the tall grass, patiently waiting for his prey. A herd of antelope lopes into view, pausing at the local waterhole. The Tiger watches and waits until one not too bright antelope wanders away from the herd. Lunchtime!

But that's only one aspect of the Tiger. There is also an impatient side, the "bounce-bounce-bounce energy" we saw in

Tigger, the Tiger of Winnie the Pooh fame. This Tiger is the impulsive, leap-before-you-look energy.

Those born during the year of the Tiger have a personality combining these two aspects. They are both patient and spontaneous. For instance, they can be very patient when they are stalking something they want. But when they find it, they jump in, completely committing themselves to having it, with no thought to the consequences.

The Tiger is a powerful sign, the second most powerful (and also second most popular) of all the Chinese Zodiac. People born under this sign are rebellious and unpredictable, but they command our respect. They are ready for anything. Overall, they love life, and they want to experience it fully. Sometimes this sits well with those around them, and sometimes it doesn't.

Those born in the Year of the Tiger are suspicious. They don't trust easily. When their suspicions are confirmed, they are quick-tempered and will say whatever is on their mind. Be cautious of a Tiger's temper—after all, they have sharp claws.

Tiger also has a gentle side. Tigers are very affectionate and devote themselves to those they care about. They can hug, snuggle and purr, just like a soft little kitten.

Tigers are dreamers and artists at heart. At the mere suggestion of it, they are ready to fly off to Bali with you. They will join your band. They will audition when the reality show comes to town looking for contestants. Everything is possible!

Tiger people may spend their entire lives running after exciting adventures. Or they may have short periods of rebellion when they quit their job, leave their relationship, and throw caution to the wind. The rest of us watch and hope the Tiger succeeds.

Tigers are emotional; their highs are really high, and their lows are very low. When the low periods happen, Tiger needs a shoulder to cry on. It will tempt others to offer advice, but

Tigers won't listen. As a Tiger, you've learned it's better to stick with who you are and know that tomorrow is another day.

Tigers can be very charismatic and influence others when they put their mind to it. They make compelling speakers, teachers, and politicians. Tigers are charming; potential lovers fall for their flattery. The passion will burn hot—at least for a while.

But when the initial excitement is over, Tiger can fall out of love just as quickly as they fell into it and just drift away. If the object of their attention strays away from them, Tiger is quickly back on the hunt, eager to renew the chase.

Tiger: Predictions for 2022

How to use your High-Energy Days: On these days, plan to take action for your most important goals, make vital phone calls, send important emails. Your high-energy days are when your energy and luck are the strongest for the month.

January 2022: *January 2 is the new moon. January 14 has Mercury going retrograde. January 17 is the full moon. On January 18, Uranus goes direct. On January 29, Venus goes direct. Your High-Energy Days are 4, 10, 16, 22, and 28.*

January begins as some of the dust settles from the changes of the past month. Tiger natives who are dating can now move toward a committed, monogamous relationship. Happiness grows as you focus on communicating with each other and having fun together. For those Tiger natives in an established relationship, positive energy abounds—especially in every aspect of your intimate life. There is a lot of fun behind closed doors.

January 2 brings the new moon, and you may be impatient for the fresh energy to begin next month. However, you're in the last month of the Metal Ox year, and it is time to finish up the little bits left from the previous 12-year cycle. It's a good idea to project possibilities and plan where you want to be a year from now, three years from now, and five years from now. Sit down with trusted friends (choosing some of the most adventurous ones) and talk about your plans.

On January 14, Mercury goes retrograde, slowing down the energy. Now, be careful about leaping too soon. You're still in the planning stages for the future, so even if you want to jump into a business or a new relationship, now is the time to be patient. (It's rare when things move as quickly as a Tiger native wishes!)

There is a full moon on January 17, and if you're in school, things are in full swing. You pay a lot of attention to your projects right now. Consider investing and passive income sources. You could make money by getting a real estate license or other professional certification.

On January 19, the energy shifts, and your luck is very strong now. You feel the synchronicity as things come together. However, it may still not exactly be the energy you're wishing or waiting for. Perhaps a job comes your way, but it may not offer the right pay or the actual duties or type of work you're looking for. You may have to wait just a few more weeks to find yourself in the full flow of Tiger energy in 2022.

February 2022: *February 1 is the new moon and begins the Year of the Water Tiger. February 3, Mercury goes direct. February 16 is the full moon. Your high-energy days are: 3, 9, 15, 21, and 27.*

The Water Tiger year begins on February 1, and there may be some changes in your life right out of the gate. This is a year of new beginnings, which is no problem for Tiger natives. However, you may feel like there are obstacles in your life that weren't there before. People are saying "no," and there are sudden restrictions or unexpected hurdles. Look at it as an obstacle course you would do for fun, as these challenges are indications you're going in the right direction. This is just the Universe's way of helping you blaze a new trail.

There is a new moon on February 1. Now, you may have a better idea of what you want to pursue. But you may feel you don't have the proper training or that you need an official certificate. There will be many projects you want to start this year, but there will always be obstacles—some real and some imagined. Maybe you want to get a degree, but the question is, do you need the degree? There may be a way to go forward without it.

February 3 brings the Water Tiger month, and Mercury moves direct. This is the most potent "seed planting" time you will experience this year. This means the more new things you try, the more opportunities will manifest throughout the year. 2022 is about changing big things in your life, but you may start by shifting some small things. For example, change brands of shampoo, give up soda pop and just drink water, take an alternate route to work, etc. The seeds you plant now will grow into something you can harvest later.

The full moon is on February 16, and you may receive some recognition at your job. There's a possibility of a promotion or a new position within your company that you can apply for. You can also assume a leadership role, move into management, or hire more employees if you own a business. You're very noticeable in all aspects of your life, so you may gain a board member position in a networking or community group.

March 2022: *March 2 is the new moon. The full moon is on March 18. Your high-energy days are: 5, 11, 17, 23, and 29.*

March shows a lot of emphasis on your career and reputation. If you own a business, you might do more marketing, rebranding, or update your website. If you're looking for a job, your prospects are excellent. This is also an excellent time to ask for a raise, as you are likely to receive more responsibilities at work.

March 2 brings the new moon, and Tiger native, you might have a big announcement to make to the family. You could get engaged or get married. You and your sweetheart may buy a house together or lease an apartment to share. This is an exceptional time to make a big proclamation, especially on social media or to your friends.

March 5 begins the Water Rabbit month, and in the next four weeks, Tiger native, you could be fairly busy. There are lots of opportunities and projects to chase. You could feel you're juggling many options for your life. This is an excellent time to focus on financial goals. There could be an additional source of revenue available to you, or you may get a windfall from selling off stuff you already own.

The full moon is on March 17, and, Tiger native, there's a focus on home and family. You may finish up some renovations on your dwelling or finally unpack from a previous move. Because this is a Tiger year, you may move again over the course of the next three years. So if you haven't moved recently, a move is probably going to happen relatively soon. This is also a time when you may deal with difficult relatives or have arguments within the family.

In some parts of the world, there will be a second new moon on March 31, and for other time zones, it will be on April 1. This new moon brings a focus on technology. You might look at getting a new computer or update your skills on a software platform or tech device. This is also a time when there is more interaction in the community. You might join a group of like-minded people or do some charity work around this time.

April 2022: *April 1 is the new moon. The full moon is on April 16. On April 29, Pluto goes retrograde. There is a partial solar eclipse on April 30. Your high-energy days are: 4, 10,* 16, 23, and 28.

April focuses you on friendships and acquaintances of all kinds. This is a great time to do some professional networking and meet people who can help you in your career. You may also expand your circle of friends by meeting friends of friends or by joining group activities. Tiger native, you're totally gregarious, and people will often seek you out to make your acquaintance.

On April 4, the Wood Dragon month begins, and a romantic opportunity may open up for you. If you're looking for love, you can find someone with whom you have great chemistry. This might be a whirlwind romance, one that is passionate and so intense it makes your head spin. If you're already in a committed partnership, you may feel quite passionate over the next four weeks.

The full moon is on April 16, and Tiger native, there's an emphasis on children and fertility. If you're looking to add to the family (or adopt a pet), you can find people who are pretty helpful now. If you already have children, you are likely to spend more time with them than usual. You might help them with school or help them choose a college.

There is a solar eclipse on April 30, and over the next two weeks, something you thought was done may come back to show you it needs more work. This could be a completed project returning to you or a debt you thought was already paid. This solar eclipse gives you a chance to deal with it once and for all. This is also a time where your words can go viral. Be careful what you post on social media, as your posts may get a much wider viewership than usual.

May 2022: *On May 10, Mercury goes retrograde. There is a total lunar eclipse on May 16. On May 30, there is a new moon. Your high-energy days are: 4, 10, 16, 23, and 28.*

During May, you may look for some downtime. You may be working behind the scenes on a huge project. Or you're out of the office for some much-needed time off. This is also an excellent time to take a step back and look at how the year is going. Consider updating your goal board and renewing your commitment to your big goals.

May 5 brings the Wood Snake month, and over the next four weeks, there is a lot of energy focused on home and family. Kids may get out of school, or you might graduate. You could think about moving in the next few months, and so you could make some preparations such as selling off excess stuff and packing what you're taking with you. Also, home renovations and home repairs are possible during this time.

On May 10, Mercury goes retrograde. Tiger native, there's a lot of emphasis on relationships now. You may revisit a relationship from your past. Or a relationship you thought was over now seems to ignite again. It's also possible that a connection you walked away from, a relationship, friendship, or partnership, now returns to ask for another shot. Mercury retrograde is a temporary aspect. However, it is your time to look at what you have let go of and see if you want to reconsider your decision.

There is a lunar eclipse on May 15, and Tiger native, there can be some changes at your job. An essential coworker may leave, and now the team is shorthanded. Or there may be new procedures that are not to your liking. It can feel like there are emotional blocks and substantial obstacles in your life now. You generally might like your job, but you may be unhappy with specific aspects of it. You're likely making some decisions about your position over the next few weeks.

The new moon is on May 30, and you are in the spotlight. You're more noticeable now and can gain help and resources. This energy is for relationships in general. You can meet someone new for a love relationship or meet someone who becomes a close friend. You can take an existing partnership and strengthen it through more communication and doing more activities together.

June 2022: *Mercury goes direct on June 3. On June 4, Saturn goes retrograde. On June 14, there is a full moon. Neptune goes retrograde on June 28. The new moon is on June 29. Your high-energy days are:3, 9, 15, 21, and 27.*

In June, Tiger native, you may start new projects or take a leadership role within a group or organization. The battle cry is "full steam ahead." You may not be sure of how you're going to accomplish your goal, but as soon as you start moving forward, things just click into place. It's time to check your feelings of hesitation at the door.

June 5 brings the Fire Horse month and romance on its way. If you're already in a relationship, you could strengthen your bond by complimenting and encouraging each other's finer qualities. If you're looking for love, this is one of your best months for connecting with someone with whom you have a lot in common.

The full moon is on June 14, and you may connect with a new business partner, mentor, or be collaborating with an influencer. You may sign a contract outlining all the details of this agreement. This could give your career or business quite a boost. It's a good idea to clear up some space in your schedule so you have time to devote to this connection.

June 28 is the new moon, and a financial windfall is possible. Your business could have an increase in sales, or you might get more hours at your job. Receiving a promotion with a salary increase is also entirely possible. There's a slight chance that this was money you were expecting, but it's more likely these funds come to you suddenly and could be a sign of a new, steady flow of revenue.

July 2022: *July 13 brings the full moon. There is a new moon on July 28. Also, on July 28, Jupiter goes retrograde. Your high-energy days are:3, 9, 15, 21, and 27.*

In July, you might be totally enthusiastic about a business idea or a new hobby. You could think about this night and day, gather the resources you will need, and tell your friends all about it. Tiger, it's well known you jump in without hesitation. This is one time when you should completely immerse yourself.

July 7 brings the Fire Sheep month, and over the next four weeks, it's a good idea to implement new systems to get more things done. Some people procrastinate out of fear, but typically you procrastinate out of boredom. You don't enjoy doing the same thing repeatedly. Look at how you can make your daily tasks more interesting through innovative thinking.

The full moon is on July 13, and over the next two weeks, there are challenges when trying to fund a loan, refinance a house, or sell off an investment. You'll have to push against this vault door to get it to open and show you the money. It doesn't necessarily mean you are going in the wrong direction. It's just going to take more time and effort than you thought. Try to be patient with the process.

The new moon is on July 28, and over the next two weeks, new opportunities are coming from some unexpected sources. It's possible you are signing a contract or doing a handshake deal that could be entirely beneficial in the future. You may think about moving forward in your life in a literal sense and look for a new car or truck to buy. It's possible to get a good deal now.

August 2022: *August 12 brings the full moon. Uranus goes retrograde on August 24. There is a new moon on August 27. Your high-energy days are: 2, 8, 14, 20, and 26.*

In August, you're brimming with ideas. You're making plans and possibly travel reservations. It's possible that you're going back to school or you're sending children off to college. Tiger, this is your year, a time for breaking new ground and planting seeds. The more you can learn and explore, the bigger your harvest will be.

August 7 brings the Earth Monkey month, and relationships may be a little challenging for the next four weeks. You're busy. Your partner is busy and important things are falling through the cracks. As you break out of your routine, this could disturb the delicate dynamic of the household. But this is temporary. When the commotion settles down in a few weeks, not only will you have weathered the storm, you will be a better sailor.

August 11 is the full moon, and you may have travel plans. You may plan a vacation, a camping trip, or to attend an out-of-state conference. There could be some delays along the way. It's wise to get refundable tickets as you may need to make changes midstream. Remember to keep your sense of humor as things go wrong. You will find that the Universe has a grand plan, and you will see it unfold.

The new moon is on August 27, and now there's a focus on home and family. You may have visits from out-of-town relatives, or you may visit family members who live far away. You also may have a strong interest in genealogy or have your DNA tested to see where "your people" come from. Family members may pass family heirlooms to you. You may discuss shared property rights with siblings.

September 2022: *On September 10, there is a full moon, and Mercury goes retrograde. On September 25, there's the new moon. Your high-energy days are: 1, 7, 13, 19, and 25.*

September puts the focus on getting things done. You're like the Energizer Bunny right now, blazing through tasks, especially tasks around the house. You may have decided to go minimalist, and you're getting rid of excess stuff. Or you are looking at organizational systems and putting everything in its proper place. This is a good time to sell off goods on a service like eBay or Poshmark.

September 7 begins the Earth Rooster month, and over the next four weeks, there's a lot of attention on investments, debt, and how to save for retirement. You may shift money around as the market has done some gyrations lately. There's a possibility of consolidating debt at a lower interest rate, especially student loan debt. But read everything carefully before signing to make sure you're getting the best deal.

The full moon is on September 10, and the same day, Mercury goes retrograde, and someone from your past returns. This could be an old lover or close friend. And now you can see how much you've grown and changed through their eyes. Soon you're rehashing old times and laughing together. It feels like no time has passed between the two of you.

The new moon is on September 25, and there's a great deal of focus on creativity, fertility, and children. You may look at your legacy from now on. If you want to add to the family, you have positive energy for finding help with medical issues as well as help with adoption (this includes adopting pets). If you already have kids, you are spending more time with them, perhaps as they are debuting in the school play or trying out for a sports team.

October 2022: *Mercury goes direct on October 2. On October 8, Pluto goes direct. There is a full moon on October 9. On October 23, Saturn goes direct. On October 25, there's a partial solar eclipse. On October 28, Jupiter goes retrograde. Mars goes retrograde on October 30. Your high-energy days are:1, 7, 13, 19, and 25.*

October can be rather a fun month for Tiger natives. Mercury goes direct on October 2, and this could bring some adventure. You might be out four-wheeling, going skating, or doing indoor rock climbing. There's a sizable list of physical activities you might do now. If you're looking for love, it's entirely possible to meet somebody doing one of these bold, exhilarating activities.

October 8 brings the Metal Dog month, and there's an emphasis on spirituality. You may look within and discover more about yourself. This could be in conjunction with a personality test, some psychotherapy, or an astrology reading. You'll likely find a new sense of confidence as you learn more about yourself. Now you're discovering that the things your friends say about you are all true.

The full moon is on October 9. You look like you're connecting with a charitable organization or group of people who need assistance. You may volunteer some time at a food bank or teach seniors how to use their computers to talk to family members. You may step up to take a leadership role in an organization you belong to. This is also a suitable time to start a book club or other hobby club to gather like-minded people.

The solar eclipse is on October 25, and there are some issues around your job. A key person may be leaving to go to another company, and this means you are picking up extra responsibilities. There's also a strong possibility that the company you work for isn't as solid as it has been in the past. There could be some downsizing going on, or there could be cuts in hours or pay. You may have to look at this job and decide whether this is a place you want to stay or if it's time to move on.

November 2022: *November 8 brings the total lunar eclipse. On November 23, there is a new moon, and Jupiter goes direct. Your high-energy days are: 6, 12, 18, 24, and 30.*

November shows substantial opportunities for improvement in your health. You may get a great report from a medical professional or find benefits with alternative medicine. You could shift your diet to healthier fare or jump on the bandwagon with a new type of exercise. All of this can be beneficial for your body, mind, and spirit. You start reaping the benefits almost immediately.

November 7 brings the Metal Pig month, and a career opportunity is entirely possible. Over the next few weeks, you may get an offer for a new job. Someone you worked with previously may reach out to you about a position open in their current company. If you own a business, you are likely expanding your team and territory. More profits are flowing your way.

The lunar eclipse is on November 8. Over the next two weeks, you may notice you are falling back into old bad habits especially staying up too late, watching a lot of TV, or playing video games late into the night. This also may be connected to people you are associating with. If you feel drained after seeing a particular person, it may be time for you to move on from that relationship.

The new moon is on November 23, and you may hear clinking champagne glasses as you attend a celebration, special anniversary, or wedding. There could be a birth in the family, bringing joy to the household. You may attend a friend's bridal shower, baby shower, or a happy retirement party. Your datebook may be filled with different celebrations over the next couple of weeks.

December 2022: *Neptune goes direct on December 3. The full moon is on December 8. There is a new moon on December 23. Mercury goes retrograde on December 29. Your high-energy days are: 6, 12, 18, 24, and 30.*

December brings positive and exciting relationship energy. If you're looking for love, you may meet somebody while doing something for a charity, with your church, or through your extended family. You could receive several party invitations which bring an opportunity to meet someone new. Allow your friends and family to fix you up on dates, as they would like to see you in a happy relationship.

On December 7, it's the Water Rat month. Additionally, it's also the full moon. There's very positive energy around friendships. You're absolutely magnetic with new connections, and you can attract people into your life, even people of high standing like celebrities. At the same time, some work/life balance is necessary now. If you have been working too hard, it's time to take a little time off.

December 23 is the new moon, and this energy lends itself to end of the year tax planning. This is a good time to look at investments, and you could get tips from an investment-savvy uncle or a well-to-do friend. You may also get some assistance with your business in the form of extra funding. This could come through family, close friends, or someone who believes in you and your vision.

On December 29, Mercury goes retrograde, and over the next couple of weeks, use caution when purchasing online to make sure that your credit card is not compromised. Take some time to change passwords on banking websites and financial apps. This is an excellent time to get a document safe for the home to ensure all your important papers are in one place.

January 2023: *January 6 brings the full moon. Mercury goes direct on January 18. The year of the water rabbit begins on January 22. Your high-energy days are: 5, 11, 17, 23, and 29.*

In January, there's a lot of energy around an intimate relationship. You and your partner may heal some old issues. The two of you could have some deep, meaningful conversations or get a little outside help through counseling to tackle some challenges in your relationship. If you're looking for love, you can find someone very easy to talk with and stay up all night talking together.

January 5 begins the Water Ox month. The next couple of weeks, you may be more introspective, looking at the year and seeing what changed and what still needs to change in your life. As you review the year, you may see how much you've grown and the new directions that are opening up. Tiger year is almost over, and the spotlight will move off of you. But you're still in a seed planting time, and many new opportunities will come over the next two years.

The full moon is on January 6, and a financial opportunity presents itself. It's a little outside your comfort zone. That rarely makes you nervous. However, your schedule is pretty full right now, so you may weigh how you're going to handle the additional responsibilities. Delegating some tasks may be the solution.

On January 18, Mercury goes direct, and a love relationship suddenly comes together. Someone you were pursuing suddenly turns and starts pursuing you. At the same time, your phone could ring with someone from your past. Your popularity is rising, and now the fun can begin.

The new moon is on January 22, and this brings the Year of the Water Rabbit. You are now entering the second year of your seed planting period. This means you have many new opportunities on the horizon. Additionally, all the new things you started last year start to blossom, ripen, and get harvested by you. But now you have to shift gears. Water Rabbit energy of 2023 is much slower, more sedate than the previous year, 2022. It's wise to harmonize with this peace-loving energy. Take a breath, slow down, and let things come to you in their own time.

Attract New Love

For Tiger natives, the year of the Water Tiger represents new beginnings of all kinds, and this certainly includes attracting a new love relationship. You will have multiple opportunities throughout the year to find a suitable match. There will likely be an intense physical attraction between the two of you as well as spiritual compatibility. It's out with the old and in with the new. It's essential to let go of past heartbreaks and disappointments, especially if you are pining for someone who is no longer in your life. Clear out the old energy, box up pictures from the past, or even erase old phone numbers. In 2022, a clean slate is what you need to attract a love that makes your heart sing.

Bell, Sweet: When attracting a new love, call that person's energy to you with the sweet sound of a bell. The bell can be made of metal, porcelain, or any material, but it must have a sweet sound. You don't want to attract love with a bell that's off-key. Hang the bell from a yellow ribbon. Yellow is the color of friendship and mutual understanding.

Put the bell in your bedroom, where you can ring the bell at least once a day. (Do not hang the bell where you're going to bump your head into it.) If you want the relationship to start as a friendship and move slowly, hang your bell in the living room. Then move it to your bedroom when you want the relationship to become intimate.

Enhance Existing Love

In 2022, if you're already in a love relationship, things could be a little bumpy. Some of this is because there could be many aspects of your life that are changing. You could soon have a new job, move to a new location or start new projects. All this could create some stress in your current relationship. If you and your partner are born in the Year of the Water Tiger, you'll need a lot of open and honest communication to get the two of you going in the same direction; otherwise, you both could take different paths. If your sweetheart is not a Tiger, they will need to be extra understanding of the changes going on with you and your life circumstances. Regarding sexual compatibility, there is very positive energy. Everything's fine behind closed doors, but when the morning sun appears, that's when trouble can begin.

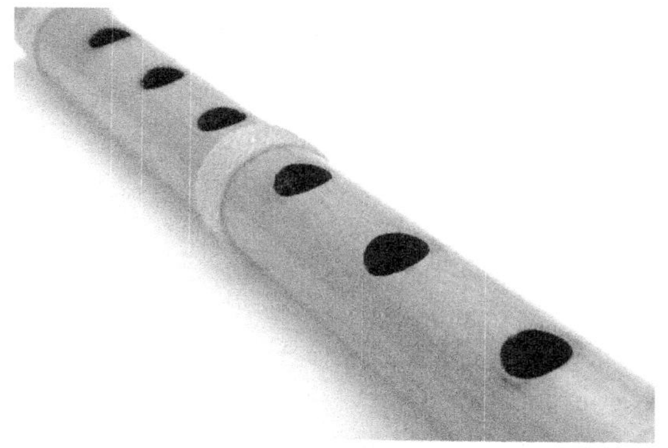

Flute: The sweet, soft sounds of a flute have been used in Feng Shui for ages to bring harmony to the energy in a home. This year, create harmony in your existing love relationship by hanging flutes. Simply take a pair of wooden flutes and hang them in the bedroom. Use a piece of red ribbon or string and tie the ends around each end of the flute. This will give you an easy way to hang the flute. See the diagram for hanging flutes below.

Looking to Conceive?

Rabbits: Rabbits are a universal symbol of procreation, so using the image of a rabbit will help bring fertility energy. Choose a figurine, hanging artwork of rabbits, or place a couple of little stuffed bunnies on the bed. But remember, you need two rabbits to make things happen, so make sure there's more than one hare depicted in the bedroom.

What would be even better than a figurine of a pair of rabbits? Chocolate bunnies, of course. Chocolate has long been known for its aphrodisiac qualities. These delicious rabbits will put you both in the mood.

(From Donna Stellhorn's book, Fertility Feng Shui)

Family and Kids

Good communication is key during the Year of the Water Tiger. Old traditions and ways of doing things will no longer cut the mustard for yourself and any other Tigers in the household. In 2022, you might look for a new place to live or look at your house in a new way. This might mean renting out part of your home, refinancing your mortgage, or doing some major renovations. With so much activity at home, this can be rather disruptive, especially to those non-Tigers in the household. Here's where open communication comes in. If you're tight-lipped about the changes you want to make, you might end up shocking and disturbing the entire family.

Hematite: For extra protection energy, those born in the year of the Tiger can carry a piece of hematite with them. Hematite is an unusual stone that looks like metal and feels like it weighs more than it should. You can carry this stone with you in your purse or pocket or find a pendant or bracelet to wear made with hematite. Hematite is naturally magnetic and is made into lots of kinds of jewelry. Wear the piece anytime you want to feel a little extra courage.

Money

Money flows in slow and steady at the beginning of the year. Then the flow picks up speed as the year goes on. In the Year of the Water Tiger, you're likely starting some new money venture or investment, which could mean some initial start-up costs. You might start a business or go back to school. While these types of activities could pay off in a few months or a couple of years, initially, it can feel like there's much more going out than coming in. That said, the second half of the year is much stronger for income. You are getting better at budgeting, being thrifty, and mindfully using your money. 2022 is also good for creating passive income sources. However, these may not pay off until later in the year, or you may have to wait until 2023 to see profits.

The Lucky Money Cat is an example of a cultural symbol that effectively shifts the energy of a home and brings in prosperity opportunities. The story of the lucky cat is told of a poor priest whose job it was to maintain a temple in the woods far from the village. No one came to visit the temple, and so the priest had no income, and yet he dutifully maintained the temple, keeping it clean, lighting the incense, and praying.

One day a cat came to the temple, and even though the priest had hardly enough food for himself, he divided his dinner each night and fed the cat. So the cat stayed. What the priest didn't know was this was a magical cat.

Months later, a nobleman was riding his horse through the forest to a neighboring town. There was a great storm, and the nobleman got off his horse and took shelter under a tree. In the flashes of lightning, he could see the temple. On the temple steps sat a little cat. To his surprise, the cat sat up on his haunches and motioned for the nobleman to approach. Intrigued, he left the shelter of the tree and went to the temple.

At that moment, lightning struck the tree. The nobleman recognized he would have died if not for the little cat. So he spent his life and his fortune supporting the cat, the temple, and the priest.

To attract more income this year, place a Lucky Money Cat in your living room or home office. Place it in the far corner of the room and have him face the door. The Lucky Cat has his hand raised to call in money. Often these little statues are banks. Remember to feed him with coins and keep feeding him until the little bank is full. Then dust him regularly to re-energize him.

Job or Career

There is a lot of positive energy in the Year of the Water Tiger for Tiger natives regarding career. If you are looking to move up in your current company or get a new job, you have a lot of support to achieve your goals. You may get a better job because you passed a professional exam or recently finished some education. It will be a struggle this year to stay in your current position without some sort of change. This is a year of change, so trying to stay in an old job is tempting fate. You also prove adept at gaining company stock, maxing out your 401(k), or getting other perks from your company.

Gold Flakes remind us of wealth accumulation and abundance through seemingly small actions. You can attract positive money energy by placing a vial of actual gold flakes on a table near your front door. (Gold flakes are available in gem and mineral shops and online.)

Write out your money goals and place them under the vial of gold flakes. Every few days, as you pass the table, pick up the vial and shake it; watch the gold flakes sparkle in the light and think about your goals for a moment. This will increase the positive money energy.

Education

You may have a compelling desire to go back to school this year. You may want to get a traditional education—go to a well-known school, get a four-year or graduate degree as you study hard, write reports and take exams. If you do some research, you could gain low-interest loans, grants, or scholarships in 2022 to help you pay for your education. You also show good energy around accelerated programs, especially those given by very reputable persons or companies, to leapfrog your way to success.

Legal Matters

Tiger natives need to be careful about legal matters in 2022. Unless you do legal activities for a living (in which case, you will be successful this year), you may find bringing suits or trying to get remedies through legal matters fairly difficult. In the Year of the Water Tiger, you will want to take any talk of lawsuits absolutely seriously. Avoid leaving everything to your lawyer. Instead, get involved and really be aware of what's happening. When getting permits, contracts signed, or a professional license, you show good energy in 2022. Legal activities such as these that you prepare for will go really well. But legal matters you try to do off-the-cuff could turn in the other guy's favor.

Health and Well-Being

For Tiger natives, your health and well-being are excellent for you in 2022. You do well when there is excitement and change, and this year is chock-full of both. You may wake up with lots of energy, be busy throughout the day and then sleep peacefully as a kitten at night. You may adopt a new sleeping routine they find works for you. With your health, there's an improvement as well. You may try out new exercises or new ways of eating that are very beneficial to your health and well-being. You might take up cooking, start growing vegetables in the garden, or you might find a healthy eating establishment that you frequent often. You bounce back from health issues, and in 2022, the Year of the Water Tiger, you're stronger and more energetic than usual.

Gourd: The Feng Shui gourd is a symbol related to health, longevity, and well-being. The gourd can be made of wood, metal, glass, or stone. It can also be a natural gourd that's been painted or otherwise decorated. You cab find gourds like these in Asian markets and art & crafts festivals.

Place the gourd in the bedroom or family room. You can tie a red ribbon around the center of the gourd to increase the energy. But do this only if no one living in the house is ill. If someone in the house is recovering from illness, place the gourd in the family room and not a bedroom.

Rabbit

January 29, 1903–February 15, 1904: Yin Water Rabbit
February 14, 1915–February 2, 1916: Yin Wood Rabbit
February 2, 1927–January 22, 1928: Yin Fire Rabbit
February 19, 1939–February 7, 1940: Yin Earth Rabbit
February 6, 1951–January 26, 1952: Yin Metal Rabbit
January 25, 1963–February 12, 1964: Yin Water Rabbit
February 11, 1975–January 30, 1976: Yin Wood Rabbit
January 29, 1987–February 16, 1988: Yin Fire Rabbit
February 16, 1999–February 4, 2000: Yin Earth Rabbit
February 3, 2011–January 22, 2012: Yin Metal Rabbit
January 22, 2023–February 9, 2024: Yin Water Rabbit

Rabbit Personality

It may surprise many, but I consider Rabbit one of the strongest Chinese Zodiac signs. Most imagine him as a fluffy bunny, an animal who cannot speak has no claws and short little legs to hop away with. But the Rabbit sits between the Chinese Signs of the Tiger and the Dragon in the Chinese Zodiac wheel, and he alone keeps these two powerful forces apart.

Rabbit (also called Hare in some translations) generally serves as the sign of kindness and sensitivity. People born under this sign have good manners, common sense, and the ability to soothe and comfort others. For this reason, Rabbit often winds up in a leadership position.

The Rabbit personality is neither forceful nor rash, and they have a way of bringing people together. Rabbit is the perfect arbitrator, networking expert, negotiator, or diplomat. They always have something positive to say about and to everyone.

Because of Rabbit's love of peace, people mistakenly view them as weak or even self-indulgent. Rabbit prefers to apply brain over brawn and will avoid a confrontation whenever possible. Often perceived as thin-skinned, Rabbit is merely cautious—after all, they don't want to be on anyone's menu! Rabbit can be a treasured friend, adept at keeping secrets and offering very sensible advice.

Rabbit people run in the best circles. They enjoy the finer things in life—everything from the restaurant's best table to the best parking space at the mall. Rabbit natives seek the easy way to do things, which often leads to the best side of town. They are often a little flashy, which helps them fit in perfectly with their A-list friends.

Rabbit is realistic yet sympathetic. They will listen to your troubles, and while they offer brilliant advice, they never push an agenda. As a parent, they are neither the disciplinarian nor are they given to criticism. They are optimistic and rarely embarrass their children in public.

In business, Rabbit's quiet, unassuming air can cause others to think they are not paying attention. But there's more to Rabbit than meets the eye. Before you know it, you have signed the contract or sealed the deal—with Rabbit taking the lion's share of the rewards. Despite this (and because of Rabbit's impeccable manners), you come away feeling grateful Rabbit was even willing to do business with you.

Rabbit: Predictions for 2022

How to use your High-Energy Days: On these days, plan to take action for your most important goals, make vital phone calls, send important emails. Your high-energy days are when your energy and luck are the strongest for the month.

January 2022: *January 2 is the new moon. Mercury goes retrograde on January 14. January 17 is the full moon. On January 18, Uranus goes direct. On January 29, Venus goes direct. Your High-Energy Days are 3, 9, 15, 21, and 27.*

January is the final month of the Metal Ox year, and it brings good relationship energy for Rabbit natives. This means you can connect with new friends and find suitable business partners. Those Rabbit natives currently in a love relationship enjoy an abundance of harmony at home. And if you're looking for love, it can come from a surprising direction or because of a chance meeting or a blind date.

On January 2, there's the new moon and a lot of connections with friends. People are calling you out of the blue, looking to reconnect. Invitations come in, and you may connect with many people you haven't seen in some time.

On January 14, Mercury goes retrograde and brings an emphasis on your finances. It's now time to evaluate what has been coming in and what has been going out. Check your bank statements and make sure there's been no fraudulent activity on your accounts. (Pull your credit report and see how you're doing on that front.) This is an excellent time to take classes in investing.

On January 17, there's a full moon, and you feel more confident and self-assured. You have been working hard on relationships and doing a great deal of inner work on yourself. You've been through a lot over the past two years, and you have every reason to be proud of how you've grown. You find you're more confident when doing job interviews and interacting with others in general. This attracts a lot of positive attention. For those Rabbit natives looking for love, this can make finding the right someone much more effortless.

On January 19, the energy shifts, and you may receive a windfall or financial benefit from investments. Consider how you can expand passive income sources or build your own business. This is not a time for taking significant risks; it's about doing what you know how to do and allowing more money to flow in. This is a great time to refresh your Feng Shui cures to bring prosperity.

February 2022: *February 1 is the new moon and begins the Year of the Water Tiger. February 3, Mercury goes direct. February 16 is the full moon. Your high-energy days are: 4, 10, 16, 23, and 28.*

The Water Tiger year begins on February 1, beginning the last year of your 12-year cycle. This is when you take everything you've learned over the previous 12 years and capitalize on it. There may be a desire to move forward, to jump into new projects, but this is a time of cleaning up and finishing up things from the past. Rabbit native, as the year moves forward, there will be opportunities to begin new things. But this month, focus on what needs to be finished.

This new moon energy on February 1 brings a focus on finances. There are considerable resources for you this year and especially this month. This means you can gain credit at a low interest rate or find an official to help you with a complex financial task. This is an excellent month to speak up and ask for help. Rabbit native, you like to be self-reliant, but consider how beneficial a little assistance could be this month.

February 3 brings the Water Tiger month, and Mercury moves direct. You may feel a considerable energy shift. Your intuition tells you that most people around you are feeling impatient, wanting to rebel against imaginary cages. You're likely standing back and observing this behavior, knowing you have the key to release yourself when you wish.

The full moon is on February 16, and Rabbit native, you might gain a financial windfall. Maybe a bonus, a raise, or a sum of money finds its way to you. You have a wonderful opportunity to create a passive source of income or start a side business with a cousin, sibling, or close friend.

March 2022: *March 2 is the new moon. The full moon is on March 18. Your high-energy days are: 6, 12, 18, 24, and 30.*

In March, you have a desire to accumulate more friends, resources, and knowledge. This is a great time to practice your ability at manifesting. Consider sitting down daily this month to meditate and visualize what you want. Avoid thinking negatively. This month, you might practice manifesting small things like parking places or beautiful sweaters that are half-price. But by the end of the year, you could manifest some major benefits in your life.

March 2 brings the new moon, and there's a great deal of focus on education. You might take a test for school or a professional license. You could help your kids get ready for a standardized test. You may realize you need to work on your concentration and stick to a schedule. You're getting back into studying, now side-by-side with your kids. Rabbit native, this is also when you could consider tutoring other people's kids to make some extra money.

March 5 begins the Water Rabbit month. This is your month. This marks the beginning of a 12-month cycle for you. What you do this month sets the tone for the next 12 months. Take a trip to somewhere you've never been before. If you're looking for a new job, this is one of the better months when you could get an offer pretty quickly. This energy will last for about four weeks.

The full moon is on March 17, and there is a strong emphasis on communication. You may receive a contract you need to review and sign. You have good energy for negotiating some points of this agreement to make it more favorable for you.

This is also a good time to notice how you communicate with yourself. Are you kind to yourself? Rabbit native, are you an advocate for yourself?

In some parts of the world, there will be a second new moon on March 31, and for other time zones, it will be April 1. This new moon brings some possible recognition for you, Rabbit. You might be on stage performing music, acting in a play, or being the host of the festivities. You may watch with pride as one of your kids takes a bow for a piano recital or when they score a home run.

April 2022: *April 1 is the new moon. The full moon is on April 16. On April 29, Pluto goes retrograde. There is a partial solar eclipse on April 30. Your high-energy days are: 5, 11, 17, 23, and 29.*

The month of April has you being more outgoing than usual. You may have more social events to attend and more people to see. The energy of springtime is pulling you out into the world. It's also possible you are doing some charity work. Your job could become more high profile. Others are seeing what you're doing and sending compliments.

On April 4, the Wood Dragon month begins, and you have an opportunity to bring in more money. This may come from items you're selling to clear space in your garage. If you're in sales, your job could be progressing fairly well now. You reap benefits from letting go of excess in your life. Rabbit native, you may look for ways to save money through cutting out cable TV or doing a phone sharing plan. Things like these put cash right back into your pocket.

The full moon is on April 16, and Rabbit natives feel an increased emphasis on home and dwellings. One of your older kids may move back into the house. Or you make room for a relative to have an extended visit. Rabbit native, you're great at hospitality, and so this may be a happy occasion for you even though it brings more work for you in the long run. This is also an excellent time to do home renovations.

There is a Solar Eclipse on April 30, and Rabbit native, there could be an issue with a close friendship. This person might need your help with a problem they are struggling with. But this may be challenging for you as they may not live very close to you or are just not ready for the help you have to offer. You'll have to proceed with caution in this situation. You are a compassionate person and hate to see when one of your friends has difficultly, but the solution here is to wait and be ready to help when they ask.

May 2022: *On May 10, Mercury goes retrograde. There is a total lunar eclipse on May 16. On May 30, there is a new moon. Your high-energy days are:5, 11, 17, 23, and 29.*

During May, there's a lot of focus on the community and how your town is changing. Some of these alterations are for the better, but there are some changes you're not happy with. This month, you may get active in the community, protest some changes, speak at a City Council meeting, or even run for office. You may belong to a spiritual group and work to shift the energy through meditation or prayer. You are an asset to the community, especially when you take an interest in local affairs.

May 5 brings the Wood Snake month, and there's a lot of contact with siblings or younger relatives. You may get together with someone you haven't seen in a long time. Rabbit native, there could be talk of moving back to your home town, or you might visit your ancestral lands and seeing where your people came from.

On May 10, Mercury goes retrograde, and you might have more dream. You are more intuitive now (which is saying something). You could pick up vibrations from other people, animals, and the Universe. At the same time, Rabbit native, you might consider getting a new pet.

There is a Lunar Eclipse on May 15, which could be a bumpy time for your love relationship. You and your sweetheart may not be seeing eye to eye. You might like a little more certainty in life. On the other hand, your partner may look for more change and excitement. You might crave the quiet of country life, and they want to be in the big city. You can work things out, but open communication will be necessary. It's good to express your feelings now.

The new moon is on May 30, and Rabbit native, you're working behind the scenes right now. You might take a break from some group obligations or a vacation from work. You might travel to a tropical island that few people visit, or you decide on a staycation at home, closing the door to the world and doing self-care. This is a good time to have a massage. Consider seeing a chiropractor, acupuncturist, or other alternative practitioners.

June 2022: *Mercury goes direct on June 3. On June 4, Saturn goes retrograde. On June 14, there is a full moon. Neptune goes retrograde on June 28. The new moon is on June 29. Your high-energy days are:4, 10, 16, 23, and 28.*

In June, you have a lot of luck, especially around your career. You may think of making a shift in your career. This may not happen overnight. In fact, it may not happen this year. But this is a time to map out the journey to a major career shift. Maybe you're considering going back to school, or perhaps you're finishing up school. The clearer and more vibrant you can make the picture of this new journey, the more help the Universe will send.

June 5 brings the Fire Horse month, and there's a lot of activity at home. Rabbit native, you might think about moving or redecorating. You could be finally unpacking boxes from your previous move, hanging up pictures, and putting up drapes. You may settle into a home you really love and get the garden just the way you like it. You could have parties in your yard with friends and family.

The full moon is on June 14, and there's a lot of emphasis on your physical health and well-being. You may start a new eating plan or a great meal prep service. It's possible that you are gathering vegetables from your garden or visiting the local farmer's market. You might prepare meals from scratch. You're also likely exercising more now, possibly walking, running, or cycling. Rabbit native, you might want to do tai chi in the park with friends.

June 28 is the new moon, and over the next two weeks, there's a lot of beginning energy once again for Rabbit natives. This means you might start new things, just testing the waters for the significant changes coming to you in 2023. Rabbit native, this is when you might eat new foods, shop in different stores, and meet new people.

July 2022: *July 13 brings the full moon. There is a new moon on July 28. Also, on July 28, Jupiter goes retrograde. Your high-energy days are:4, 10, 16, 23, and 28.*

The month of July brings relationship energy. Rabbit native, you could meet someone new for an epic romance. You could meet this person through a personal introduction (as your friends and family have wanted to fix you up for some time). Or you may have a matchmaker who helps you find a soul connection.

July 7 brings the Fire Sheep month, and positive relationship energy continues. Over the next two weeks, you might take a relationship to the next level by discussing moving in together, buying property, or getting engaged. Rabbit native, you could introduce this person to family and friends. If you're already in a love relationship, you will find it gets stronger during this time.

The full moon is on July 13, and now you're meeting many new people. You might be involved in a group or attending social functions. Rabbit native, people are approaching you, wanting to be friends and connect with you on a deeper level. You can find a mentor or someone who wants to do a business partnership with you.

The new moon is on July 28, and Rabbit native, you might realize just how much stuff you have. You might empty a storage unit, participating in a neighborhood garage sale, or selling your stuff on eBay. Some of these things are more valuable than you knew and can fetch a reasonable price. But other items should be bagged up and sent to Goodwill just to save time.

August 2022: *August 12 brings the full moon. Uranus goes retrograde on August 24. There is a new moon on August 27. Your high-energy days are: 3, 9, 15, 21, and 27.*

In August, you have quite a few obligations with work and in the community. You might be the treasurer of a professional group or help with a fundraiser for a charity. You may let go of these positions because your schedule is filled with responsibilities and time commitments. But many people are counting on you, so you'll likely stay on well past this month.

August 7 brings the Earth Monkey month, and work heats up. Your team at the office may be shorthanded because someone's out on leave. Rabbit native, you're taking up the slack, which means added responsibilities (and possibly some overtime). You're learning new skills like what you can delegate or eliminate to help get things done. Mostly, you operate at your own speed. But now you're surrounded by people who need you to accelerate.

August 11 is the full moon, and there's a lot of emphasis on your investments and saving for the future. You may be less pleased with the results from the unpredictable shifts in the market of late. And over the next two weeks, you might do a thorough analysis of your finances. And this could put you on the road to prosperity. Rabbit native, now is the time to sit down with your financial planner to discuss your future.

The new moon is on August 27, and there's a lot of energy around vehicles and transportation. Your car might be in the shop for routine maintenance or major repairs. Rabbit native, this might be the time you're considering upgrading, getting an electric vehicle or perhaps a larger vehicle because you have a family to ferry around. You may also consider how you can use your vehicle less. You might ride your bike more or get more things delivered.

September 2022: *On September 10, there is a full moon, and Mercury goes retrograde. On September 25, there's the new moon. Your high-energy days are: 2, 8, 14, 20, and 26.*

The month of September has you focused on keeping your balance. You might be pulled in a lot of different directions, everyone needing something from you. But there's no reason for you to rush from thing to thing when you know everything will get done in its time. Spend a little bit more time at home, journaling, doing yoga, or reading a good book. Rabbit native, you don't have to keep up with the pace everyone else seems to be setting.

September 7 begins the Earth Rooster month, and relationship energy is powerful now. If you're already in a love relationship, you may feel you're closer than ever. There is a balance between the two of you. You each bring essential skills and positive qualities to this relationship. If you're looking for love this month, you could find someone with whom you have great chemistry. Consider doing some online dating if you've had trouble finding someone to go out with in the past.

The full moon is on September 10, and the same day, Mercury goes retrograde. You might travel to see an old friend or past lover. Rabbit native, this might mean you are returning to a place you've been before, where you can see how things have changed. But mostly, you're focused on the relationship and how you are either growing closer together or growing apart.

The new moon is on September 25 and brings a lot of information from family members. Someone in the family may need some help with moving or some career advice. Rabbit native, you might gather up family memorabilia, putting pictures in albums, or making virtual albums. Look at your genealogy and find out how far back you can trace your family line.

October 2022: *Mercury goes direct on October 2. On October 8, Pluto goes direct. There is a full moon on October 9. On October 23, Saturn goes direct. On October 25, there's a partial solar eclipse. On October 28, Jupiter goes retrograde. Mars goes retrograde on October 30. Your high-energy days are:2, 8, 14, 20, and 26.*

The month of October can be quite an intense month for Rabbit natives. Additionally, Mercury goes direct on October 2. There's a great deal of focus on career. You're likely doing something that's very high profile. This could mean you're finishing a project or leading a team meeting where the CEO sits in the room. This can be a great success. The CEO and your supervisor could be pretty impressed with your performance, giving you leverage for your next review.

October 8 brings the Metal Dog month, and you're paying a lot of attention to getting out of debt and being frugal. Perhaps you have started a debt snowball or have recently paid off a debt, and now you're enthusiastic about getting the rest paid off. You may focus on paying off the mortgage, saving every penny so you can be debt-free as soon as possible.

The full moon is on October 9, and you might be involved in a big event either for yourself or for the family. Rabbit native, you might be involved in a wedding, helping a family member or friend get down the aisle. There could be a big celebration, needing lots of planning and coordination with others.

The Solar Eclipse is on October 25, and there is very intense energy for Rabbit natives regarding love relationships. You might fall head over heels for someone who's not necessarily your type. Or you may be pursued by someone so intensely that you feel like running. In some ways, this is the love you asked for (just a bit more intense than you were expecting). But if you stay true to yourself, it will all work out.

November 2022: *November 8 brings the total lunar eclipse. On November 23, there is a new moon, and Jupiter goes direct. Your high-energy days are: 1, 7, 13, 19, and 25.*

The month of November shows you having fun. As the energy of the holidays begins, you might settle down to enjoy your favorite time of the year. Your focus is on family and home and just having a good time. You're pushing work aside and giving time to those people who mean a lot to you. This is a good time for adjusting your work/life balance.

November 7 brings the Metal Pig month, and a legal matter clears up. Rabbit native, something you have been working on for a while regarding contracts or a lawsuit now settles, and you have a reason to celebrate. It's not a total victory because it took a lot of time and energy, but overall the results are pretty happy.

The Lunar Eclipse is on November 8, and you may have some trouble with a piece of technology that you rely on. Rabbit native, your laptop might fizzle, or your toddler drops your phone in the toilet. Now you're scrambling to get this item replaced. If you're reading this ahead of time, make sure you have all your backup systems in place before this date.

The new moon is on November 23, and life settles down considerably. Life feels more peaceful even though you still have a lot to do. You're doing things you enjoy, especially involving family, friends, and charitable endeavors. Rabbit native, your life is running on a tight schedule, but things are getting done, and you enjoy the results.

December 2022: *Neptune goes direct on December 3. The full moon is on December 8. There is a new moon on December 23. Mercury goes retrograde on December 29. Your high-energy days are: 1, 7, 13, 19, and 25.*

In December, you're sliding into some old habits. Some of these are honored traditions like sending greeting cards or putting out special decorations. But you may also fall back into some bad habits that you thought you had moved on from. This is the next thing to let go of. In this last year of your 12-year cycle, it's imperative to let go of many things, and now you only have a few months left. This month, Rabbit native, let go of a bad habit.

On December 7, it's the Water Rat month. Additionally, it's also the full moon. Rabbit native, you're very noticeable. Maybe you're posting more on social media, or your podcast is going viral. But during this time, you want to keep your message very uplifting and positive. Stay away from anything controversial, or you could get into some hot water.

December 23 is the new moon. Rabbit native, you have excellent relationship energy. You could meet someone new at a party or charitable event. If you're already in a love relationship, your friends and family are talking about how good your relationship is going and how your relationship is inspiring others. You are communicating well with your sweetheart and doing small, romantic things for each other.

On December 29, Mercury goes retrograde, and you likely have a reunion with someone you haven't seen in a long time. Rabbit native, this could be a person you knew in high school or college. You might marvel at how much they've changed. This reminds you of how you have changed, and now you're thinking of the past and comparing it with the future.

January 2023: *January 6 brings the full moon. Mercury goes direct on January 18. The year of the water rabbit begins on January 22. Your high-energy days are: 6, 12, 18, 24, and 30.*

January brings the last month of your 12-year cycle and emphasizes letting go of as much from the past 12 years as you can. You might do some journaling and then burn the pieces of paper when you're finished. Look at recycling old clothing, kid's toys, and books. Also, you could look at things you have gathered, maybe for a hobby, and decide to donate the entire lot. Letting go is the focus this month.

January 5 begins the Water Ox month, and you have a lot of help and assistance around you. Rabbit native, others are stepping up to give you a hand. That is everything from teaching you how to use some new software to help you move a sofa. All you need to do is ask.

The full moon is on January 6. Over the next two weeks, the last moments of your 12-year cycle come into play. You might become quite reflective, wanting to hide from the world. But a spotlight is already on you. People are calling you out of the blue. Rabbit native, your manager notices when you're five minutes late. It's like there's a big sign over your head that says, "look at me."

On January 18, Mercury goes direct. And during this time, a relationship that you thought was damaged now heals. The other person comes to you and apologizes. They may say that they were wrong. Now you can start communicating again (much to the relief of both of you).

The new moon is on January 22, bringing the beginning of the Year of the Water Rabbit. You are now entering your first year of seed planting. This will last for three years, and during this time, many things in your life will change as new opportunities flow in from every direction. Rabbit native, the important thing this year is to plant as many seeds as possible. This means doing many new things. And that is big things as well as small things. Even changing the type of toothpaste you use can lead to unexpected opportunities. This is going to be a great year.

Attract New Love

For you, Rabbit, the Year of the Water Tiger brings a lot of positive relationship energy. This could be your year for meeting somebody who is an excellent match. You do this by focusing on your excellent qualities and what you have to offer. You are also are interacting with more people this year than you were in the previous year. In 2022, you appear more confident and self-assured, and this is like a love potion, bringing opportunities to you. As you let go of some of the stuff in your life and release an old relationship, new love comes and finds you.

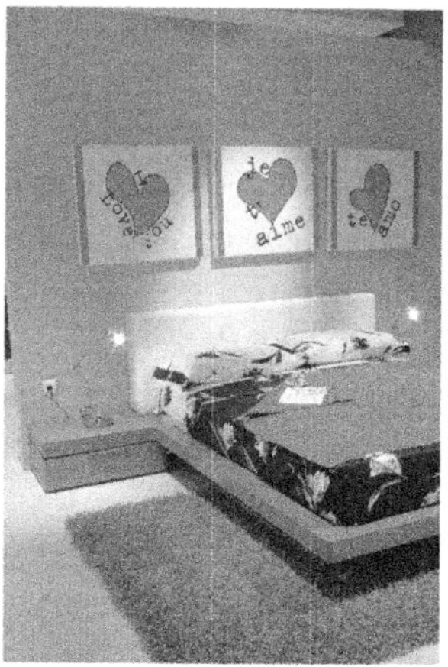

Bedspread, Red: It's easy to attract new love energy when you add a big splash of red to the bedroom. Consider getting a red bedspread. Red is the color of excitement and passion. Choose a shade of red that appeals to you. The spread can include other colors in a pattern, stripes, or floral design.

Enhance Existing Love

2022 has good energy for Rabbit natives for your existing love relationship. You can settle down and be quite comfortable with each other this year. There may be a storm raging outside, but the two of you know and trust each other, and so you know you will be fine. Towards the end of the year, there will be an energy of things shifting, which you'll need to discuss with your partner. If you're both born in the year the Rabbit, the Year of the Water Tiger means you should look around and see what to let go of. What no longer serves your partnership? But if you're born in different years, let your partner know that this is your year of letting go. They may be in a different place in their cycle, and so they need to be extra understanding of what you're going through.

This year, consider getting a moonstone to increase love energy. It can be part of jewelry or a loose, polished stone. Reasonably priced moonstones are available in mineral shops and online. It's said if you light a red candle on the night of the full moon and place the moonstone by the candle so that the moonstone will gather the moon's energy and bring you luck with love.

There are also stories of how the energy of moonstone can smooth out trouble in a relationship. Give a moonstone piece of jewelry or a tumbled stone to your beloved and let the moonstone's loving vibrations bring peace to the relationship.

Looking to Conceive?

Pine cones are a great fertility symbol. Think of how a tiny seed grows between the hard petals of the cone. You can display a basket of scented pine cones in your family room or bedroom to promote conception energy. Eating pine nuts is also said to bring on good sexual relations, leading to a future happy event.

You can add the nuts to a salad or create a decadent dessert with honey and increase your odds of getting pregnant.

(From Donna Stellhorn's book, Fertility Feng Shui)

Family and Kids

Regarding home and family, you might feel pushed in different directions, and no Rabbit native likes to be pushed. You might be encouraged to move closer to your parents or your older children when you're actually quite happy with the place you have. In 2022, your routines and how you structure your life may be at odds with other people in the family. And this can cause them to give you lots of unsolicited advice. But, in general, everything goes along pretty smoothly with family matters. Disagreements are slight, and there's always some sort of compromise that can be reached. In the Year of the Water Tiger, it could be a good year at home.

Succulents are a type of plant that stores water and can thrive in arid conditions. This is about using resources wisely and being able to handle whatever circumstances are thrown at you.

It's also said succulents represent an enduring love. For this Feng Shui cure, find succulents without spikes or thorns. Place small succulent plants around the house, near the entry, in the kitchen, and in the family room. If you have a yard, you can plant succulents in areas close to your front and back door. This will help bring this positive, resourceful energy to your family.

Money

In 2022, when you get serious about your finances, your money picture improves significantly. This is the year you can get out of debt or make a significant dent in student loans and other obligations. Rabbit native, you might go to a written budget or a cash envelope system to get this started. In the Year of the Water Tiger, many people will play fast and loose with finances, but you can be calm and level-headed. You can watch other people make mistakes and learn from them. Overall, you have some great opportunities ahead for your finances when you are a good steward of your money. Take care of the pennies, and the dollars will accumulate.

When you want to attract money in abundance, hang or display a pair of fish by the front door. The fish may be crafted out of fabric, glass, wood, or metal. The symbol of the two fish represents the saying, "May you have so much money, you have left-over money!" In Feng Shui, fish are used to attract wealth because the Chinese word for fish sounds like the word for "abundance." Displaying a couple of fish this year will help the money flow in effortlessly.

Job or Career

While there are some job opportunities for Rabbit natives in 2022, the energy lends itself to staying where you're at. Most of the changes will occur within the company rather than having you jump into a new profession (that's more likely in 2023). So you may get a different office or have a change of supervisor. You could shift laterally within the company or move to a different department with new duties, but overall, the transition is pretty peaceful. And because this looks like a good money year, you are likely to stay employed for the entire year. During the Year of the Water Tiger, others are making lots of sudden changes, but you seem to be in the eye of the storm.

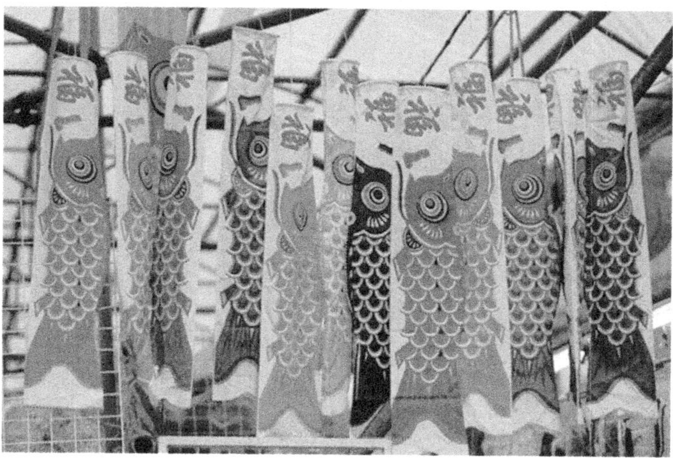

Even though you have lots of positive energy this year for career, you want the energy to flow smoothly and continuously. Hang a windsock or flag outside, either by your front door or on your patio/balcony. Choose a colorful one, something bright that makes you happy when you see it; you might also switch out the banner for each holiday or at the change of every season. Or, you can choose one in the form of a fish (fish represent abundance). This will attract a constant flow of energy and bring you more opportunities.

Education

Rabbit native education opportunities seem to be hinged on others. You may strike an agreement with your partner to take some time off work to go back to school. Or perhaps you are delaying your education, again by mutual agreement. Additionally, your school applications are highly assisted by others. Notable and influential people may write testimonials on your behalf. If you're already in school, you're likely meeting lots of new friends and having a good time in 2022. However, an important test may have to be taken twice.

Legal Matters

In the Year of the Water Tiger, you have a lot of luck in legal matters. If you enter into a lawsuit or have one continuing from a previous year, things can be settled in your favor this year. You're able to find good counsel and other helpful people to help protect you legally. Your good luck extends to contracts, and you may get to negotiate or renegotiate an important agreement. With small legal matters like getting a building permit or professional certification, you can breeze through red tape. You can pass your test, bar exam, or get the credentials you need.

Health and Well-Being

In the Year of the Water Tiger, there could be a lot of focus on your health and well-being, especially around gaining new information and new ways to take care of yourself. By the end of the year, you could do substantially better because of the steps you've taken during the year. 2022 could bring a breakthrough regarding your health when you see a different doctor or get a new form of treatment. You are more likely to pay attention to your diet and exercise, taking better care of your physical self, bringing you many benefits. This is also a good year for prioritizing rest and sleep. You may crack the code on getting a good night's sleep, which gives you the energy and positive attitude to make positive health choices. Overall, Rabbit native, you have outstanding energy regarding health and well-being in 2022.

A pagoda is a many-tiered sacred building popular in the far East. They are often religious or spiritual structures, some dating back to BCE times. Often the very top pinnacle comes to a point and was made of metal to channel lightning strikes. In Feng Shui, the pagoda symbolizes peace and harmony. You might display a small replica pagoda or have a picture of a pagoda. Place this in your living room or family room to attract positive, healthy energy. You can also find stone pagodas to place in the garden for the same purpose.

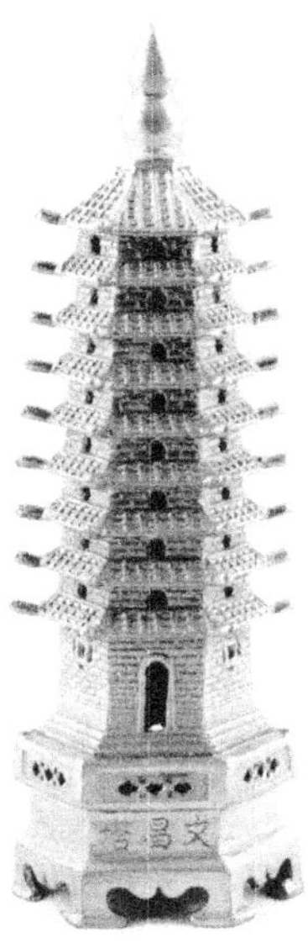

Dragon

February 16, 1904–February 3, 1905: Yang Wood Dragon
February 3, 1916–January 22, 1917: Yang Fire Dragon
January 23, 1928–February 9, 1929: Yang Earth Dragon
February 8, 1940–January 26, 1941: Yang Metal Dragon
January 27, 1952–February 13, 1953: Yang Water Dragon
February 13, 1964–February 1, 1965: Yang Wood Dragon
January 31, 1976–February 17, 1977: Yang Fire Dragon
February 17, 1988–February 5, 1989: Yang Earth Dragon
February 5, 2000–January 23, 2001: Yang Metal Dragon
January 23, 2012–February 9, 2013: Yang Water Dragon
February 10, 2024–January 28, 2025: Yang Wood Dragon

Dragon Personality

When considering Chinese Zodiac animal qualities, it helps to examine the animal's traits, behaviors, and personality—except there are no dragons to study (at least not anymore). Dragons are listed in the Shuo Wen dictionary (200 AD). It describes this creature: The Dragon has "the will and power of transformation and the gift of rendering itself visible or invisible at pleasure."

It is said there are three types of Dragon: one, the most powerful, inhabits the sky; the second lives in the ocean, and the third resides in dens (or caves) in the mountains. Some say a dragon can shrink to the size of the silkworm, or expand in size, lie down and fill up an entire lake! These powers describe the traits belonging to Dragon and explain why so many people envy the Dragon native.

The Dragon seems not to be of this world, and likewise, Dragon natives are thought to exist "above it all." They have big ideas and the power to make them happen. Even when young in years, Dragon will take on and carry enormous burdens and responsibilities.

Dragon natives can tap into a seemingly endless supply of energy, and they are eager to talk about their ideas. The Dragon has the potential to accomplish great things—or simply to fly around in the heavens, never allowing their feet to touch the ground.

Despite this magical power, people born in the Year the Dragon can have violent tempers (and explosive temper tantrums) when things don't go their way. Sometimes a Dragon is not diplomatic. They would much rather say what they want to say than tell others what they want to hear. When a Dragon breathes fire, everyone in the vicinity gets singed!

The Dragon native requires a clear purpose in life, a cause to champion, a wrong to right. No matter what Dragon does for a living, they will have their pet projects and dreams. Without these, Dragon becomes listless and depressed.

The Dragon is very skillful in finance and management. Dragon sensibly looks at long-term investing to protect their assets. Good at spending money, Dragon is always on the lookout for an innovation to adopt. Dragons rise to the top of whatever field they choose. They are often chosen to be the leader, even if they're new to the organization.

Dragons hate to be trapped, with no options for change. If stuck behind a desk or saddled with a long list of rules, Dragons will revolt. For all their seeming confidence, the Dragon can feel insecure on the inside. There is a constant struggle between the desire for success and the fear of success. They're status-conscious and don't like to fail, especially in the eyes of others. This sometimes causes them to shoot for small goals rather than pursue big dreams.

Dragon is by far the largest personality of the Chinese zodiac. As the only mythical animal of the twelve, a Dragon can take on many forms.

Traditionally, a Dragon could manifest as a creature the size of a gigantic cloud formation to one as small as a butterfly. Because of this remarkable ability, Dragon holds the vision for our future in this world. They see where we are heading and are aware of where we should be going.

Dragon's confidence is as big as its personality. They motivate everyone around them. They undertake the greatest adventures, eager to experience wild success—or will endure crushing failure. There is no stopping a Dragon once their mind is made up. They will push right to the edge to see if they can make something happen. If things go wrong, well, that's when Dragon truly shines as a leader, the one to lead everyone out of danger.

Dragons have nothing to hide—Why should they? They have nothing to fear! Their feelings are out in the open for everyone to see. Dragons do not keep secrets. After they share the news, the Dragon will tell you they were right to reveal everything. So, if you have a Dragon as your confidant, be aware that whatever you tell them will come out, eventually.

Dragons are sensitive to the climate. Calm in pleasant weather; when a storm comes, they become rattled or irritated. When a storm is on its way, it's time to steer clear of Dragon! Dragon doesn't mind either way—although nearly always surrounded by friends, they are perfectly happy spending time alone.

Dragon natives need a mission or a life purpose. Dragon can soar to heights other animals couldn't even dream of reaching when their life purpose is clear. Dragon is very decisive. Once they've chosen a path, it's tough to dissuade them from continuing along it.

However, sometimes Dragon is not particularly smart in the realm of business. They don't pick up on the cunning of others. Dragon natives are often unaware of the plots and schemes surrounding them. Dragon is more concerned about reaching their goal and not willing to play the petty games of others.

The most challenging thing for a Dragon is the stubborn desire to do everything on their own! They never call for help, never ask for support. Dragon is powerful and can be intimidating; natives have a fiery temper and a fixed idea of the ways things should be. Dragon often speaks without editing, letting people know exactly what they think.

Dragon: Predictions for 2022

How to use your High-Energy Days: On these days, plan to take action for your most important goals, make vital phone calls, send important emails. Your high-energy days are when your energy and luck are the strongest for the month.

January 2022: *January 2 is the new moon. January 14 has Mercury going retrograde. January 17 is the full moon. On January 18, Uranus goes direct. On January 29, Venus goes direct. Your High-Energy Days are 6, 12, 18, 24, and 30.*

On paper, January looks a lot like a new beginning. However, the old energy of the Metal Ox is still lumbering along for the entire month. For Dragon natives, there's a focus on putting paperwork in order, de-cluttering, organizing the garage, and rearranging things—striving to make life better. You may change your diet by eating healthier meals and perhaps doing more cooking at home.

January 2 is the new moon, and this splits the energy between finishing up old projects and starting brand-new things. You may wrap up seasonal work or organizing things for your job (like taking the annual physical inventory). At home, there's similar energy involved in putting away the holiday things and cleaning up after extended holiday visits.

New energy is abundant all around you. Single Dragon natives may meet someone new and quickly fall in love. This person seems so familiar to you, and it feels comfortable to slip into a serious partnership. If you're already in a love relationship, you discover more wonderful things about each other—helping to draw you closer together.

On January 14, Mercury goes retrograde, possibly derailing a lot of resolutions and plans. Fortunately, Dragon natives can change directions pretty quickly. You will hear many people complaining and griping because things they want to do are delayed or canceled entirely. This is an excellent time to stay flexible and adapt.

On January 17, the full moon introduces an excellent two-week period for Dragon natives. Now you can expand your circle of friends and supporters. This is an excellent time to find mentors, teachers, or advisors. If you see someone you're interested in working with, don't hesitate to send them a message.

The energy shifts on January 19, and now it's time to evaluate your current work-life balance. You may have to delegate or even eliminate some tasks in your life so you can enjoy some much-needed quality free time. When you have free time, make sure you are spending it mindfully, not merely frittering it away on something that brings you nothing of value.

February 2022: *February 1 is the new moon and begins the Year of the Water Tiger. February 3, Mercury goes direct. February 16 is the full moon. Your high-energy days are: 5, 11, 17, and 23.*

The Water Tiger year begins on February 1, and the shift of energy is palatable. Even the air seems alive with possibilities as you're ready to spread your wings and take flight. This is a year when people are more open to change and can listen to big ideas (of which you have many). But you are almost at the end of your twelve-year cycle, so this is not a time to start new things but for you to complete projects. Consider what you want to finish this year.

The new moon energy is on February 1. There is a focus on relationships of all kinds, especially long-term friendships. A friend of yours may call you for some help. They may have had a recent loss in their life and need a shoulder to lean on. Dragon, you have wisdom and an understanding of what people need. This can help you strengthen many of your relationships.

February 3 brings the Water Tiger month, and Mercury moves direct. Everything now picks up speed. It will feel like a freight train of energy coming at you. People will be impatient, and this can make them erratic and unpredictable. Be careful when commuting as there will be careless drivers on the road.

The full moon is on February 16, and the spotlight is on you. You may lead a meeting, teach a class, or be on stage holding the microphone. Others are looking to you for guidance. You may instruct others one on one, or you could teach groups. Dragon, you have a natural ability as a teacher, even if it's not your favorite thing to do.

March 2022: *March 2 is the new moon. The full moon is on March 18. Your high-energy days are: 1, 7, 13, 19, 25, and 31.*

In March, you have the likelihood of accumulating money. This could be through business or passive income sources. It's like you're cracking the code for making more money. This is also a a favorable month to plug up holes in your spending. Sometimes, Dragon, you like to give lavish gifts. But for this month, you'd do better accumulating cash for an investment opportunity coming later this year.

March 2 brings the new moon, and there are some romantic possibilities over the next two weeks. You might be in an intimate relationship where it feels just like a honeymoon. You may close the door to shut out the world so the two of you can spend more time together. If you're looking for love, this is a great time to find someone with whom you have great chemistry.

March 5 begins the Water Rabbit month. You might need a little downtime. Over the next four weeks, it would be great to take some time off to rest and recuperate. Dragon, you might see an alternative health practitioner such as a chiropractor, acupuncturist, or cranial sacral specialist. Or you may do something more physical like rock climbing, hiking, or biking. The important thing is to do something enjoyable while taking care of your body.

The full moon is on March 17, and you're meeting a lot of new people. This could be connected to your job, but it's also possible you are involved in a group that is helping you to meet like-minded people. Dragon, you could do some political canvassing, teaching, or attending a convention. There's more than one interesting person you're likely to meet over the next couple of weeks.

In some parts of the world, there will be a second new moon on March 31, and for other time zones, it will be April 1. This new moon brings a possibility of travel. You might go a long distance on a trip you have been saving up for. This could be to visit your ancestral lands or to a place you've never been before. You might consider a car-camping trip, where you are taking your SUV to some public lands to be among wildflowers and under a canopy of tree branches.

April 2022: *April 1 is the new moon. The full moon is on April 16. On April 29, Pluto goes retrograde. There is a partial solar eclipse on April 30. Your high-energy days are: 6, 12, 18, 24, and 30.*

In April, positive relationship energy continues. You may attend a wedding (or perhaps more than one wedding). You might have to travel to this event. This event could involve a close family member, and maybe you are part of the wedding party. It's a joyous occasion, and the romantic energy seems to be contagious. Dragon, you and your sweetheart may consider renewing your vows.

On April 4, the Wood Dragon month begins, and now you start four weeks of new beginnings. Plant seeds for what you want to manifest this year. It might be time to update your resume, start a business or upload your novel to Amazon. Look at what you can do that is new and fresh and could manifest sometime this year.

The full moon is on April 16, and your financial picture improves considerably. Some investments you made are improving, and income from your business seems more robust than ever. You may collaborate with someone to expand your territory. If you work for somebody else, you might find you are entitled to some shares of stock or other perks of great value.

There is a solar eclipse on April 30. Now there is some uncertainty in your job, or your company could go through a rough time. Dragon, there could be changes in management or your company may be acquired by a larger firm. This could lead to some downsizing within the company. It may be necessary to do some networking and perhaps transfer into a different role. On the other hand, this could be your signal that it's time to move on to greener pastures.

May 2022: *On May 10, Mercury goes retrograde. There is a total lunar eclipse on May 16. On May 30, there is a new moon. Your high-energy days are:6, 12, 18, 24, and 30.*

During May, you are easily seen. When you post on social media, your memes and pictures will probably reach more people than usual. People are reading what you're writing. They may retweet or repost what you send out. At this time, it's good to avoid controversial topics. Consider posting uplifting things, information to inspire people. If you want to start a YouTube channel or a podcast, this is a time to consider it.

May 5 brings the Wood Snake month, and it's time to put your finances under a magnifying glass. Consider pulling your statements together to make sure the numbers balance. Gather your records to file what you want to keep. Then shred the rest. This is a good time to unsubscribe from catalogs, so you are not tempted to buy things you don't need. Dragon, benefits come when you get back on budget and make your financial goals a priority.

On May 10, Mercury goes retrograde. Rumors at your job now are confirmed. Promised changes that were delayed now start to happen. During this time, it could be difficult to change jobs. Ideally, you wait till Mercury begins to move forward again on June 3.

There is a lunar eclipse on May 15, and a member of your family may have a troublesome time. Fortunately, you have had experience with this issue and are ready to give advice. This is much easier to deal with when you pull together as a family unit. In a few weeks, this energy will pass, and the sun will shine again.

The new moon is on May 30, and now you're surrounded by friends. Dragon, you may throw parties celebrating a graduation or welcoming summer. You may consider traveling to see friends who live a long distance away. Life feels fun and exciting again. Your circle of friendships is growing as you meet friends of friends. You may get a handful of invitations to great places to visit in the upcoming months.

June 2022: *Mercury goes direct on June 3. On June 4, Saturn goes retrograde. On June 14, there is a full moon. Neptune goes retrograde on June 28. The new moon is on June 29. Your high-energy days are: 5, 11, 17, 23, and 29.*

In June, you have several opportunities connected to your career. If there have been changes at your company, a new position could open up for you. Dragon, you may be transferred to a new department or taking a management role. If you want to leave this company, you have several opportunities for work elsewhere. There is a strong possibility that you can make more money in the process.

June 5 brings the Fire Horse month, and there's a lot of attention on your vehicle. You may decide to get a new car or truck. You may have your old vehicle detailed, so it looks brand new. Your vehicle reflects the inner you to the world outside. Whether your car is flashy or your truck is utilitarian, it says something about you.

The full moon is on June 14, and there's a lot of energy around children and creativity. Dragon, you may take the kids on a camping trip or theme park vacation. It's also possible you are in joining some creative activities such as painting or playing music. This is a great time to take some classes in enjoyable activities.

June 28 is the new moon, and your intuitive ability is very strong. Dragon, you may have dreams that reveal the future. You might investigate different spiritual tools such as tarot cards or dowsing rods. This is an excellent time to have an astrology reading or have someone read your palm. This is an ideal time to do some feng shui and use symbols like coins and dragons to bring in positive and prosperous energy.

July 2022: *July 13 brings the full moon. There is a new moon on July 28. Also, on July 28, Jupiter goes retrograde. Your high-energy days are:5, 11, 17, 23, and 29.*

The month of July is a quieter month for Dragon natives. You might consider taking some time off work to spend more time at home. If you're feeling energetic, you're likely to clean out the garage, closets and get rid of excess stuff. This will help with the feng shui of the house as well as bring in some cash.

For the moments when you're not so energetic, take time for reflection, meditation, and to recharge your batteries.

July 7 brings the Fire Sheep month, and over the next four weeks, there's a lot of emphasis on the family. There could be a celebration going on, such as a wedding or birth. Dragon, you might explore local activities such as hiking or visiting the community swimming pool now that school is out, and the sun is shining. You may help a family member move. You could go with them as they look for a house or apartment and help them unpack at their new place.

The full moon is on July 13, and there's a great deal of emphasis on habits and habit-forming strategies. You might release negative habits as well as cultivating some positive ones, especially around diet, exercise, or stress management. Over the next couple of weeks, you can completely transform your life through some simple day-to-day activities.

The new moon is on July 28, and over the next two weeks, the spotlight is on you. You are attracting positive relationship energy. Dragon, you might meet a new friend or an intriguing individual for a romantic relationship. If you're already in a committed relationship, things can go very well. The two of you feel closer and more aligned in your goals.

August 2022: *August 12 brings the full moon. Uranus goes retrograde on August 24. There is a new moon on August 27. Your high-energy days are: 4, 10, 16, 23, and 28.*

In August, your work, education, and your finances are all moving up on your priority list. You might begin a new job or starting at a new school. You're making a good impression and connecting with people who have influence. At the same time, cash flow is a little tight. Dragon, you may have spent extra money for necessary expenses, and now you're watching your pennies. Dragon rarely likes to do this, but it is helpful this month to monitor the small things.

August 7 brings the Earth Monkey month, and over the next four weeks, there's a lot of emphasis on creativity and children. If you have kids, most of your time and energy is going to them (more than usual) as you get them ready for school or send them off to college. Dragon, you also may work on a creative project and feeling very compelled to get it done this month. This is a good time for finishing things.

August 11 is the full moon, and there's an emphasis on solidifying a partnership or relationship. If this is a love relationship, you may take it to the next level, such as living together or getting engaged. But if this is a business partnership, you could put things on paper and sign a partnership agreement.

The new moon is on August 27, and now a financial windfall can come in. Finances, in general, look better, and now money is flowing into your accounts. You may have sold an object of value, and that's put a chunk of money into your account. Dragon, you also may see some financial increase from your career either through a bonus or more sales from your business. At these times, you could feel quite generous, but you want to make sure you replenish your accounts before buying a round of drinks for everyone to celebrate.

September 2022: *On September 10, there is a full moon, and Mercury goes retrograde. On September 25, there's the new moon. Your high-energy days are: 3, 9, 15, 21, and 27.*

The month of September continues the focus on education as well as bringing opportunities to make more money. It's possible you are learning new skills through a formal course curriculum, or you are picking up some new skills through trial and error, as well as YouTube videos. At the same time, a potential new job or side business opens up a source of income for you. Dragon, you could do something you enjoy while making money.

September 7 begins the Earth Rooster month, and over the next four weeks, you could find yourself quite busy. Now is the time to work on your productivity and finding better ways to schedule your time. Make sure you put leisure time in your calendar; otherwise, your days could be all work and no play this month. On the other hand, you could conquer procrastination and make significant progress on some long-term projects.

The full moon is on September 10, and the same day, Mercury goes retrograde. This could throw a monkey wrench into your plans to get a loan, refinance the house, or fund a business. The process is going to take longer than you expect. But it can go through if you take careful steps. The other party involved may lose some of your paperwork or be relatively slow to respond. But overall, if you're looking to gain financially during this time, you're heading in the right direction.

The new moon is on September 25. Over the next two weeks, there's a lot of energy around communication, siblings, and younger relatives. Dragon, you might spend time with a sibling who lives far away or talk to your cousin about starting a business. There's also some energy now with neighbors. A challenge you had with a neighbor could resolve, either by the neighbor moving away, or they suddenly become more neighborly.

October 2022: *Mercury goes direct on October 2. On October 8, Pluto goes direct. There is a full moon on October 9. On October 23, Saturn goes direct. On October 25, there's a partial solar eclipse. On October 28, Jupiter goes retrograde. Mars goes retrograde on October 30. Your high-energy days are:3, 9, 15, 21, and 27.*

The month of October can be quite an active month for Dragon natives. Mercury goes direct on October 2. Many things you have been waiting for now start to trickle in, first slowly and then pick up speed towards the middle of the month. This can include an employment contract or a purchase and sales agreement. You could be more active during this time as you go out dancing, cycling, or training for a marathon.

October 8 brings the Metal Dog month, and relationships are highlighted. This energy is especially strong for intimate relationships and long-term friendships. You could strengthen your partnership through active listening and spending more time together. Dragon, you are always there for your friends, ready to give advice or some help materially. But over the next four weeks, it would be helpful for you to open your arms to receive support as well.

The full moon is on October 9, and there's energy around travel. You may take a brief trip or visiting a nearby town. You could go by car or by train. There are likely some delays if you're flying, or you may find that it's much more expensive than you were expecting. Otherwise, good things are coming from trips you take over the next two weeks.

The solar eclipse is on October 25, and there can be some issues at home. You may deal with broken appliances, a leaky roof, or difficulties with your landlord. Dragon, you also may have some more stress with siblings fighting, or you and your partner are not getting along as well as you usually do. The focus on this energy is about control. Someone in the family likes to control external circumstances and possibly is trying to control you. Recognize that you may become quite frustrated with one of your closest relationships.

November 2022: *November 8 brings the total lunar eclipse. On November 23, there is a new moon, and Jupiter goes direct. Your high-energy days are: 2, 8, 14, 20, and 26.*

The month of November shows continued activity at home. You may finish repairs or get ready for the upcoming holidays by laying out decorating. It is also possible you may have a large celebration at home (perhaps for Thanksgiving). You may consider some new furniture, or you are busy unpacking from a recent move.

November 7 brings the Metal Pig month, and a financial matter that starts bumpy gets much better over the next four weeks. Dragon, now suddenly, the road ahead seems to open up, and you have opportunities where none existed before. You could refinance the house at an amazing rate or find a lucrative investment. Some of this positive energy is connected to your intuition. You feel when to push forward, when to hold back, and when to wait for the other person to make their decision.

The lunar eclipse is on November 8, and there could be some changes at your job. This may involve the entire company and result in a merger or top-down reorganization. This can trickle down to affect your job in particular. You may end up reporting to a different manager or have your team consolidate with another team. At this time, there's also energy affecting where you work. You may change offices or work at home more often.

The new moon is on November 23, and love relationship energy is powerful. You could find a person for a romantic partnership. Dragon, you might discover someone through an online dating app or a matchmaker. When you meet this person, you find that the chemistry between you is unmistakable. This could be a whirlwind romance, bringing you together immediately. You could go from dating to living together in record time.

December 2022: *Neptune goes direct on December 3. The full moon is on December 8. There is a new moon on December 23. Mercury goes retrograde on December 29. Your high-energy days are:2, 8, 14, 20, and 26.*

In December, good relationship energy continues, especially with intimate relationships. If you're already in a committed partnership, you might find that you are spending more time behind closed doors, with the two of you feeling frisky. Over the next four weeks, fertility energy is also quite robust. If you're looking to add to the family (children or pets), the stars are aligning in your favor.

On December 7, it's the Water Rat month, and also the full moon. You have quite a few social engagements on your calendar. It seems like everyone wants you at their party. You're in high demand even with friends who live some distance away. Dragon, you may have to pick and choose which event to go to, or you may attend more than one event on the same day. It's good to be popular.

December 23 is the new moon, and your busyness continues. You are likely finishing up some important tasks at work for the end of the calendar year. You may also work on some projects at home. While other people are resting and taking a break, your schedule may not allow much time off. Dragon, you could do some last-minute health appointments, shopping, and visiting friends.

On December 29, Mercury goes retrograde, and you may notice you have fallen off the healthy eating wagon. Now there's a lot of positive energy for getting back on track. Over the next two weeks, you may be hit in the gym or clean out the fridge, giving away delectable desserts to friends and family.

January 2023: *January 6 brings the full moon. Mercury goes direct on January 18. The year of the water rabbit begins on January 22. Your high-energy days are. 1, 7, 13, 19, 25, and 31.*

The month of January has you focused again on education. You might return to school or help kids get back into the swing of things. It's possible you are studying for a professional exam or getting certification from a government agency. This is an excellent time for learning new things. You can be pretty successful in passing a test and getting the kids back into the study groove.

January 5 begins the Water Ox month, and you may receive some recognition in your career. This could be an award, or you are mentioned in the company meeting. There can be the talk of promotion, but, likely, you will not be implementing these plans for a few months. Mostly, this is the boss or the CEO reaching out to pat you on the back and say, "good job."

The full moon is on January 6, and the calendar year may have just begun, but you feel you could use some time off. The holiday season was so busy that now you need a break. You have an opportunity to work behind the scenes for a little while. This is the perfect time to shift your schedule, so you quit work at a reasonable hour and shut off your computer for the weekend.

On January 18, Mercury goes direct. During this time, some paperwork you've been expecting now comes through. His could also mean an offer letter or contract. Dragon, you may have some excellent results from health tests.

The new moon is on January 22, and this brings the Year of the Water Rabbit. Dragon, you are now entering your third year of seed saving. This period will last for three years in total, and during this time, you're likely to connect with a lot of new people. What you post on social media can go viral. Your artwork and creativity, in general, take on a whole new dimension. But the focus for 2023 is on finishing projects rather than starting things. So think of what you want to get done and put yourself to the task.

Attract New Love

In the Year of the Water Tiger, you may feel some frustration, especially at the beginning of the year when you are looking for a new love relationship. You are likely to be pursued by someone very interested in you, but you may not feel a connection with this person (or people, as there could be several). It's helpful for you to be quite clear about what you're looking for in a love relationship. Picture how you would meet this person and how the relationship could progress from dating to a commitment. In the second half of the year, it gets easier for Dragon natives to find someone for an intimate relationship. This is especially true if you allow your friends and family to fix you up on dates.

Garnet: A good Feng Shui cure this year for Dragon natives is a gemstone. Gemstones have powerful energy. To attract a new love into your life, use the gemstone: Garnet. For centuries, this deep red gemstone has been used to attract worthy partners. You can carry a polished stone with you or choose to wear garnet jewelry—perhaps earrings or a pendant.

If you already have the garnets and want to use them now to attract a new love, it's a good idea to clear the stone. See the section in this book for instructions on clearing stones and crystals.

Enhance Existing Love

There is a great deal of positive energy in 2022 for Dragon natives already in a love relationship. Communication is improved between the two of you. You see eye to eye on many issues. There's more support for each other and commitment for the long haul. Also, there is more fun behind closed doors. You may find a hobby that you enjoy doing together, such as ballroom dancing, indoor rock climbing, or couples massage. If you haven't yet tied the knot, the Year of the Water Tiger is a great time to make it official. Or you may renew your vows this year.

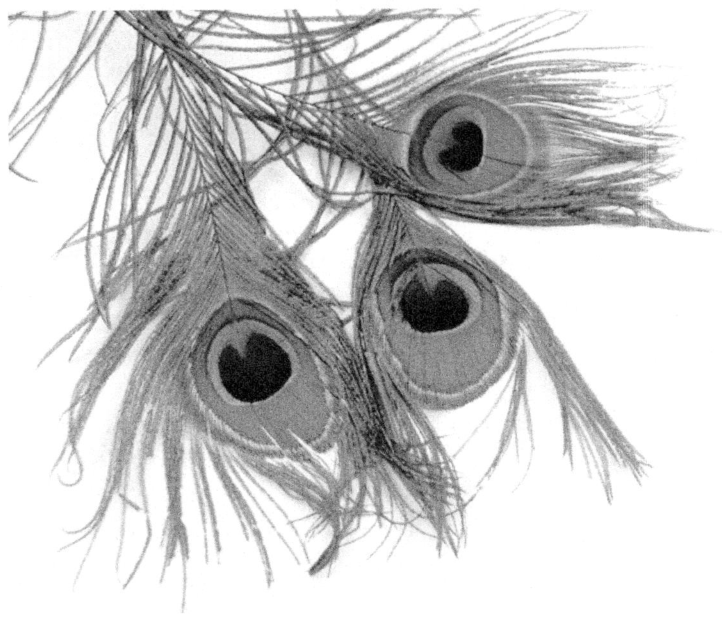

Peacock Feather: Display a peacock feather to increase your fertility energy. In Indian folklore, the peacock dances to attract a mate, and so its feathers are associated with abundance and fertility. Place your peacock feather on the wall at the head of your bed. You can attach it to the wall or the headboard. Use more than one peacock feather if you really want to make a statement. The more feathers, the more positive energy.

Looking to Conceive?

For those born in the year of the Dragon, it's a year to deepen your existing love relationship. You are independent, but everything is easier with someone who cares about you. This year find some pearls to bring into the bedroom. It can be a strand of pearls or a single pearl. People in many countries have worn pearls to increase happiness in marriage. Pearls are said to increase loving vibrations in the people around them.

(From Donna Stellhorn's book, Fertility Feng Shui)

Family and Kids

You and your family may be much more social this year, seeing other families, extended family, or visiting with friends. Your house may be a social center where people come and go, some staying briefly and others for extended stays. The house is lively with much discussion and some disagreement, but eventually, a happy ending is achieved. There's a lot of energy around working on the house this year. You might do some renovation projects or redecorating. This extends to the garden as well. You might do some landscaping or building an outdoor room.

Lavender is a wonderfully scented herb, popular and easy to find. It is known to clear energy, promote healing, and bring positive feelings into a space. Here are several ways you can use lavender this year. Plant lavender in the garden, as it is said that brings longevity energy to a property and its owners. You may fill bowls with lavender buds and place them on the entryway table, the dining table, or the kitchen island. Of course, you can use a lavender-scented room spray to attract peaceful, harmonious energy for the family to enjoy.

Money

Dragon, this year you have plenty of money opportunities, but most of them are tied to effort of some sort. You may have passive income coming in, but you have worked hard to get it. Your business may take off, bringing you multiple streams of income. But in the Year of the Water Tiger, you are at the center, juggling meetings, keeping track of spreadsheets, and perhaps hiring or firing help. So more money is flowing into your account in 2022, but it's because of the efforts you're making. Only that opens the floodgates of finance.

Around the world, seaports are still the most popular places to live and work. Even though we no longer rely on ships for personal transportation, much of the goods we use come into the country via boat. For this reason, one Feng Shui cure is the 'Wealth Ship,' representing prosperity sailing into your life. This is one of the most potent symbols for attracting what you want.

When using the symbol, you can choose a model of a wealth ship or find a picture or painting of a ship. If you're feeling ambitious and craft-minded, you can build a model ship from a kit. Or, if you have the inclination, you can paint a picture yourself of your own wealth ship. Any of these would make a fine Feng Shui cure.

Place your cure near your front door or in your home office. Position the ship or picture, so it appears to be sailing into the room, not out the door. If the ship is sailing out the door, it will take a lot longer for it to return and for wealth to find its way to you.

Job or Career

The Year the Water Tiger is a busy year for Dragon natives. You are likely 100% employed for the entire year. Even if you change jobs, there's very little space between the old and new jobs. You may have more than one job as you build a lucrative side business in 2022. That said, there can be substantial changes in your company or in the industry itself. This could mean mergers, or your company is seeing a decline in business. The reason that you are gainfully employed throughout the year is because of your networking skills. If it's necessary for you to change jobs, a friend or colleague will open that door for you. Or, as others are downsized out of their jobs, you remain in your position by doing the work of three people.

Sometimes, in Feng Shui, we combine multiple symbols to create a powerful cure. The symbol of a bowl is used to "welcome something new into our space." If the bowl is made of brass, we have the energy of success and prosperity.

So, for this cure, place a small brass bowl on your entryway table. You can leave the bowl empty or put coins and crystals in it. You can also place a list of your wishes describing your new, awaited career.

Education

Dragon, you rarely pass up a time to learn new things, and so it's likely you are taking classes on top of your already busy schedule. These could be self-study or accelerated programs. You may do video courses or one-on-one tutoring. If you are studying in a four-year university, it may be challenging to get assistance or get all the classes you want. Schools look like they are overflowing with people wanting to learn, so it's more challenging to take the conventional route in 2022. But no matter how you gain your information, you absorb it quickly and do well on exams.

Legal Matters

Legal matters can be challenging in the Year of the Water Tiger. People can be more contentious in general, and since you don't tolerate disrespect or deceit, you may be tempted to bring a lawsuit against someone. However, you do not have luck in this area this year. It would be better to see if you could settle out of court or just walk away from the situation. Dealing with government agencies for licensing, building permits, or certifications can be challenging. You may find incompetent people or individuals who refuse to help you for no apparent reason. So don't rush to do any legal matters if at all possible in 2022.

Health and Well-Being

There is a lot of positive energy around health and well-being in 2022. This is some of the best energy you've had in a long time. This can mean you are back on track with healthy eating and regular exercise. You can find a friend to go with you to the gym or be your accountability partner as you train for a marathon. It's easy to get a good diagnosis and to get in to see expert medical personnel when needed. You can also get helpful information as you are tapped into the positive energy this year.

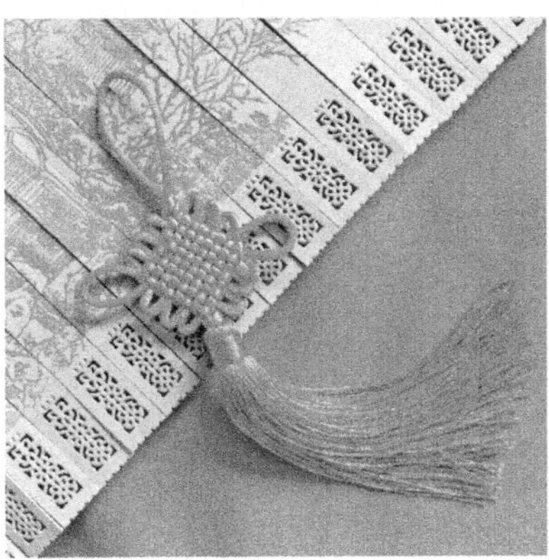

Many cultures know about the mystic knot. The knot is known throughout Asia and the British Isles and is even mentioned in Greek mythology. The mystic knot is a decorative knot tied in such a way it seems to go in an endless loop. It represents eternity or longevity.

Mystic knots come in various colors and various materials, such as rope, wire, or yarn, but the best for our purposes is bright red. Hang your mystic knot in the kitchen, bedroom, or family room to bring positive health energy to everyone in the home.

Snake

February 4, 1905–January 24, 1906: Yin Wood Snake
January 23, 1917–February 10, 1918: Yin Fire Snake
February 10, 1929–January 29, 1930: Yin Earth Snake
January 27, 1941–February 14, 1942: Yin Metal Snake
February 14, 1953–February 2, 1954: Yin Water Snake
February 2, 1965–January 20, 1966: Yin Wood Snake
February 18, 1977–February 6, 1978: Yin Fire Snake
February 6, 1989–January 26, 1990: Yin Earth Snake
January 24, 2001–February 11, 2002: Yin Metal Snake
February 10, 2013–January 30, 2014: Yin Water Snake
January 29, 2025–February 16, 2026: Yin Wood Snake

Snake Personality

When considering a Chinese Zodiac animal's qualities, it's a good idea to examine the animal's traits, behaviors, and personality. At first glance, it may seem Snake is at a disadvantage, having no hands or feet. But Snakes use their sense of smell to track their prey. Their sense of smell comes from using their forked tongue to collect airborne particles. You may already be aware your sense of smell is more acute than the average person. This is one of your advantages.

The scales covering a snake's body allow them to grip things tightly and to move swiftly along the ground. These scales are shed periodically, revealing new skin beneath as the snake literally crawls out of its old skin. This means you can reinvent yourself whenever you want. When your life needs to change, you can change it in a big way.

People born in the Snake Year rely on their intelligence and wisdom to make their way through the world. They have a very keen intuitive sense of other people. They easily attract people and keep them near for as long as they need. Snakes can also enjoy spending time alone when they wish.

Snakes cope well with making significant life changes. It seems they can renew themselves at will. They may change careers or move to a new city, leaving everything behind. They are reborn. Snakes admire power and look to gain control for themselves. When Snake realizes they're stuck in a situation or feel limited in their choices, they will move on.

Snake is the wisest of the zodiac signs and relies on their judgment. They're excellent with money and have a a great sense for investments. They have a computer-like brain that never stops calculating. They are incredibly tenacious when they want to achieve something. They never forget a broken promise. Some say the Snake is paranoid, but that doesn't mean people are not plotting against them.

While Snake natives always have money in the bank, they are cautious about speculating and should avoid gambling. If they gamble, they need to make safe bets.

Snakes are passionate lovers (not necessarily limited to one person). Snakes are loyal, but they will wander if they suspect the other person is not entirely devoted. When wronged, they like to crush their enemies completely. Snake natives will strike without warning, although they can be patient until the time for revenge is right.

People born in the Year of the Snake keep their feelings a well-guarded secret. Often seen as detached and cool, but in reality, Snakes feel things deeply. If surrounded by negative people, it breaks their concentration, and Snake becomes wary. But Snake has the power to win people over, and many fall into line with whatever Snake wishes.

Snake: Predictions for 2022

How to use your High-Energy Days: On these days, plan to take action for your most important goals, make vital phone calls, send important emails. Your high-energy days are when your energy and luck are the strongest for the month.

January 2022: *January 2 is the new moon. January 14 has Mercury going retrograde. January 17 is the full moon. On January 18, Uranus goes direct. On January 29, Venus goes direct. Your High-Energy Days are 6, 12, 18, 24, and 30.*

January brings one of the best relationship periods of the year for Snake natives. If you are looking for a new relationship, find someone you connect with beyond the surface attributes. You can find a special person to share true compatibility with you. It's a good idea to put yourself out into the world in as many ways as possible during this month to capitalize on this energy. This could mean going on online dating sites, letting friends and family know that you're looking, or even contacting a matchmaker.

January 2 brings the new moon, and your creative, courageous energy is very high. You recognize all you've been through and how you've weathered storm after storm. In a sense, you are now an expert sailor. So as things come up, you can remind yourself you've been through storms before, and you will get through this one as well.

January 14 has Mercury going retrograde. It's imperative to make sure work projects are securely backed up. If you are carrying a company computer, keep an eye on it. On a positive note, a a substantial opportunity could come back into your life. You may be selected to lead the team this time.

January 17 brings the full moon and emphasis in your personal realm of money derived from career. You will probably receive recognition. Be sure to use this opportunity to ask for a raise. You may get a "No," but it's more likely you'll get positive feedback.

On January 19, there's a shift of energy, and your thoughts turn towards health and well-being. You may have started the year with some resolutions and possibly found it was difficult to follow through. But now information about an alternative method of taking care of yourself through diet or exercise comes to you and piques your interest. This can be centered on martial arts or some sort of dance.

February 2022: *February 1 is the new moon and begins the Year of the Water Tiger. February 3, Mercury goes direct. February 16 is the full moon. Your high-energy days are: 6, 12, 18, and 24.*

The Water Tiger year begins on February 1, and so does a plethora of opportunities for Snake natives. This will be a busy year. Of course, Tiger energy is much more erratic and variable than your own energy. But while people rush around, change directions, and make quick decisions, you will see many opportunities to gather resources and make great connections. It's not that these options drop in your lap, but if you're willing to spend a little effort, you can achieve much.

This new moon energy on February 1, and you are spending extra energy at work. You may have a new computer system, or you may train new personnel. Snake native, if this is a new job for you, you might be in training yourself. At the same time, your side business could take off, which could mean your schedule is packed.

February 3 brings the Water Tiger month, and Mercury moves direct. You may have a big announcement for friends and family. You may have met somebody new, and now you're establishing the relationship or moving in together. Snake native, if you're already dating, you may declare an engagement or that you are purchasing a home together. Some Snake natives could announce a pregnancy or birth.

The full moon is on February 16. Over the next two weeks, your intuition is stronger. You may see evidence of your angels and guides working in your life. There could be signs and symbols such as repeated numbers or animals crossing your path. Snake native, you may study how to improve your psychic ability or read tarot cards. This is a great time to start a dream journal.

March 2022: *March 2 is the new moon. The full moon is on March 18. Your high-energy days are: 2, 8, 14, 20, and 26.*

In March, you're juggling work and relationships. You may be very concerned with work/life balance. You could miss a special occasion due to work obligations. Your weekends may be filled with projects. There is little time to relax. However, things will settle down in a few weeks, and you will be more in tune with the energy flow.

March 2 brings the new moon, and over the next two weeks, you could meet a lot of new people. You may connect with your partner's family. You could meet new colleagues by working in a different office. During this time, you could meet some new friends.

March 5 begins the Water Rabbit month, and over the next four weeks, you have a lot of new ideas. You're very clever and like to solve problems. Snake native, you may come up with something that is patentable or that you want to trademark. This is an excellent time to discuss ideas with an ambitious and trustworthy friend.

The full moon is on March 17. You may have more energy for the rest of the month. This could be because of some new health regimen you're doing or a change in your daily eating habits. You may decide to wake up earlier to get in some exercise. Snake native, you might also do some introspective work by journaling and clearing out old blocks.

In some parts of the world, there will be a second new moon on March 31, and for other time zones, it will be April 1. This new moon brings a real emphasis on investments and saving for the future. Over the next two weeks, you may get an intriguing investment tip or discover a new, exciting category of investments. You might focus now on paying down debts and get an opportunity for lower interest rates or a bill consolidation loan. Snake native, you're naturally good with money so that you could see tangible improvements in your accounts.

April 2022: *April 1 is the new moon. The full moon is on April 16. On April 29, Pluto goes retrograde. There is a partial solar eclipse on April 30. Your high-energy days are: 1, 7, 13, 19, and 25.*

April brings the continued emphasis on finances and keeping your resources safe. Over the next four weeks, it's good to monitor your accounts. Change passwords for banking or investment accounts. Snake native, you might diversify holdings to grab some profits from a potentially volatile market. Upgrade your antivirus software to keep your data safe.

On April 4, the Wood Dragon month begins, and over the next four weeks, it's a good idea to take a break. You might schedule yourself a long weekend or perhaps take a spring trip to see family and friends. This is a favorable time to put some boundaries on your workday. You may shut off your computer at 5 PM or stop working on the weekends, so you have time to unwind.

The full moon is on April 16, and over the next two weeks, you and your sweetheart might think of making a large purchase. This could be something for the home or buying a dwelling itself. You're now taking stock of what you have and perhaps looking at selling or donating some of the excess stuff. It looks like you are creating a more peaceful and comfortable home.

There is a solar eclipse on April 30, and over the next few weeks, there could be a struggle connected with education for you or one of your kids. If you're in school, you may rush to finish a project or have trouble getting a meeting with an advisor. There could be problems with your financial aid or student loans. Snake native, this may be when your child is struggling in school or perhaps deciding which college to attend. Eclipses can be bumpy times. The best bet is to take everything one step at a time.

May 2022: *On May 10, Mercury goes retrograde. There is a total lunar eclipse on May 16. On May 30, there is a new moon. Your high-energy days are: 1, 7, 13, 19, and 25.*

During May, there will be more than one surprise that occurs. A legal matter could rapidly change course. A case could be suddenly dismissed. Threats of a lawsuit could fizzle and disappear. On the other hand, it's not beneficial for you now, Snake native, to pursue a lawsuit as a turn of events could go against you. Additionally, over the next four weeks, be extra careful when signing contracts.

May 5 brings the Wood Snake month. This is your month, Snake native. Over the next few weeks, things you begin, like projects, side businesses, or relationships could grow into something real and substantial in the next 12 months. You're planting seeds by doing new things. Try to sow a lot of seeds during this time.

On May 10, Mercury goes retrograde, and a work project could be delayed. There could be substantial changes in the project, causing you to feel you're starting over. If you're expecting a promotion or raise, this also could be delayed. Information is being reviewed, or decision-makers may be out of town.

There is a lunar eclipse on May 15, and there's some adverse energy around transportation or your vehicle. It doesn't help that Mercury is retrograde and so if you need to take your car into the shop, make sure you get a warranty for the work done. Be careful when driving. Snake native, if you get one traffic citation over the next two weeks, you could get a second one very soon.

The new moon is on May 30, and now the energy gets substantially better. Over the last few weeks, there have been some problems, but clever Snake native, you have come up with some excellent solutions. You've also grown spiritually, and you may recognize that you can handle quite a bit. This means that you will grab hold of many more opportunities before the year is done. Over the next two weeks, you may receive some accolades or an award for the work you've been doing.

June 2022: *Mercury goes direct on June 3. On June 4, Saturn goes retrograde. On June 14, there is a full moon. Neptune goes retrograde on June 28. The new moon is on June 29. Your high-energy days are: 6, 12, 18, 24, and 30.*

In June, there's an emphasis on accumulating knowledge. You may finish up school and now finally read books and study for fun. You might take an online course or engage a tutor. Topics might include investing, photography, horseback riding, golf, or learning a foreign language.

June 5 brings the Fire Horse month, and over the next four weeks, there is a great deal of emphasis on your finances as you gain some additional income. You may have a new stream of revenue that, with little effort, could become permanent. You may pay a lot of attention to tracking your money. Snake native, you might put yourself on the "envelope system" or use an app to track your spending. Suddenly you realize how much money you can save just by paying attention to your cash spending.

The full moon is on June 14, and over the next two weeks, there's a lot of activity going on at home. You may have guests come over, or perhaps you are doing some redecorating. You could build an outdoor room or refit your balcony with plants and comfortable seating so you can spend more time outside enjoying the pleasant weather. Snake native, this is an excellent time to make some home improvements.

June 28 is the new moon, and a close friendship could turn romantic. If you're looking for love, you may connect with a friend or the friend of a friend. A family member may fix you up on a date with someone they know from their job. If you're already in a love relationship, you might be double-dating with friends or having people over for dinner parties and backyard barbecues.

July 2022: *July 13 brings the full moon. There is a new moon on July 28. Also, on July 28, Jupiter goes retrograde. Your high-energy days are: 6, 12, 18, 24, and 30.*

July brings intense energy connected to the people around you. While you are generally staying calm and collected, friends and family may dial up the drama. Snake native, so much is happening you might feel a desire to control external circumstances. But it would be better to maintain your usual hands-off approach. As you stand back and observe, you'll see the Universe orchestrate things to bring about the most appropriate outcome magically.

July 7 brings the Fire Sheep month and an emphasis on communication and thinking process. This is an excellent time for you to take up a meditation practice. Snake native, this could be mindfulness meditation, transcendental meditation, or the meditation of loving-kindness. You might want to download an online class on improving communications, reading body language, or micro-expressions. The slight changes you make over the next four weeks could make a tremendous impact on your life.

The full moon is on July 13, and over the next two weeks, you may be pursued for a romantic relationship. You could meet someone and fall head over heels. If you're already in a love relationship, you may spend more time enjoying each other's company and expressing your affection behind closed doors.

The new moon is on July 28, and you may work behind the scenes. You could work from home, or close your office door so you can finish a project. Snake native, you may say "no" to some social engagements because you've over-committed yourself. At the same time, you may be procrastinating, getting caught up in binge-watching a TV series, or playing a video game.

August 2022: *August 12 brings the full moon. Uranus goes retrograde on August 24. There is a new moon on August 27. Your high-energy days are: 5, 11, 17, 23, and 29.*

August brings an emphasis on travel, education, and knowledge in general. You may travel to help one of your kids get settled at college. Or perhaps you are gathering the family for an end-of-summer vacation. This is an appropriate time to do some camping or travel across the country. Meet some new people and see the sights.

August 7 brings the Earth Monkey month, and over the next four weeks, you may have more contact than usual with family, extended family, and distant relatives. You may work on the family tree and genealogy to discover more about your heritage. Snake native, you could exchange family heirlooms with siblings or cousins. You may help an older family member relocate to a new home.

August 11 is the full moon, and you may learn something new at work. There could be a new computer system, or you might have a new position within the company. It's also possible you have a new device such as a phone or laptop that you are learning how to optimize. Now is a suitable time to look at new software platforms for content publishing, video editing, or making music.

The new moon is on August 27, and there's a lot of attention on you. You might be on stage announcing speakers or giving a lecture. This is an apt time to audition with a theater company, a church choir, or join an improv group. Snake native, you also may change your physical appearance over the next two weeks by getting a new hairstyle or adding a tattoo.

September 2022: O*n September 10, there is a full moon, and Mercury goes retrograde. On September 25, there's the new moon. Your high-energy days are: 4, 10, 16, 23, and 28.*

September brings a substantial opportunity. This could be the one you have been waiting for; however, it is outside your comfort zone. That said, you have the skill set to do this, and you can gather resources to help you. Several people could lend you their knowledge and experience to bring this opportunity to fruition. This month you could land a whale.

September 7 begins the Earth Rooster month, and there's a lot of emphasis on creativity and fertility. Creative ideas flow at this time. You might be inspired to do art or music. You may finish up a craft project you have been working on for some time. If you're looking to add to the family (children or pets), you have very positive luck at this time.

The full moon is on September 10, and the same day, Mercury goes retrograde. Relationships and partnerships are highlighted for the next two weeks. Snake native, you may meet someone for business collaboration. You could meet a mentor or influencer. You might bump into a celebrity. There's good energy for friendships, especially if you want to find someone to travel with.

The new moon is on September 25, and you could receive a windfall. Some extra money may come into your account via a bonus from your job or from selling a high-ticket item. You may also win money in a raffle or contest.

October 2022: *Mercury goes direct on October 2. On October 8, Pluto goes direct. There is a full moon on October 9. On October 23, Saturn goes direct. On October 25, there's a partial solar eclipse. On October 28, Jupiter goes retrograde. Mars goes retrograde on October 30. Your high-energy days are:4, 10, 16, 23, and 28.*

October can be a profitable month to 6 for Snake natives. Mercury goes direct on October 2. If you have been looking for a new job, you could sign an employment contract or even start a new job now. In your current job, you can get more hours or get a salary increase. If you own a business, you can receive funding, especially if you do crowdsourcing.

October 8 brings the Metal Dog month, and over the next four weeks, it's a good idea to take care of your physical self. You might want to change up your exercise routine or look at different herbs/vitamins to take to support your health. Consider doing some yoga or a moving meditation for a holistic approach. Snake native, you do well with exercises that involve stretching.

The full moon is on October 9, and over the next two weeks, you may have a strong interest in investments. Look at opportunities through your employer, such as a 401(k) match or discounted stock purchase plans. You have luck with investments now, so this could be a good time to diversify your portfolio.

The solar eclipse is on October 25. In the next two weeks, there could be some challenges in communication, especially with siblings and younger relatives. A misunderstanding could lead to an argument and hurt feelings. Snake native, you're highly intelligent, and in a debate, you can run circles around most people at this time. You will want to go easy on family members.

November 2022: *November 8 brings the total lunar eclipse. On November 23, there is a new moon, and Jupiter goes direct. Your high-energy days are: 3, 9, 15, 21, and 27.*

November begins rather bumpy but smooths out towards the end of the month. There could be some issues around your vehicle or how you get around town. There could be construction or delays due to weather. You may be snowed in and stuck at home when you want to be somewhere else. The energy settles down at the end of the month, and you can get back to normal.

November 7 brings the Metal Pig month, and you have good relationship energy for the next four weeks. If you're dating, you may move the relationship forward to make it official by changing your relationship status on social media. Some Snake natives will get engaged. You may also establish a business partnership at this time, drawing up a contract for both parties to sign.

The lunar eclipse is on November 8, and over the next two weeks, travel could be difficult. This is probably due to weather or crowds of people causing traffic or long lines. You need to be patient if you're on the road and consider a backup plan just in case.

The new moon is on November 23. Now a sense of peace and harmony can flow in. Arguments are smoothed over and hurt feelings are mended. You have a deep and clear understanding of the people in your life. The family pulls together stronger than ever. You may gather to celebrate the season and each other.

December 2022: *Neptune goes direct on December 3. The full moon is on December 8. There is a new moon on December 23. Mercury goes retrograde on December 29. Your high-energy days are: 3, 9, 15, 21, and 27.*

In December, you see happier times at home. If you're dating, introduce your sweetheart to your friends and family. This is an excellent time to bring friends into the family circle to celebrate the holidays or for an open house. You may get together with coworkers for some festivities.

On December 7, it's the Water Rat month. and it's also the full moon. You may receive some recognition from your job. A customer could write a glowing review or the CEO notices your performance. Snake native, you may receive an award for top sales or for contributing significantly. This could come with a bonus or a cash prize.

December 23 is the new moon, and there is energy around having fun and doing creative things. You may take some time off to do some art or music. You might have some fun excursions with the kids. You may gather with friends to celebrate the end of the year.

On December 29, Mercury goes retrograde, and a lover could return to you. Someone from your past may knock at your door. They could find you through social media. Snake native, this might be someone you went to high school or college with. And while you may not be available for a relationship, this offers a chance to get reacquainted.

January 2023: *January 6 brings the full moon. Mercury goes direct on January 18. The year of the water rabbit begins on January 22. Your high-energy days are. 2, 8, 14, 20, and 26.*

January brings a desire to take risks and live a bigger life. You might be ready to start a business or buy a franchise. You might look at a lifestyle change, possibly downsizing to live in a tiny house or living in a foreign country. This is a suitable month to write down your goals, no matter how wild and audacious they might be. Then see what the Universe brings you in the way of opportunities.

January 5 begins the Water Ox month, and this month, you may take action on an important goal. Snake native, you could take a class or contact knowledgeable people to learn how others do what you want to do. This could mean that you are watching a lot of YouTube videos or doing tutorials. You are soaking up information like a sponge.

The full moon is on January 6, and you may be involved in the community over the next two weeks. You could network for your career or join a mastermind group to brainstorm ideas for business. It's also possible to connect with a local charitable organization to help seniors, promote the library, or build a better town center.

On January 18, Mercury goes direct. This is an excellent time to upgrade equipment such as a printer, laptop, or cell phone. Snake native, you might get additional equipment such as a better microphone, camera, or lighting to do YouTube videos.

The new moon is on January 22, bringing the beginning of the Year of the Water Rabbit. 2023 will be your second seed-saving year. This is a more relaxing year where you're in harmony with the energy. You understand the peace-loving nature that Rabbit energy brings. Snake native, being one of the most intuitive signs, you will have an innate understanding of what people want. If you're willing to take action, it will be easy for you to capitalize on opportunities this year. At the same time, you're nearing the end of your 12-year cycle, and so it's better to finish things rather than to start new projects in 2023.

Attract New Love

The year of the Water Tiger could be a very romantic year for Snake natives. You may have more than one possibility for a love relationship. It looks like you're communicating with several potential love matches, and you may juggle dates in your calendar. By the end of the year, you may have chosen your sweetheart, or you could still decide between two suitors. 2022 looks like an exciting year.

We are more sensitive to scent than any of our other senses. Odors are known to influence our emotions and behaviors. Scent triggers memories in our brains and associations with those memories. We then act even if we're not fully conscious of the reasons. Those small actions add up, bringing us closer to our goals.

The scent of vanilla is wonderful for attracting new love. Vanilla extract can be found in most grocery stores. Place a drop or two on cotton balls and place these in your bedroom. These can be placed behind a picture or on a small dish on your bedside table. You can also spray vanilla-scented air fresheners—however, the more natural the scent, the better. Or place a small amount of vanilla in a pot of boiling water on the stove and allow the aroma of vanilla to fill the house. At the same time, visualize the love relationship you want readily coming to you.

Enhance Existing Love

There's a lot of positive relationship energy for Snake natives in 2022. You are working on projects together like home renovations or a small business. You're also more likely to agree on matters regarding the children. This year, the only snag is that you may spend a little time apart when one of you is traveling or needs to help a family member for a time. But overall, the Year of the Water Tiger is good for your committed love relationship.

If you're in an existing relationship and want to increase the fidelity energy and overall happiness, you can place a pair of Mandarin Ducks on your bedside table or dresser. These ducks are known to mate for life, and they are a symbol of marital bliss. These ducks can be so attached that when separated, they will pine away and die.

Mandarin ducks are primarily used, as they are considered the best of the species in intelligence and beauty. Their energy symbolizes felicity. They are usually displayed with the lotus blossom, which emerges from the mud pure and clean.

Looking to Conceive?

Geode: One of the gemstones associated with pregnancy is the geode. A geode is a hollow mineral mass with gemstones growing inside the shell. A geode often looks like an egg on the outside, and when cracked open, reveals the sparkling gemstones.

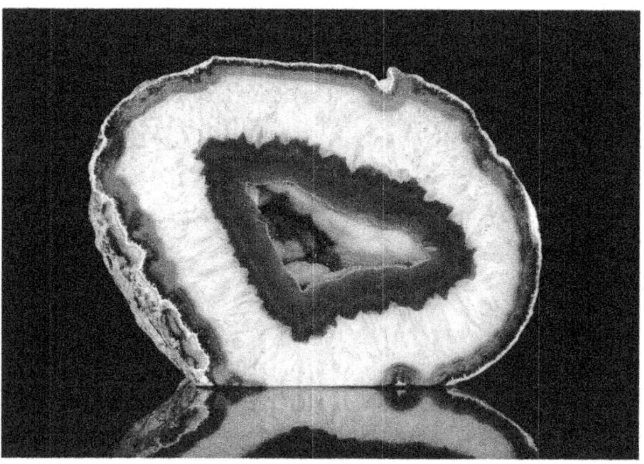

Geodes range from a couple of inches in size to several feet in diameter. When you find a geode you like, place it in your bedroom to enhance the pregnancy energy.

(From Donna Stellhorn's book, Fertility Feng Shui)

Family and Kids

Life at home is good in 2022 for Snake natives. You may do a lot of work on the house, including kitchen or bath renovations or redecorating your bedroom. Older children may come to stay with you for a time or perhaps move back in for the year. You could have a multigenerational household. Single Snake natives may get a roommate or add a pet. There's also a strong possibility you are working out of the home, doing your own business, or telecommuting.

The Chi-Lin is a magical creature, a chimera, part horse, part dragon with the scales of a fish. Statues of this creature are displayed in the living room or dining room to protect the home and family. Place him up high where he can watch over everyone. The statue need not be large but should be a size that can be seen on its high shelf. The Chi-Lin can be plain or colorfully decorated.

Money

There are several outstanding financial opportunities in 2022 for Snake natives. While some of these opportunities may feel outside your comfort zone, you have the necessary skills to take on these investments or business opportunities. You can find knowledgeable people to help you with these opportunities if you want to pursue them further. In the Year of the Water

Tiger, some Snake natives may just want to put on the cruise control and sail through the year. As long as you keep your spending in check, this could work out just fine.

To capitalize on your luck, consider creating a "Money Tree." You can make one using any large house plant. Using pipe cleaners or twist ties, attach dollar bills like leaves to the plant. You can also hang Chinese coins (the coins with the square hole in the center) from the branches.

As you decorate your Money Tree, choose an odd number of bills or coins. From the perspective of Feng Shui, odd numbers are more powerful than even numbers. You can select bills of any denomination, but dollar bills work just fine.

Display the money tree in your home office, your living room, or in view of your front door. And make sure you take care and water the plant—you want it to stay healthy and happy.

Job or Career

2022 could be quite a busy year for Snake natives. The Year of the Water Tiger brings a lot of opportunities. You may get a promotion or take on a management position. If you own a business, you might hire employees. You may have two jobs during the year, or your side business is really taking off. This year, you may decide how long you want to stay in your current profession. It's good to review your company's financial fundamentals and notice whether your industry is changing. So, while you are most likely employed all year, you may look at ways to transfer out of your current job in the future.

To welcome new opportunities in your career, get a new welcome mat for your front door. Choose a simple mat. It can be black and made of rubber (representing the water element and flow of opportunity) or natural grass (representing the wood element and growth). It can say the word "Welcome" or "Home," but it shouldn't have pictures on it (no pictures of kittens, flags, or clever sayings that could have negative connotations).

About once a month, weather permitting, take the time to clean up the porch to welcome new positive energy. Shake out the mat to stimulate the energy flow. If the mat becomes worn, then replace it.

Education

With education in 2022, you are laser-focused. You are collecting educational credits and knowledge by the bucketful. You may be well on your way to finishing up a degree or certification. You may take advantage of free certification programs or YouTube videos to learn new skills. You may make a change in your education this year. The Water Tiger energy facilitates change so you could go to a different university or move from a traditional program into an accelerated course.

Legal Matters

In 2022, legal matters can be unpredictable and costly. This is not an area where you have a lot of luck this year. It's wise to stay clear of lawsuits if at all possible. If you're currently in a difficult lawsuit, you may benefit by trying to settle or extending out the time beyond this year. If you're looking to test to renew a professional license, be aware that the program requirements could have changed. Don't leave this to the last minute, or you may be caught unprepared. Your best area for legal matters is contracts. Your ability to negotiate agreements is strong this year, so be sure to ask for what you want.

Health and Well-Being

Your health and well-being show a lot of improvement this year as you put more time and effort into your physical self and wellness in general. Snake native, you are pretty good about taking care of yourself, and now you are taking it to a whole new level. In 2022, you're implementing a lot of the ideas you've been thinking about concerning exercise, healthy eating, meditation, and other things related to self-care. By the end of the year, you could be transformed.

Consider adding the fragrant flower, jasmine, to your front yard or, if this is not possible, place a picture of jasmine in your bedroom. You can also have cut jasmine flowers in the bedroom about once a month. Artificial or silk flowers will work energetically for a few months but need to be cleaned or replaced to renew the energy. This pretty, night-blooming flower is said to bring sound sleep and prophetic dreams. In the morning, you will feel both rested and have an inner knowledge of what the day will hold.

Horse

January 25, 1906–February 12, 1907: Yang Fire Horse
February 11, 1918–January 31, 1919: Yang Earth Horse
January 30, 1930–February 16, 1931: Yang Metal Horse
February 15, 1942–February 4, 1943: Yang Water Horse
February 3, 1954–January 23, 1955: Yang Wood Horse
January 21, 1966–February 8, 1967: Yang Fire Horse
February 7, 1978–January 27, 1979: Yang Earth Horse
January 27, 1990–February 14, 1991: Yang Metal Horse
February 12, 2002–January 31, 2003: Yang Water Horse
January 31, 2014–February 18, 2015: Yang Wood Horse
February 17, 2026–February 05, 2027: Yang Fire Horse

Horse Personality

When considering a Chinese Zodiac animal's qualities, it's a good idea to examine the animal's traits, behaviors, and personality. There are many myths and legends about horses in our culture. Humans domesticated horses around 3000 BC. Many cultures have horse stories and traditions that help us identify these beautiful animals' specific traits and behaviors.

Horses are sensitive creatures; they can sense danger and know how to flee. They can sleep standing up, giving them the ability to run at a moment's notice. Even baby horses—foals—can run soon after birth. Horses have enormous endurance and are highly intelligent.

Those born in the Year of the Horse are attuned to the moods and motivations of others. They are quick to take offense and can explode with anger. But once Horse feels safe again, they quickly forget their rage. Horses want to move things forward, sometimes rushing others. They become impatient when results manifest too slowly.

They prefer things done their way. While they believe in the pursuit of happiness for everyone, their way is the best. They will become aggressive if you try to block them or pull them off their chosen direction.

Horse natives are great at business—primarily from the perspective of sales and promotion. They are social beings eager to connect people for the benefit of all. However, they're not good at sticking to a schedule, nor do they like adhering to procedures. The more stimulating the job, the better! Once involved in their tasks, Horse prefers to keep working on a project until it's done, then take time off to play.

Horse natives are better at short-term projects; they may not have the staying power to tackle lengthy processes. Break goals down into quick steps. Horses are great at solving problems. They love to get things done—no endless projects, please! Horses are curious and enthusiastically interested or not interested at all. Once they lose interest, they're out the door. (This goes for love as well as business.)

Horses need both mental and physical exercise. They are graceful and elegant in their movements (and in their decision-making). They can be defiant nonconformists. When you try to put them in a box, they become hot-tempered and headstrong.

Their biggest problem is their lack of focus and their readiness to jump to another project when things seem to move too slow.

They will abandon the original goal and wonder why they are not making much progress.

Horse natives excel at making money. They are strong leaders but allow people the freedom to work on their own. They can be extremely generous with their time and energy, but if Horse doesn't like what you're saying (or doing), he won't think twice about trampling you.

Horse: Predictions for 2022

How to use your High-Energy Days: On these days, plan to take action for your most important goals, make vital phone calls, send important emails. Your high-energy days are when your energy and luck are the strongest for the month.

January 2022: *January 2 is the new moon. January 14 has Mercury going retrograde. January 17 is the full moon. On January 18, Uranus goes direct. On January 29, Venus goes direct. Your High-Energy Days are 2, 8, 14, 20, and 26.*

While the calendar year begins, there is still Metal Ox energy to contend with. Many Horse natives are ready to charge forward, but you can feel held back. This is the perfect time to finish things up. Look at what was left incomplete at the end of 2021 and see if you can put any final touches on it. This mainly includes creative projects like screenplays, home renovations, or website creation.

The new moon falls on January 2. For Horse natives, the emphasis is on home and family, and now to an even greater extent, on your extended family. You may help someone move or get settled into a new place. Someone may travel to you to stay for a while. Some Horse natives will send off older children back to college. If the weather permits, clean up around the outside of your house. For those who are homebound because of the weather, consider working on your entryway to make it warm and inviting.

On January 14, Mercury goes retrograde in your area of romance and fun. You may be contacted by a lover from your past, someone who wants to rekindle things. Or you might reach out to someone you knew a long time ago. You can track this person down through Facebook and see how they're doing. Communication with friends or distant relatives you haven't spoken to in a while is also a good idea.

January 17 brings the full moon, and you may find there is a work-at-home opportunity, or the business you run out of the house is expanding. Financially, things improve, and while you may have put a lot of money into furnishings or repairs at home, you're also able to put some into your savings account.

The energy shifts on January 19, and there are opportunities for happy relationships for Horse natives looking for love. You can meet someone new through friends or an online dating app. Over the next few weeks, you could connect with someone who becomes a long-term relationship for you.

February 2022: *February 1 is the new moon and begins the Year of the Water Tiger. February 3, Mercury goes direct. February 16 is the full moon. Your high-energy days are: 1, 7, 13, 19, and 25.*

The Water Tiger year begins on February 1. You may immediately sense the positive energy shift, as this is more harmonious energy for you. The sluggish, blocked energy of the previous year is now quickly dissipating. It's being replaced with vibrant energy of people wanting to be social. There will be connections to make and opportunities everywhere you look. Horse native, this could be a very exciting year.

This new moon energy on February 1, and for the next two weeks, there' are a lot of positive romantic possibilities for Horse natives. If you're looking for love and want a long-term relationship, this is good energy for meeting someone new. If you're dating, you could take your relationship to the next level by announcing to friends and family that you are officially a couple.

February 3 brings the Water Tiger month, and Mercury moves direct. A troublesome matter regarding education or a legal issue now clears up. Someone steps in to help you and clear up a misunderstanding. Even though it will take a little while for this whole matter to resolve itself, you can see genuine progress over the next few days, where you didn't see any before.

The full moon is on February 16, and a friend comes to your rescue. You may discuss a significant decision you have to make. They'll sit with you and go over the pros and cons. Horse native, while they encourage you to trust your judgment, it's wonderful to have them as a sounding board.

March 2022: *March 2 is the new moon. The full moon is on March 18. Your high-energy days are: 3, 9, 15, 21, and 27.*

In March, some changes are going on with your job. Maybe you have switched positions or have a new person on your team. Horse native, you might train someone, or you are learning a new system. In this process, you are gaining new skills.

March 2 brings the new moon, and you may receive a good health report from your doctor. Your personal trainer may tell you how well you're doing. This is an excellent time to get information on a medical issue as you can find good, clear advice now.

March 5 begins the Water Rabbit month. This month you could receive recognition from your job or the community. If you do some volunteering, you could receive an award and gratitude from the people you work with. If you're connected with the City Council, you may receive accolades for your service.

The full moon is on March 17, and over the next two weeks, there's powerful relationship energy. You and your sweetheart may set up house together or do renovations on the property.

If you're looking for love, you could find someone with whom you have great chemistry. The relationship could become intimate quickly.

In some parts of the world, there will be a second new moon on March 31, and for other time zones, it will be April 1. This new moon brings opportunities with relationships as well as partnerships. You could find a person to do business with, perhaps a mentor in your field. Horse native, you may connect with a celebrity or get a backstage pass. Now is the time to reach out to someone you admire through direct messaging.

April 2022: *April 1 is the new moon. The full moon is on April 16. On April 29, Pluto goes retrograde. There is a partial solar eclipse on April 30. Your high-energy days are: 2, 8,* 14, 20, and 26.

The month of April brings your attention to your work/life balance. Horse native, consider how emails and texts for work keep seeping into your free time. This is your opportunity to put things back into balance. It's time to set clear boundaries and express to your coworkers that you have particular hours for answering emails. The rest of the time is yours.

On April 4, the Wood Dragon month begins, and you may find several friends reaching out to you to get together over the next four weeks. Some may travel and come to see you. You may also receive invitations to visit friends who live far away. There are opportunities to make new friends as well as you meet the friends of your friends.

The full moon is on April 16, and your charisma and popularity increase. Several people go out of their way to make your acquaintance. They've heard lots of good things about you. These individuals may be willing to collaborate with some profitable results. Horse native, one of these connections could lead to a great job opportunity.

There is a solar eclipse on April 30, and there could be some difficulty around your finances, credit, or investments. Make sure that your insurance policies give you adequate coverage. It's a good idea to change passwords on banking and brokerage websites. Be wary of emails you get from financial institutions, as they could be fake. Over the next two weeks, you want to be extra careful with your data.

May 2022: On *May 10, Mercury goes retrograde. There is a total lunar eclipse on May 16. On May 30, there is a new moon. Your high-energy days are: 2, 8, 14, 20, and 26.*

During May, you sort out the financial difficulties that came up last month. Towards the end of the month, money and finances improve considerably. Your investments are doing better, and extra money is flowing into your accounts from multiple sources.

May 5 brings the Wood Snake month. Horse, you could use some time off. It's a good idea to take a break during your busy month. If you can't take a vacation, consider taking a long weekend. Maybe take a meditation class or go someplace beautiful where you can sit by a swimming pool and sip a cool beverage.

On May 10, Mercury goes retrograde, and there's an emphasis on education. Your child or younger relative graduates from high school, college, or maybe kindergarten. You may be around extended family, taking pictures, and socializing.

There is a lunar eclipse on May 15, and you could have fascinating moneymaking ideas. Perhaps you've been mulling over some of these ideas for a while. Now it's time to take action. You may start a side business or get funding for your concept. Horse native, if you're uncertain, find a friend who happens to be a lawyer or has experience in business. They can lend a hand.

The new moon is on May 30, and Horse native, things have settled down considerably. A lot of the issues from earlier in the month have dissipated. Now you enter a time of increased spirituality. Horse native, you may feel more connected to God, the Universe, and nature. It's a good idea to be outside when you can to receive messages through animals and nature itself.

June 2022: *Mercury goes direct on June 3. On June 4, Saturn goes retrograde. On June 14, there is a full moon. Neptune goes retrograde on June 28. The new moon is on June 29. Your high-energy days are: 1, 7, 13, 19, and 25.*

In June, you have an opportunity to be more visible. You might be on stage or be in front of your coworkers showing off a PowerPoint presentation (just when the CEO happens to stop in). Horse native, you may receive some recognition from clients or customers as written testimonials.

June 5 brings the Fire Horse month, and this begins your 12-month cycle. This is an opportune time to do new activities and meet new people. Each new thing you do is a seed you plant that could later grow into a bountiful harvest. Look at new things to try—everything from brands of tomato sauce to where you shop for groceries to buying land to starting your own farm. Big changes or small, each could grow into an abundant opportunity.

The full moon is on June 14. Horse native, there's a great deal of activity around agreements and contracts. A contract you've been waiting for now is likely in your hands, but it's not exactly what you had thought it would be. Some adjustments or an addendum may be needed. Horse native, there could be negotiations back and forth before this agreement is finalized.

June 28 is the new moon, and you have some good news from your job. If you have been looking for a new position, now you have the green light. You will probably receive your start date. If you're staying in your current job, you may get some positive feedback from your supervisor as well as coworkers. A colleague who has been quite difficult may be leaving.

July 2022: *July 13 brings the full moon. There is a new moon on July 28. Also, on July 28, Jupiter goes retrograde. Your high-energy days are: 1, 7, 13, 19, 25, and 31.*

In July, there is excellent relationship energy. If you're already in a love relationship, you and your sweetheart are getting along better and seeing eye to eye more often. If you're dating, this might be the time to introduce your sweetheart to your friends and family. You could make a big announcement about your plans for the future. If you're looking for love, you have a great opportunity now to meet someone with whom you feel genuine closeness.

July 7 brings the Fire Sheep month, and you may receive a financial windfall. Horse native, some money could come into your account from a bonus, salary increase, or perhaps you have sold a valuable item. This money may come from an unexpected source.

The full moon is on July 13, and Horse native, you're needed at home. There could be some difficulty with an appliance, power, or plumbing. You may have to call in a professional to work on it. Or you may deal with your landlord about the issue. But this energy could turn positive, and you may end up receiving more benefits than you were expecting.

The new moon is on July 28, and a friend may help you upgrade your technology. Horse native, you might upgrade your website by adding a shopping cart or making it a membership website. Perhaps you are starting your YouTube channel or putting out a podcast. Look into getting the equipment your business needs to move forward.

August 2022: *August 12 brings the full moon. Uranus goes retrograde on August 24. There is a new moon on August 27. Your high-energy days are: 6, 12, 18, 24, and 30.*

The month of August has you working behind the scenes though this can pay off quite handsomely. You could do investment research or flip a house for profit. You can find suitable investments at this time. But a friend may feel the investment is too risky or too safe and may try to talk you out of it. You'll have to weigh their opinions with your research.

August 7 brings the Earth Monkey month, and over the next four weeks, there's a focus on communication. Horse native, you may take a class on how to communicate your ideas to coworkers. Or you may sit down with your teenagers for important life discussions. This is a good time for writing or journaling.

August 11 is the full moon, and this could be quite a romantic time. But this is not the energy for a one-night stand. This is for meeting and connecting with someone for the long haul. If you're dating, take your relationship to the next level. Change your relationship status on social media to let the world know that you're in a serious relationship. Horse native, a friend may introduce you to someone who is quite impressive.

The new moon is on August 27, and over the next two weeks, there's a lot of positive spiritual energy for you. Your psychic ability is more robust. You may have dreams with vivid messages for you. This is an excellent time to learn to read tarot cards, find water through dowsing, or have a past life regression done.

September 2022: *On September 10, there is a full moon, and Mercury goes retrograde. On September 25, there's the new moon. Your high-energy days are: 5, 11, 17, 23, and 29.*

The month of September brings some discordant energy. While you are sailing through your days, people around you may feel easily irritated or blocked. You may see your partner or your kids struggle with the same issue over and over. It's hard for you to explain it to them because they have blinders on. Horse native, you'll need a lot of patience during this time.

September 7 begins the Earth Rooster month, and there's a lot of energy around dwellings. It's possible you are moving, or perhaps one of your neighbors is moving. Someone you know well could move across the country. You may also get a new roommate or have someone stay with you for a while.

The full moon is on September 10, and the same day, Mercury goes retrograde. A miscommunication at work could cost you some extra hours. A document that you need may get lost even though you are sure it was saved to the hard drive. Be extra careful when dealing with flash drives and make a note of filenames as you save documents.

The new moon is on September 25. Over the next two weeks, there is joyful relationship energy. You may attend a wedding or milestone anniversary celebration. You and your sweetheart are likely getting along very well. Horse native, your friends may look to you as an example of having a good relationship.

October 2022: *Mercury goes direct on October 2. On October 8, Pluto goes direct. There is a full moon on October 9. On October 23, Saturn goes direct. On October 25, there's a partial solar eclipse. On October 28, Jupiter goes retrograde. Mars goes retrograde on October 30. Your high-energy days are: 5, 11, 17, 23, and 29.*

October can be a month when you are very noticeable. Additionally, Mercury goes direct on October 2. Horse native, you might be recognized in a grocery store, or someone might approach you at the post office. An old high school friend may reach out to you through social media. If you have social media followers, you may connect with a follower in real life.

October 8 brings the Metal Dog month and a lucky period for Horse natives, especially if you're willing to take some risks. Take a chance on romance by asking out someone you admire. Or say "yes" to someone who asks you out. You may also take risks in business or investing. By trusting your abilities and having confidence in yourself, you could have success.

The full moon is on October 9. A former supervisor or colleague may reach out to you with a job opportunity. If you own a business, you can find someone to collaborate with for advertising or marketing promotion. Horse native, if you're looking to buy a business, move forward slowly as the energy will shift towards the end of the month.

The solar eclipse is on October 25, and you may spend a sizeable chunk of money. You might invest or buy a business. You may shell out money for your kid's education. Horse native, you might invest in a video course for yourself. Make sure what you are purchasing is worth the money. Don't make a purchase in haste.

November 2022: *November 8 brings the total lunar eclipse. On November 23, there is a new moon, and Jupiter goes direct. Your high-energy days are: 4, 10, 16, 23, and 28.*

November has you looking at what you own and decide whether you can let go of some of it. If you have a storage unit, you might move items to the house to be sorted. You could distribute some of your things to relatives, especially antiques or family heirlooms.

November 7 brings the Metal Pig month, and over the next four weeks, there's a lot of emphasis on your routines and habits. Horse native, you may let go of a nasty habit or instilling new positive habits, especially exercising and healthy eating. You may find faster ways of doing everyday things. You might get the dishes done in half the time or delegate your laundry to a laundry service.

The lunar eclipse is on November 8. You may work with a banker or credit card company to gain more credit or lower interest rates. You could refinance your mortgage. If you are looking to change apartments, you may check your credit score. Horse native, this is a good time to do any credit repair that might be needed to dispute erroneous data.

The new moon is on November 23, and there's a lot of contact with siblings and younger relatives. You might get together for the holidays or attend your kid's school play. You may babysit other people's kids as your children invite their friends to your house. You also may be pet sitting.

December 2022: *Neptune goes direct on December 3. The full moon is on December 8. There is a new moon on December 23. Mercury goes retrograde on December 29. Your high-energy days are: 4, 10, 16, 23, and 28.*

In December, a misunderstanding with a family member or close friend is cleared up. You're compassionately listening to each other and noticing that your love languages are different. You will probably grow closer together and appreciate each other more.

On December 7, it's the Water Rat month. It's also the full moon. You may travel over the next four weeks. Horse native, you might visit some relatives or travel to a warm and sunny destination. Even if you're just getting in the car to go to the next town, a change of scene is very beneficial.

December 23 is the new moon, and you are surrounded by friends and family. You have many invitations and different things you can do. There is also intense energy for doing charity work within the community. You may distribute care packages or do a fundraiser.

On December 29, Mercury goes retrograde, and something at home that you thought was fixed breaks again. It may be covered by a warranty if you can just lay your hands on it. If this is something to do with plumbing, it can mean some overflowing emotions in the house. Horse native, you may want to have a family meeting.

January 2023: *January 6 brings the full moon. Mercury goes direct on January 18. The Year of the Water Rabbit begins on January 22. Your high-energy days are. 3, 9, 15, 21, and 27.*

In January, you might be torn between staying at home or visiting someone who lives outside your town. There are benefits on both sides, and you could be indecisive now. Your choice can be made when you see which option will bring more money to your accounts. There is a splendid business opportunity this month.

January 5 begins the Water Ox month, and a potential love relationship could turn romantic. You might have thought it was just a friendship, but it's taken a sensual, sexy turn. Over the next four weeks, this could grow into a serious love relationship. Horse native, if you're already in a love relationship, you may have someone who is tempting you.

The full moon is on January 6, and you may get a promotion at work or a new team. You could fill in for your boss, who is away. With all this added responsibility now, you can ask for a raise in the next few months. It's a good idea to keep track of what you're doing now so you can bring it up at your next review.

On January 18, Mercury goes direct. Issues around the house are now solved, and things are running much more smoothly. Someone who recently left the house is returning to live with you again or coming for a visit.

The new moon is on January 22, and this brings the Year of the Water Rabbit. You are now entering your first year of seed saving. This is the easiest year of the three-year seed saving period. Now you can gain recognition for your accomplishments. You can find jobs and opportunities worthy of your skills. Over the course of the year, you have an opportunity to gather resources. Horse native, this could include helping people, knowledge, and actual cash. Your investments could grow, and you could find additional sources of revenue that last beyond this year. It's time to open up your arms to receive.

Attract New Love

The Year of the Water Tiger brings some fantastic opportunities for Horse natives in the area of love. Not only can you find romance, but you can find someone to settle down with for a long-lasting relationship. Some Horse natives may get engaged this year. But there is also the possibility of moving from one relationship to another. When the energy is this good, you have choices. The blocks of the previous year are fading away, and now, in 2022, you can meet new people and connect with someone extraordinary.

If you are looking for a serious relationship with someone to settle down with, consider using the Wedding Ring cure. Find a replica wedding ring (you can often find these at party stores in the bridal section). Place the ring under the mattress on the unoccupied side of the bed. Just lift the mattress and slide the ring underneath.

If you're not ready to settle down, but you still want a romantic new love in your life, then instead of the ring, put a copy of your house key under the mattress. Put it under the side of the bed where your new lover will rest their head. If you decide later to make the relationship more permanent and official, change out the house key for the replica wedding ring.

Enhance Existing Love

2022 is the healing year for your existing love relationship. Horse native, you have better communication, and you understand each other. A lot of the external distractions of the previous year are gone, and now you can focus on loving and caring for each other. The Year of the Water Tiger also brings some opportunities for romance no matter how long you've been together. You could explore some new ways to have fun behind closed doors.

Amethyst is the purple quartz stone of peace. It's said to raise hopes, calm the mind, and bring soothing energy to your life. Amethyst can help you be more intuitive and connect spiritually. This is a good gemstone for Sheep natives who are looking to improve their love relationship.

Place a specimen of amethyst in your bedroom. Place it on the dresser or on a table where you can see it from the bed. You can also wear amethyst jewelry this year to help you connect with your partner in a deeper, more meaningful way.

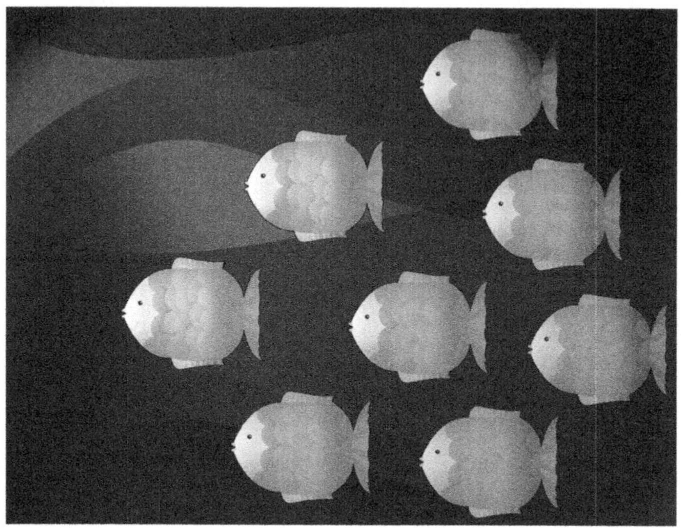

Looking to Conceive?

As well as being a symbol of money and abundance, fish are a Feng Shui symbol of fertility because fish have been so abundant in our waterways, lakes, and the sea. You could choose to have a fish tank in the bedroom (keep brightly-colored fish, or a school of fish, not fighting fish). Or, if live fish sounds like too much work, consider hanging pictures of fish (such as koi or goldfish in a pond) or brightly colored fish swimming through a clear sea. You could also place colorful glass fish figurines in a group on a surface in the room or find some cute fish-motif pillows to put on the bed.

(From Donna Stellhorn's book, Fertility Feng Shui)

Family and Kids

There's a great deal of activity at home for Horse natives in 2022. It's possible you are thinking about moving, or the family is unpacking from a recent move. There's good energy for renovating the house, especially adding a room, redoing the kitchen, or building an outdoor room. The family is coming together very positively. You may have out-of-town guests, or an adult child may move back into the house to help you. While the Year of the Water Tiger can cause unpredictable energy, things look peaceful and quiet at home.

Your symbol of protection this year is the Dragonfly. Dragonflies are associated with harmony, good luck, power, and adaptability. When dragonflies are in your life, they remind you of joy and letting the wind guide you. In ancient Japan, dragonflies were a symbol used by Samurai warriors to represent agility and victory.

Find dragonfly symbols to place near your front door. You can place them inside the home or on the front porch. The dragonfly motif can be in wind chimes, painted on pots, or be metal sculptures hung, so they seem to fly on their own. You can use one or use many. Odd numbers are best.

Money

There are definite money opportunities for Horse natives in 2022. You may have your own business or have a side business that is taking off. The Year of the Water Tiger can bring some volatility in the financial markets, and you could scoop up some extra profits. You may be tempted by risky investments this year, such as buying a business or experimenting with highly leveraged investments. Make sure you do your due diligence before plunking down your hard-earned cash. Overall, there's positive energy for making money, but you want to be conservative regarding investing.

In choosing a Feng Shui cure, remember the universal rule: "Like attracts like." This concept allows us to use representations of things to attract the real thing. For example, as you are looking for your new job, visualize that you will be showered with money when they make you the offer.

To complete the picture, find a wind chime made of Chinese coins. Choose a chime with many coins. This is to represent a shower of money.

Hang the wind chime outside your front door or, if you're in an apartment, hang it from your balcony/patio. As you hear the coins tinkle and chime in the breeze, imagine the sound of raindrops showering money on your roof and your windows.

While it's best to hang the chime outside your front door, if this isn't a viable option where you live, hang your wind chime on your back porch or balcony.

Job or Career

Horse native, while you can be gainfully employed all year long, you need to draw attention to yourself to make actual progress in your career. Mostly, you're working happily behind the scenes. But there will be opportunities for you to take a leadership role if you're willing to step forward into the spotlight. In the Year of the Water Tiger, taking chances helps you stand out. You could find more than one career risk that is worth taking. On the other hand, you could be happy keeping a low profile, so you have time and energy for friends and family.

If you are looking to change positions, get a new job, move up in the company you currently work for, or expand your market share for your business, consider displaying a globe. The globe can be small-paper-weight size or a larger standing model (though it should be in keeping with your décor, so if a large globe looks out of place in your home, choose a smaller version). The globe can be of any color, but should display the continents clearly. Place the globe in view of your front door. Once you have your new job, you can move the globe to your family room or home office to help maintain the positive energy.

Education

2022 shows you continuing your education towards a degree or certification. This could be through a formal institution, or you may pick up certifications by doing online studies. Your ideal situation in the Year of the Water Tiger is not to incur a lot of additional debt for your education. There are some options for you for scholarships, grants, or low-interest loans. You may find a free program through your employer.

Legal Matters

Horse native, you don't show a lot of legal activities in 2022. There may be the occasional contract, but if you're in a lawsuit, things may be on hold this year. There are possible agreements for renting a flat or buying a new house. You also could receive an employment contract. Take your time and study these agreements before signing to make sure you are very aware of what you're getting yourself into. Negotiations could be complex this year, so you may have to accept the contract as is. This is one reason to be careful and not sign anything in haste.

Health and Well-Being

There is fortunate energy for Horse natives for 2022 for your health and well-being. You have access to helpful people, knowledgeable medical professionals, and when you want an appointment, one seems to appear magically. This is an excellent time to take care of your health and to exercise through dance, swimming, or cycling. You may give yourself a boost through juicing or making homemade soups. Meditation, prayer, and connecting spiritually benefit your mind, body, and spirit in the Year of the Water Tiger. By the end of the year, your health picture is very positive.

If you've been healing from past injury or illness, you'll see improvements. Consider lighting a green candle once a month to focus your mind and spirit on your healing process. Often Pig natives will do all the physical things required for personal healing, but they skip the mental effects and stress of injury and illness. Speed you're healing by exploring mental and emotional issues while you're working on your physical health.

Sheep/Goat/Ram

February 13, 2007–February 1, 2008: Yin Fire Sheep/Goat/Ram
February 1, 1919–February 19, 1920: Yin Earth Sheep/Goat/Ram
February 17, 1931–February 5, 1932: Yin Metal Sheep/Goat/Ram
February 5, 1943–January 24, 1944: Yin Water Sheep/Goat/Ram
January 24, 1955–February 11, 1956: Yin Wood Sheep/Goat/Ram
February 9, 1967–January 29, 1968: Yin Fire Sheep/Goat/Ram
January 28, 1979–February 15, 1980: Yin Earth Sheep/Goat/Ram
February 15, 1991–February 3, 1992: Yin Metal Sheep/Goat/Ram
February 1, 2003–January 21, 2004: Yin Water Sheep/Goat/Ram
February 19, 2015–February 7, 2016: Yin Wood Sheep/Goat/Ram
February 6, 2027–January 25, 2028, Yin Fire Sheep/Goat/Ram

Sheep/Goat/Ram Personality

When considering a Chinese Zodiac animal's qualities, examine its traits, behaviors, and personality. For this sign, we need to consider several animals—Sheep, Goat, and Ram. They have distinctive qualities. We'll start with Sheep.

There are many traditions and stories about Sheep. (A ram is a male sheep, a ewe is a female sheep, and lambs are both the male and female young.) Sheep are gregarious creatures who enjoy living in a flock. They can become stressed when separated from others in their flock. They have a natural inclination to follow a leader. Sheep are not territorial, but they do like to stay in familiar spaces. They flee from danger, but when cornered, they will charge and "ram" you.

Even though the traits of Ram represent the masculine expression of the sheep family energy, people born under the sign of Sheep appreciate the more "feminine" expression of their essence. By this, I mean qualities such as shyness, sensitivity, tolerance, and compassion. Sheep natives represent these attributes.

While Sheep can come across as thin-skinned, they will willingly forgive when they sense the honesty in an apology. Sheep dislike getting hemmed in, preferring not to be under someone else's rule or schedule. Neither do they care to rule—often opting for the supporting role.

Sheep is a generous sign; known for their kind heart. Despite their generosity—or perhaps because of it—they always have a pleasant home, plenty of food, and money in the bank. Sheep spend their life helping others and are generously reciprocated.

When Sheep make a list of their material goals and share it with others, people step up to help Sheep make these goals a reality. Sheep often receive legacies from people not related to them.

The only time a Sheep is straightforward in word and deed is when they are angry. They will take a circuitous route to tell you what they want or think most of the time. They may tell you their story in the most expressive and creative terms, yet never come right out to say what they need or expect of you.

Sheep are devoted to their families and their friends. They remember birthdays, celebrate occasions, and are quick to send help when they sense trouble for the people they care about. Often not reciprocated, their birthdays or special events are often forgotten by those around them, which profoundly hurts the kindly Sheep.

Sheep natives show a tendency to worry and perceive future events as being dark and potentially disastrous. They can spend many hours—even days—stuck in a dark depression. They benefit hugely by talking over their difficulties with others, but many Sheep try to hold everything inside, causing physical issues such as fatigue and low energy.

Sheep can receive money, but they often spread it around quickly, leaving themselves with just the minimum to meet their needs. They often attract money in the first place because of someone else—someone they love needs it. It's imperative that Sheep plan for their future financial security, although they rarely do so.

Sheep are astute in business and are masters of soft sell. They're able to get beyond objections and help others decide.

People born under the sign of the Sheep wait for the right moment to take action on their goals. They can wait for quite a while to get what they want. Committed to doing things the "right way," things seldom get done at all.

Sheep are hypercritical of their own actions (and sometimes the actions of others.) This leaves them feeling vulnerable and causing them a great deal of suffering. They need to take chances more often—they are more sure-footed than they realize.

In some parts of the world, the creature symbolizing this section of the Chinese Zodiac is the Goat—not Sheep or Ram. While many of the qualities ascribed to Goat are similar to those of Sheep or Ram, the energy of Goat has some unique attributes overall. A person born in the year of the Sheep/Goat can access the attributes of both the Goat and the Sheep.

While a Goat is a different animal than a Sheep, goats are a sub-family of sheep. A simple way to tell the difference is by noting a goat's tail points to heaven and a sheep's tail points to earth. When you act more goat-like, you can focus on climbing to new heights; you seek to get to the top and see the view below. When you are more Sheep-like, you want to stay home and stay in your comfort zone, your routine.

Goat forages for its meal; sheep graze on grass. People born in Sheep/Goat years may find they investigate lots of new things, new foods, new places, and new people. They might then spend months doing the opposite—sticking to a routine and the places and people they know well.

One of the valuable qualities of Goat we see in people born in Sheep/Goat years is curiosity. This quality allows you to explore and examine various opportunities and determine whether they may be viable for you to pursue. Curiosity keeps you interested in the motivations of the people around you. Your life is enriched as you find yourself entranced by new topics and ideas. This keeps life very interesting.

For clarity in this book, we will refer to Sheep, Goat, or Ram as Sheep.

Sheep/Goat/Ram: Predictions for 2022

How to use your High-Energy Days: On these days, plan to take action for your significant goals, make vital phone calls, send critical emails. Your high-energy days are when your energy and luck are the strongest for the month.

January 2022: *January 2 is the new moon. January 14 has Mercury going retrograde. Jan+uary 17 is the full moon. On January 18, Uranus goes direct. On January 29, Venus goes direct. Your High-Energy Days are 3, 9, 15, 21, and 27.*

Our familiar calendar year begins in January, but a full month of Metal Ox energy remains. You may have a desire to travel, but there are some limitations now due to work obligations or the family schedule. However, short trips are highlighted. You may consider a drive to the next town, an opportunity to explore local theater or check out new restaurants.

The new moon comes in on January 2, and energy highlights your area of education. You may be in school, or your children could be ready to go back to school, so it's time to crack the books and get to work. Some Sheep natives will benefit by creating a designated study area, clearing off the workspace, and getting all the necessary tools ready to go. If you're not in a traditional school, you may take online courses. Carving out a little time each day, even if it's just 10 minutes, can help you feel you're making progress.

On January 17, there's a full moon, and in these last couple of weeks of the Metal Ox energy, put yourself forward and make sure you're getting recognition where it's due. This may even mean letting your manager know how much you are contributing to the team's efforts. Maybe you need to standing up at your local PTA meeting and reminding people of what you bring to the table. This is the lesson Sheep natives have been working on for the last 11 1/2 months! So by focusing on this lesson now in the final two weeks of the Metal Ox year, you are letting the Universe know you have learned your lesson and you're ready to move on.

There is a shift in energy on January 19. Now, with just days left of the old energy, you can finish up any leftover projects from last year, do a little decluttering, and get rid of things you no longer need.

February 2022: *February 1 is the new moon and begins the Year of the Water Tiger. February 3, Mercury goes direct. February 16 is the full moon. Your high-energy days are: 2, 8, 14, 20, and 26.*

The Water Tiger year begins on February 1, and almost immediately, things get easier for you, Sheep native. The opposition energy of the previous year is now dissipating quickly. While Water Tiger year can be somewhat unpredictable, you'll find that your intuitive sense guides you out of the way of excessive disruptive influences. Now you're entering the second year of your 3-year harvest. You will have many opportunities to capitalize on skills you already have and contacts you've made in the past.

This new moon energy on February 1, and Sheep native, there's a great deal of focus on home and family. You may do some renovations or finally getting unpacked from a move you made last year. It's also possible that someone is moving into your house or moving out. Now you're able to get everything in order just the way you like it.

February 3 brings the Water Tiger month, and Mercury moves direct. Over the next four weeks, you can gain some resources. This could get you a low-interest loan or money for a business idea you have. This also could bring you antique objects at a fantastic price or a family heirloom.

The full moon is on February 16, and your career is highlighted. You may ask for a raise or show interest in another position. Now you need to wait for the powers-that-be to decide. Sheep native, you can do a little feng shui to get things moving, but at this point, it's mostly a waiting game.

March 2022: *March 2 is the new moon. The full moon is on March 18. Your high-energy days are: 4, 10, 16, 23, and 28.*

In March, a chance meeting could lead to an exciting opportunity. If you're looking for love, this could bring a very interesting match. This could be someone you hadn't considered in the past or a person who is not necessarily your type, but who is very intriguing all the same. If you're already in a committed relationship, you could meet a person who becomes a good friend.

March 2 brings the new moon, and for the next two weeks, you have a lot of creative and fertile energy around you. If you're looking to add to the family, you can find helpful medical professionals. This is also good energy for adopting a pet. Sheep native, you may find a lot of inspiration during this time to finish a creative project.

March 5 begins the Water Rabbit month. Over the next four weeks, you may do something around education, perhaps taking or teaching a class. This is a good time for writing and journaling. You also have positive energy around travel. You may go to a place you've never been before and do some exploring.

The full moon is on March 17, and a friendship could become much closer or even turn romantic. Someone you know well may express their feelings for you, and suddenly a relationship could blossom. Sheep native, love could wait for you behind a friendly face.

In some parts of the world, there will be a second new moon on March 31, and for other time zones, it will be April 1. This new moon brings emphasis to your daily routines, habits, and systems. You're figuring out new ways to do things, even mundane things such as laundry or dishes. You may look at how you get work done. You might go paperless, minimize possessions, or simplify processes. In the end, you could be more productive while feeling more peaceful.

April 2022: *April 1 is the new moon. The full moon is on April 16. On April 29, Pluto goes retrograde. There is a partial solar eclipse on April 30. Your high-energy days are: 3, 9, 15, 21, and 27.*

April brings a lot of energy for health and well-being. You may get outdoors more, biking, running, or hiking. This is an excellent time to get into the garden, especially to grow your own herbs and vegetables. You may also do more in the kitchen, such as juicing or making your own bread. As you take these steps, your health improves.

On April 4, the Wood Dragon month brings some interesting career energy. You may work more hours and add to your team or get an assistant. Sheep native, if you own a business, you could find contractors to help you out.

The full moon is on April 16, and Sheep native, you need some downtime. You may take a brief vacation or working from home. This is a favorable time to change the bedroom to facilitate restful sleep, such as getting a new mattress, blackout shades, or a white-noise machine. Sheep native, this is also an excellent time to take up yoga or start a meditation practice.

There is a solar eclipse on April 30, and eclipses bring change. A person close to you may go through major changes in their life, which has a ripple effect in yours. Of course, you're always supportive and empathetic. As their life changes, you're there to help them. This can affect your long-term relationship with this individual. You might make some changes to your home because of this.

May 2022: *On May 10, Mercury goes retrograde. There is a total lunar eclipse on May 16. On May 30, there is a new moon. Your high-energy days are: 3, 9, 15, 21, and 27.*

During May, there is increased relationship energy for Sheep natives. A close relationship may be shifting. You could become closer through living together or sharing a secret. You may experience a time when you're separated. Perhaps your partner needs to go to help a family member or is called away for their job.

May 5 brings the Wood Snake month, and you may connect with your community now. You may belong to an organization that does charity work or gathers professionals together for networking. Sheep native, you might consider starting a group with like-minded people for games, walking your dogs, or sharing gardening tips.

On May 10, Mercury goes retrograde, and the stress and strain around a special relationship now settles down to a new routine. You may have set up housekeeping together, or you're getting comfortable living in two separate households.

There is a lunar eclipse on May 15, and now you may experience some changes in your own life. There could be a significant shift in your job as well as a few changes at home. You were likely expecting this change, and over the last few weeks, you've been preparing. Now that the new energy is here, it's likely to go smoothly.

The new moon is on May 30, and there are more` resources available to you. Over the next two weeks, you can get a loan or additional credit at a good interest rate. You can get funding for a business or consolidate your bills. Sheep native, there is also the possibility of winning some money now.

June 2022: *Mercury goes direct on June 3. On June 4, Saturn goes retrograde. On June 14, there is a full moon. Neptune goes retrograde on June 28. The new moon is on June 29. Your high-energy days are: 1, 7, 13, 19, and 25.*

In June, you have a sense of a new beginning. You may visit a place you've never been to before, explore new foods or new activities. A friend who lives far away may come to see you and inspire you with what they're doing. It's also possible you are signing a contract for employment or some other new venture.

June 5 brings the Fire Horse month. Over the next four weeks, you are more intuitive than usual (which is saying something, as Sheep natives are one of the most intuitive signs of the Chinese zodiac). You may explore how to increase your psychic ability through reading tarot cards, the I Ching, or you might do more feng shui. Consider getting past life regression or doing hypnosis to rid yourself of issues from your past.

The full moon is on June 14, and there's a great deal of emphasis on your finances. During this time, you may go back to a written budget or review subscription charges to see what you can eliminate. Sheep native, you may be very focused on being frugal, so you can save more money and work less in the future. What you add to your piggy bank now will benefit you later.

June 28 is the new moon, and you might look into a legal matter. You could finish up a lawsuit or deal with government paperwork. This is a beneficial time to renew a professional license or talk to the city about zoning or building permits. Sheep native, you may even attend City Council meetings or get involved in an upcoming election.

July 2022: *July 13 brings the full moon. There is a new moon on July 28. Also, on July 28, Jupiter goes retrograde. Your high-energy days are:1, 7, 13, 19, and 25.*

In July, you are very focused on routines, productivity, and simplifying your life. You may consider what you can eliminate in tasks or mundane activities, so you have more time for doing what you want to do. It's also possible you're cutting back on your hours at your job so that you can work on your own business or spend more time with your family.

July 7 brings the Fire Sheep month. This month sets the tone for the next 12 months. This is a seed planting month. The more new things you do, the bigger the harvest you will get a year from now. Sheep native, this is the time to go to new places, meet new people, and try new foods. A few months from now, you'll see what new activities have taken hold. Nurture these to grow into an abundant harvest.

The full moon is on July 13, and over the next two weeks, there's a lot of emphasis on communication and contracts. You may receive a contract for employment or to work in a business partnership. You may look to purchase a large item such as a vehicle. Now you have positive energy around negotiations regarding price and interest rates.

The new moon is on July 28, and you may receive recognition at work. Over the next couple of weeks, the boss, or perhaps even the CEO, may present you with an award for sales or exemplary service. One of your customers may write a glowing review. Sheep native, if you own a business, you may get some free publicity.

August 2022: *August 12 brings the full moon. Uranus goes retrograde on August 24. There is a new moon on August 27. Your high-energy days are: 6, 12, 18, 24, and 30.*

In August, there is a great deal of emphasis on relationships especially healing a friendship you have. There could be apologies on both sides, and you may talk out how misunderstandings and differences in communication styles created the problem in the first place. But the most important thing is that healing is taking place.

August 7 brings the Earth Monkey month, and over the next four weeks, some financial benefits are coming to you. You may gain a windfall and an additional source of income. This could be because of some investments or a side business that is starting to take off. Sheep native, you could gain more money through your job, getting a salary increase or a better commission percentage.

August 11 is the full moon, and your charisma and magnetism are pretty strong over the next two weeks. If you're looking for love, you can attract a new partner, someone with whom you have great chemistry. This relationship could become intimate quickly. Before you know it, you're not only having dinner together but also breakfast.

The new moon is on August 27, and there's an emphasis on technology. You may upgrade your phone, laptop, or desktop computer. You may add peripherals to help with a hobby, such as a good camera for photography, a keyboard for your music, or a lighting kit to shoot your videos. Sheep native, this is an excellent time to take courses on how to use different software platforms or pieces of equipment.

September 2022: *On September 10, there is a full moon, and Mercury goes retrograde. On September 25, there's the new moon. Your high-energy days are: 5, 11, 17, 23, and 29.*

In September, you have a great deal of energy for doing what you want to do and very little energy for anything else. So you may find you're procrastinating on projects for work (especially if they feel like busy work) as well as tasks around the home. But as soon as you're working on something you want to do, you could forget the clock and stay up all night.

September 7 begins the Earth Rooster month. Over the next four weeks, there's a lot of emphasis on siblings and younger relatives. You may get a visit from a sibling who lives far away. Or you may get together with a sibling to help celebrate a family member's milestone birthday or anniversary. One of your siblings or cousins may get married.

The full moon is on September 10, and the same day, Mercury goes retrograde, and an old lover could return. An ex-boyfriend or ex-girlfriend could contact you through social media. They may want to reconnect to see if there is still some flame of passion between the two of you. Sheep native, this could be an exciting couple of weeks.

The new moon is on September 25, and over the next two weeks, you seem to keep to yourself. You and the old flame may sneak off to have a rendezvous, but it is more likely that you spend time by yourself in meditation and self-reflection. Sheep native, this is a good time to journal, write, or look at your astrology chart in-depth.

October 2022: *Mercury goes direct on October 2. On October 8, Pluto goes direct. There is a full moon on October 9. On October 23, Saturn goes direct. On October 25, there's a partial solar eclipse. On October 28, Jupiter goes retrograde. Mars goes retrograde on October 30. Your high-energy days are: 5, 11, 17, 23, and 29.*

October can be quite an exciting month for Sheep natives. Mercury goes direct on October 2. Some Sheep natives may get engaged or even married. If you are single and looking for love, you could meet someone and fall head over heels. Someone may call and text you at all hours of the day and night just to hear your voice. This can be a romantic and exciting time.

October 8 brings the Metal Dog month, and there could be some changes at home. You may think about moving, selling the house, or changing apartments. Sheep native, this is a good time to do a deep declutter and get rid of the excess stuff. Consider clearing out your garage, basement, or attic. You may change your lifestyle and move from the city to the country or move from the house in the suburbs to a high-rise apartment building.

The full moon is on October 9, and a lot is going on at work. There could be some personnel changes, and someone may leave your team. There could be adjustments in the hours you're working, or you might move to a new office. Your company may have been purchased, and so new orders are coming from the top down. It's also possible that technology is replacing someone's job in the office.

The solar eclipse is on October 25, and you may feel very ready for a change. You may be prepared to throw off your old life and do something entirely different. You might consider teaching English in a foreign country, getting an RV to do the nomadic lifestyle, or buying some land for homesteading. Sheep native, you may create change through small steps by choosing to go vegetarian, signing up for the night shift, or taking in a roommate for extra money.

November 2022: *November 8 brings the total lunar eclipse. On November 23, there is a new moon, and Jupiter goes direct. Your high-energy days are: 4, 10, 16, 23, and 28.*

November shows you, Sheep native, still dealing with some decisions you made towards the end of October. You may implement some of the lifestyle changes you were considering then. You may feel great excitement at the idea of how easy it is to change your life. Now, with the snap of your fingers, you can go in a new direction. You're tapping into your own personal power.

November 7 brings the Metal Pig month, and there's a great deal of emphasis on creativity and fun. Over the next four weeks, you may explore activities you really enjoy. After working hard over the last few years, you may not be sure what fun is anymore. You might take some classes or watch videos on sewing, writing, painting, jewelry making, or how to play the guitar.

The lunar eclipse is on November 8, and there is intense relationship energy for Sheep natives. If you're in a committed relationship, the two of you could have deep discussions. Sheep native, if you are looking for a romantic relationship, you may suddenly realize the person you've been dating is the one. You just need to make some adjustments in your thinking or communication. The path forward for your love life becomes clear over the next few weeks.

The new moon is on November 23, and you may receive a financial windfall. Money is flowing in at a better rate. But cash is still flowing out, so it will be essential to check subscriptions, annual payments, or other bills can sneak up on you. But overall, your finances are looking good.

December 2022: *Neptune goes direct on December 3. The full moon is on December 8. There is a new moon on December 23. Mercury goes retrograde on December 29. Your high-energy days are: 4, 10, 16, 23, and 28.*

December is both a busy and productive month. You have lots to do, including some social functions, charity events and family get-togethers. Sheep native, you are getting everything done with time to spare. This is a credit to how organized you are, especially when it comes to social occasions. You're notably good at helping others feel comfortable and welcome.

On December 7, it's the Water Rat month. It is also the full moon. You're showing improved health because of some changes you made earlier in the year. You may visit health practitioners to get annual checkups. You may consult with alternative medicine practitioners as well as those who work in Western medicine. This is also a time when you might do more exercise.

December 23 is the new moon, and there's a lot of emphasis on communication. You might send out holiday letters or cards. You could talk to more people on social media and get caught up with friends and family you haven't spoken to in a while. People may come over to visit, and you could share potluck suppers or do a cookie exchange. Sheep native, it's a very social time now.

On December 29, Mercury goes retrograde, and now friends you haven't seen in a while come back into your life. It's great to get caught up, and you could ring in the New Year with some old friends.

January 2023: *January 6 brings the full moon. Mercury goes direct on January 18. The year of the water rabbit begins on January 22. Your high-energy days are. 3, 9, 15, 21, and 27.*

January brings an emphasis to your thinking process. You might look at how you communicate with yourself and take steps to eliminate some of the mental spirals you go through. You could do this through meditation or biofeedback. You may journal, writing down the progression of your thoughts. This helps you become mindful of your thinking and gives you the power to change when you think about something else.

January 5 begins the Water Ox month. Over the next four weeks, there is a lot of emphasis on love relationships. You and your sweetheart could do much better, being united on many fronts and understanding with each other even when you disagree. Your communication is better, as you are now kinder to yourself.

The full moon is on January 6, and there's an emphasis on education. You might be in school, or you might help your kids get through their classes. There may be some standardized tests you need to take for your profession, or you're helping your kids get through their SATs or other essential exams.

On January 18, Mercury goes direct. You might be in the market for a new vehicle, or you could look at a new way to get around town. Sheep native, you might be ready to let go of your vehicle to choose public transportation or Uber instead.

The new moon is on January 22, and this brings the Year of the Water Rabbit. This is quite harmonious energy for Sheep natives. You are now entering the last year of your harvest period. This is the easiest of the three harvest years. This is an excellent time to make more money and gather resources based on what you already know how to do and the skills you have already acquired. You can settle into resting on your laurels. However, this is an excellent time to expand the current business, get a promotion, and deepen a love relationship. If you push in these directions, the benefits far exceed the efforts.

Attract New Love

The Year of the Water Tiger could be a very romantic year for Sheep natives. You have excellent opportunities to meet someone new for a love relationship. You could meet a special person through friends, taking classes, or by random chance when you're in line at the post office or grocery store. There are some magical qualities for you this year, so consider doing feng shui cures to attract love. Visualize how you might meet a person for a new relationship. Before you know it, you could introduce your new love to your family and friends.

In Feng Shui, we often use wind chimes to call new energy. The material the wind chimes are made of will tell us what energy a specific one will attract. When looking for new love, choose a silver tone wind chime. The color silver attracts relationship energy.

Hang your wind chime on the in- or outside of your front door or outside your bedroom window. (If this is not possible, hang the wind chime in your bedroom window inside the house.) Remember to touch the chimes manually and listen to the tones every few days.

Enhance Existing Love

There's generally good energy in 2022 for Sheep natives regarding your current partnership. However, there can be short periods of change or disruption. Some of these instances could come from outside sources, such as your partner's job or obligations to their family. But you also have an opportunity to become closer as a couple (even if you are living in different houses for a time). You have better communication, empathy, and understanding of each other. In the Year of the Water Tiger, you are likely more committed to each other than ever.

To bring good luck in love, you can display the statue of an angel. Choose a depiction that is peaceful and sweet. Statues of angels with flaming swords are helpful and powerful, but not to maintain a love relationship. Display your angel figurine in the living room to promote the friendship and loving support you feel for each other.

Looking to Conceive?

All nuts represent the potential for fertility and children, but traditionally the hazelnut, in particular, represents this energy. Folklore throughout Europe says that eating the nuts would make you both wise and fertile. Hazelnuts are rich in protein, containing thiamine and vitamin B6, making them valuable food for getting pregnant. Hazelnuts can be eaten raw, roasted, or ground into a paste and mixed with chocolate for a delicious treat.

(From Donna Stellhorn's book, Fertility Feng Shui)

Family and Kids

There can be some changes at home this year. You may have an older child going off to school or leaving home to start their own family. A family member may come to live with you for some period during the year. There's also a chance you're changing residences this year. There could be alterations in your neighborhood the cause you to see your house differently. But it's also possible that for some time, you've been planning to adopt a new lifestyle, and now you see a path forward. The energy in 2022 can empower as you pull the family together to try something new.

Use a Feng Shui cure this year to add an extra layer of protection to your home. Choose a convex mirror. (A convex mirror is shaped like the back of a spoon.) You can use such a mirror to reflect negative energy back to where it originated more forcefully than a flat mirror can do. This adds additional protection for you and your family.

Hang your convex mirror in a window near the front door, in your bedroom window, or—if you have a challenging neighbor—you can point it in the direction of their home. (This can result in them moving within a couple of months). Use only one of these mirrors at a time, as they are powerful. Too many convex mirrors and you will block even positive energy from reaching you while simultaneously blocking the negative energy.

Money

Your financial picture improves during the Year of the Water Tiger. You have luck with money. You also will find more temptations to spend money. It will be important for you to pay attention to the outgo. If you plug up the holes in your spending, you can end up with much more money in your accounts by the end of the year. Throughout 2022, you may get some great tips for investments. You might sell a property or stuff around the house that adds up to more money than you expect. If you're careful with your money this year, you can do quite well.

To help attract money this year, consider placing a Lucky Money Frog by your front door. The Lucky Money Frog sits on a pile of coins and has a coin in his mouth. If you place him by your front door, he will collect money because of the energy that comes in. Place him on the floor by the front door or on a table nearby. If he's sitting inside the house (most people do place him inside the house), he should face the door, like your personal butler. If he's sitting outside the door, his back should be to the door, like your personal bouncer.

Job or Career

In 2022, your job is humming along nicely, with you likely working behind the scenes. This could mean you're working out of your home or you have a low-profile position. This could be an ideal situation. However, you need to keep an eye on the company itself to ensure that it's stable and growing. Your job could be affected by a company merger or a downturn in business. If this happens, you could easily find another position in the Year of the Water Tiger. You would quickly settle in to your new place, again retreating into the background. If you're looking for something high-profile, it will take effort to be seen this year.

Bayberry is a very popular scent used in winter and on holidays to attract prosperity energy. This year it would be a good idea to consider using it throughout the year to bring wealth opportunities your way. At the beginning of the year, you'll find bayberry candles, incense, and oils on sale. Grab a few extras for use during the summer months.

You can use these at home or in the office. You only need a small amount to increase the money energy. Also, carry a bit of bayberry scented pot-pourri or bayberry essential oil in your briefcase or handbag to bring luck and money.

Education

Education is one of the most active areas in your chart in 2022. You could go back to school, finish up a degree, or do an accelerated program to gain certification in a field. It's also possible that you are teaching this year. This could be your profession or part of a small business you own. You may also study for pleasure, learning about art or music. You might develop skills in cooking, carpentry, or website design. It is especially beneficial to learn about communication, negotiation, and reading other people's body language.

Legal Matters

For Sheep natives, you can succeed with legal matters, contracts, and official business during the Year the Water Tiger. You're likely able to negotiate contracts in your favor. If you have been working on a lawsuit, you may finalize a settlement or receive a final ruling. The best energy is around taking tests for certification or licensing, as well as dealing with bureaucratic paperwork for things like building permits for business licensing.

Health and Well-Being

In 2022, your health and well-being are improving. It's possible you are solving some issues around getting restful sleep, better nutrition, and you are taking more time for exercise this year. The Year of the Water Tiger is more active, and you can find many people to join you on walks, hikes, and bike rides. This year, you are likely tracking your improvement. As things get incrementally better, you can become excited about continuing the progress. Health solutions come this year that have eluded you in previous years.

Add Sunflowers to your home or garden this year to bring in positive health energy. In past centuries, people would string sunflower seeds and wear them as necklaces to protect themselves from diseases. Hang pictures of sunflowers or have cut sunflowers in the house, especially in the living room and bedroom. Also, if you have a garden, plant sunflowers along the edges. It's said if you have a little wish, you can cut a sunflower at sunset from your garden, and the wish will come true before the sun sets again.

Monkey

February 2, 1908–January 21, 1909: Yang Earth Monkey
February 20, 1920–February 7, 1921: Yang Metal Monkey
February 6, 1932–January 25, 1933: Yang Water Monkey
January 25, 1944–February 12, 1945: Yang Wood Monkey
February 12, 1956–January 30, 1957: Yang Fire Monkey
January 30, 1968–February 16, 1969: Yang Earth Monkey
February 16, 1980–February 4, 1981: Yang Metal Monkey
February 4, 1992–January 22, 1993: Yang Water Monkey
January 22, 2004–February 8, 2005: Yang Wood Monkey
February 8, 2016–January 27, 2017: Yang Fire Monkey
January 26, 2028–February 12, 2029: Yang Earth Monkey

Monkey Personality

When considering the qualities of a Chinese Zodiac animal, examine the animal's traits, behaviors, and personality. Of all the Chinese Zodiac animals, the most agile and adaptable is the Monkey. Monkeys can live on the ground or in the trees.

The Chinese Zodiac sign of Monkey is the sign of intelligence. This Zodiac animal rules the inventor—intelligent and innovative enough to solve complex problems with ease. Monkeys have an excellent memory and proficiency in communication. They can give you an inspirational speech that motivates you or a dressing down, which leaves you feeling about two inches tall. Monkey is a problem solver. They will not offer you sympathy but will provide you with a solution instead.

Monkeys do well in business because they are connectors. They find people who can help them achieve their goals. They know how to play the system, trading favors as part of a strategy for success.

Monkey always has a plan, often several. Monkey wants to do more than merely survive; they want to prosper! The Monkey native will avoid confrontation if you might be of assistance later. Once wronged, they will exact revenge, but only when the time is right.

A Monkey is susceptible to incentives and bribes. To get them on your side, you need to offer something they want. You can criticize the Monkey, but they pay no attention. They are incredibly confident in their talents and abilities.

Monkey can justify their actions to achieve or obtain what they want; thus, others can find it hard to trust Monkey. This can affect Monkey's career and personal life. However, On the plus side, Monkey is rarely discouraged by failure nor envious of the success of others.

Monkeys love a bargain. They're good with money but would rather save it than spend it. They prefer to find their own solution to spending cash. This choice shows up in their home, where innovative decorating ideas and creative uses for castoffs abound. They love a party at home (BYOB); if you're invited, you can expect an evening (or night) of stimulating conversation and lively music.

Monkeys are into self-preservation. This can show up as nervousness or hyperactivity. It causes them to leap out of any situation they don't feel right about. They can get themselves into trouble by trying to avoid what they perceive as "trouble."

But no matter what mistakes they may make, they are quick to rebound. Overall, the Monkey native gets what they want without too much effort or struggle. If there's no apparent benefit, they simply lose interest.

Monkeys are at one moment a passionate lover; the next moment, it seems as if they've forgotten you entirely. When in a long-term, committed relationship, they can be a devoted partner. However, they love a good time and lots of attention, and they get caught up in the moment. Monkey won't notice a partner's jealousy, and before you know, they will be back at your side as if nothing ever happened.

Monkey's love projects and can renovate their home continuously. They love to create new things and improve old ones. Sometimes they just like to move the furniture around for a different look. It's not unusual for the combination of half-finished projects and a love of new stuff can make for a very messy house.

Monkey: Predictions for 2022

How to use your High-Energy Days: On these days, plan to take action for your most important goals, make vital phone calls, send important emails. Your high-energy days are when your energy and luck are the strongest for the month.

January 2022: *January 2 is the new moon. January 14 has Mercury going retrograde. January 17 is the full moon. On January 18, Uranus goes direct. On January 29, Venus goes direct. Your High-Energy Days are 4, 10, 16, 22, and 28.*

It's January, and the new calendar year arrives, though we are still in the Metal Ox energy for the next four weeks. Monkey native, you are finishing up your three-year seed tending period. This has been a time to nurture your business prospects as well as your personal relationships. Pretty soon, you'll enter your three-year harvest time. You'll be able to capitalize on all of your experience and connections.

You need to focus on finishing rather than starting. Look at which projects need your attention and see what can be completed (even though the desire to create something new will be extreme now). Any new projects this month will probably need re-doing later in the year. Skip this frustrating step and focus on getting current issues finished up and off your desk.

The new moon on January 2 may bring trouble at home. Perhaps some relatives are taking advantage of you, or you may have been in a struggle with a landlord or neighbor. You may want to withdraw and not engage. However, the best course of action is to give deep thought to what you want and what is reasonable to expect from others. Avoid arguing during this time. It's about more than winning a debate this time. It's time to be strategic.

On January 14, Mercury goes retrograde, and things begun over the last two weeks can now unravel. You feel the new energy for change approaching, but it's better to visualize, affirm, or even create a vision board with pictures of things you want to attract. Vision Boards are a handy tool for creating a complete life change, such as leaving a job and working for yourself or moving into a yurt in the middle of a forest.

On January 17, the full moon brings several people seeking advice and help. People around you may be struggling and need your advice or even material assistance. Keep your goals in mind as you assist others. There will be situations where helping is entirely in line with your success strategy. But it's good to maintain your boundaries, especially for people with whom you've had difficulties in the past.

The energy shifts on January 19, and you may be waiting for specific paperwork or an agreement. But Mercury is still retrograde, so it's better not to push this. Even though you know different ways to move forward, it would be better to use the last bit of the Metal Ox energy to step back and allow this to happen in its own time.

February 2022: *February 1 is the new moon and begins the Year of the Water Tiger. February 3, Mercury goes direct. February 16 is the full moon. Your high-energy days are: 3, 9, 15, 21, and 27.*

The Water Tiger year begins on February 1, and there will be two prevailing energies for Monkey natives. The sign of Tiger is opposite to your own sign. This means the entire world is looking at Tiger and away from Monkey. This can be challenging because it means to be noticed or acknowledged, you have to speak emphatically and get people's attention first. Fortunately, Monkey native, you're not shy. You should have no problem speaking louder when it's necessary. Now for the good news. You are entering the first year of your three-year harvest period. This means that there are more opportunities for you this year (if you're willing to put in the work). Harvest time means abundance, but you have to get out there and start picking the fruit or digging up the potatoes to gather this abundance. So there will be many opportunities for the ambitious Monkey native.

This new moon energy on February 1, and for the next two weeks, there's a great deal of focus on communication. Monkey native, you may receive a contract to review or do a handshake deal with the business partner. If you're looking to make a large purchase, you might hold off a few days, as Mercury is still retrograde.

February 3 brings the Water Tiger month, and Mercury moves direct. For the next four weeks, there's a preview of how the year could unfold. You will see many opportunities for money and new connections. Be ready to present your resume, state your case, or make your sales pitch, and the door will open for you.

The full moon is on February 16, and over the next two weeks, you may be offered a new position at work. This could contain more responsibilities and less prestige than you want. It's also possible you're in the running for a new position, competing against someone who has less experience. Don't rest on your laurels. Monkey native, this can be a great opportunity, but you may have to sell your boss on the idea.

March 2022: *March 2 is the new moon. The full moon is on March 18. Your high-energy days are: 5, 11, 17, 23, and 29.*

March likely brings some changes in your daily life, work, or your routines. You may change your work hours, such as going to a four-day workweek or working a later shift to avoid traffic. You may adopt a new routine, perhaps exercising in the morning or doing meal prep on Sundays. Many of these changes could be very beneficial over time.

March 2 brings the new moon, and over the next two weeks, there's a lot of emphasis on home and family. A family member may come to visit, or you could help a family member move into a new dwelling. This is also an excellent time to investigate your family tree. Monkey native, you could look into genealogy or perhaps having a past life regression.

March 5 begins the Water Rabbit month, and over the next four weeks, you have some opportunities to gain more resources. You may tap into some suitable investments or see an increase in a stream of passive income. Putting your attention on debt repayment and long-term savings is an excellent notion.

The full moon is on March 17, and over the next two weeks, you could find some changes at your job have translated into a financial benefit. Or you may have a job offer from a competing company that will pay you more. Monkey native, this is your harvest year. You can parlay your considerable skill set and experience to bring you material benefits.

In some parts of the world, there will be a second new moon in March, and for other time zones, it will be April 1. This new moon brings an opportunity for romance. If you're looking for love, you have the chance to meet a new, exciting person. This individual could come through a dating app, matchmaker, or be someone you meet at a friend's party. Monkey native, you could fall head over heels for this love match. The best part is, the feeling is mutual.

April 2022: *April 1 is the new moon. The full moon is on April 16. On April 29, Pluto goes retrograde. There is a partial solar eclipse on April 30. Your high-energy days are: 4, 10, 16, 23, and 28.*

April brings an emphasis on creativity, fertility, and children. You may work on a creative project involving art or music. If you're looking to add to the family, you can find assistance for fertility treatments or adoption (this includes the adoption of pets). You may spend more time with children, including other people's children. You might babysit or host a kid's party.

On April 4, the Wood Dragon month begins, and over the next four weeks, you may do some travel. This could be for your job or a Spring vacation. It's likely this is local travel within your state or province. But there is a chance that a friend has invited you to an exotic locale where you could share a beautiful hotel suite overlooking the water.

The full moon is on April 16, and over the next two weeks, a friend may come to you with a business proposition. They have a money-making idea and could use your brilliant mind to help them strategize, write a business plan, or formulate a marketing campaign. Monkey native, all this could be quite an exciting prospect for you, but you should get the details in writing, so there's no misunderstanding later down the road.

There is a solar eclipse on April 30, and there's a great deal of focus on health and well-being. Monkey native, you are usually healthy and active. You excel at things like rock climbing, gymnastics, hiking, and other outdoor activities. The Year of the Water Tiger is quite a busy year in general. But over the next two weeks, be cautious not to injure yourself when doing a sport or exercise. If you do receive a sprain or other injury, take good care of it so it heals completely.

May 2022: *On May 10, Mercury goes retrograde. There is a total lunar eclipse on May 16. On May 30, there is a new moon. Your high-energy days are: 4, 10, 16, 23, and 28.*

May could be a hectic month for Monkey natives. You may work overtime to finish up a big project. Your side business may show a profit and require your attention on weekends or evenings. You can get some help from family members or colleagues at work if you ask.

May 5 brings the Wood Snake month, and over the next four weeks, your work can be noticed. This is a fine time to do marketing campaigns, post on social media, and send out a resume if you're looking for a new job. Monkey native, you may also be on stage giving a lecture, presentation, or as part of a production.

On May 10, Mercury goes retrograde, and someone from your past may return. This could be an old lover who wants to see if there is still some heat between the two of you. You'll need to tread carefully here if you're already in a love relationship. If you're single and looking for love, here is your opportunity to give this one more try.

There is a lunar eclipse on May 15, and your intuition is increased over the next couple of weeks. Monkey native, you may know who's calling before the phone rings. You may see multiples of numbers and animal signs. You may feel drawn to make some predictions based on your intuition. This is an excellent time to work with tarot cards, past life regression, or do some dowsing.

The new moon is on May 30, and over the next two weeks, you have terrific relationship energy. You and your sweetheart may get along better, seeing eye to eye on a lot of different subjects and making plans together. You could take this relationship to the next level by moving in together or getting engaged. Some Monkey natives may renew vows.

June 2022: *Mercury goes direct on June 3. On June 4, Saturn goes retrograde. On June 14, there is a full moon. Neptune goes retrograde on June 28. The new moon is on June 29. Your high-energy days are:3, 9, 15, 21, and 27.*

June brings new opportunities and potential investments you never considered before. These could be derivatives or some new, innovative financial instrument. This will take some research, and it would help to find someone with experience in this area before you proceed. It's an excellent idea to calculate the downside as well as the upside to see if this type of investment is a good match for your risk tolerance.

June 5 brings the Fire Horse month, and over the next four weeks, there's a lot of activity with friends. You may socialize with friends or gather together with groups to do activities such as sports, video games, or creative activities like painting or playing music. Monkey native, this is one of your most social times of the year.

The full moon is on June 14, and over the next two weeks, someone may be interested in pursuing you for a love relationship. They may have a crush on you and be quite serious about their intentions. This could be fun if you're looking for a relationship. It could be a tantalizing temptation if you're already in a committed partnership.

June 28 is the new moon, and over the next two weeks, there's an opportunity for you to make more money. Monkey native, this might involve selling a high ticket item. You might get access to credit at a low interest rate to fund a business or to do some bill consolidation. This is a proper time to refinance your mortgage or to get a rental property.

July 2022: *July 13 brings the full moon. There is a new moon on July 28. Also, on July 28, Jupiter goes retrograde. Your high-energy days are:3, 9, 15, 21, and 27.*

July brings fun, romance, and intimacy for Monkey natives. If you're looking for love, you may find someone who wants a physical relationship, like a one-night stand. If you're looking for a long-term partnership, you'll need to move slowly. On the other hand, if you're feeling spontaneous, you could have a fun and frolicking time.

July 7 brings the Fire Sheep month and has you working behind the scenes. For the next four weeks, you may find that your work is not acknowledged or, worse, attributed to someone else. It will be necessary for you to point out what you have accomplished or to claim authorship. On the other hand, if your goal is to keep a low profile at this time, you will have no trouble doing it.

The full moon is on July 13, and over the next two weeks, it's a good idea to have a firm grip on your finances. Monkey native, you want to change passwords on your financial accounts. Keep an account of what is coming in and what is going out. Look at subscriptions or annual payments to see what you can eliminate. It would be good now to direct more money toward savings and debt repayment.

The new moon is on July 28, and you may be on the road traveling, off to see friends, long-distance relatives, or to a location that is hot and exotic. Monkey native, get your paperwork in order—things like passports or travel visas. You can get a good deal on tickets even far in advance for traveling at the end of the year during the holidays.

August 2022: *August 12 brings the full moon. Uranus goes retrograde on August 24. There is a new moon on August 27. Your high-energy days are: 2, 8, 14, 20, and 26.*

August has a legal matter going in your favor. This could be something you've been working on for some time that is now settled to your benefit. Or you may deal with a government agency to get a professional license, permit, or certification.

After completing the arduous paperwork, you can pass the test and get the piece of paper that you need.

August 7 brings the Earth Monkey month, and over the next four weeks, it's a good time to start new things. Starting a business or a course of study could lead to an abundant harvest over the next 12-months, where you reap profits or gain a degree. Monkey native, the more new things you start during these four weeks, the bigger your harvest could be.

August 11 is the full moon, and there could be some challenges with a neighbor or in the community. You may not like what your neighbor is doing next door, or perhaps construction or roadwork is going on in the neighborhood. Monkey native, you may attend a City Council meeting for rezoning or a building permit. You may protest a new law or edict.

The new moon is on August 27, and there are some positive changes in your job. A new position at your company could open up that is perfect for you. This might mean you will be on a new team, or you could become a manager. If you want to change jobs, you could get a job offer from outside of your company. If you own a business, there are great opportunities for free publicity to increase your sales.

September 2022: *On September 10, there is a full moon, and Mercury goes retrograde. On September 25, there's the new moon. Your high-energy days are: 1, 7, 13, 19, and 25.*

In September, you're ready to jump into action, but there will probably be some delays. Sometimes delays are orchestrated by the Universe to help you slow down. So instead of pushing against the block, take time to pause and look again at what you're planning to do. Maybe the Universe is trying to get you to change course.

September 7 begins the Earth Rooster month, and over the next four weeks, there's good financial energy. You could make more money in your job or through a passive income source. Your investments could improve. Monkey native, you may have an opportunity to get a lower interest rate on debt or get some debt relief for a student loan. You may make extra money selling off excess stuff.

The full moon is on September 10, and the same day, Mercury goes retrograde. Over the next two weeks, there could be some technical issues in the house. Maybe the thermostat is not working, the Wi-Fi is funky, or you are having intermittent power issues. Look at your backup systems to see what you can put together, just in case. Monkey native, it's good to stock the pantry and learn how to use your phone as a Wi-Fi hotspot. Being prepared at home can give you peace of mind all year long.

The new moon is on September 25, and you are likely meeting new friends now. You could attend a social event or get involved with an organization. Monkey native, you might do some professional networking or be part of the club of like-minded people who do gardening, play video games, or do improv.

October 2022: *Mercury goes direct on October 2. On October 8, Pluto goes direct. There is a full moon on October 9. On October 23, Saturn goes direct. On October 25, there's a partial solar eclipse. On October 28, Jupiter goes retrograde. Mars goes retrograde on October 30. Your high-energy days are:1, 7, 13, 19, and 25.*

In October, you may play an essential role in a group or organization. Additionally, Mercury goes direct on October 2. This month, you could be voted into office, becoming the president or treasurer of a group you belong to. While this is more responsibility, it also can bring you some prestige. If you're already in a board member role, you might look to step down, but it will be difficult for you to leave the position as few people want to take on the work.

October 8 brings the Metal Dog month, and over the next four weeks, you could negotiate a contract or agreement. This could be for employment, apartment rental, or perhaps you're buying property. Some Monkey natives may purchase a vehicle. It's advisable to come prepared to the dealership to do serious negotiating. Or go with one of those auto services where you don't have to haggle about the price.

The full moon is on October 9, and over the next two weeks, there's a lot of energy around romance. If you're looking for love, you may find a friendship turns romantic. Monkey native, this could be someone you know very well, but you never saw that way before. Suddenly they look pretty appealing. If you're dating, this is an excellent time to introduce your sweetheart to your kids.

The solar eclipse is on October 25. Monkey native, you may feel frustrated your supervisor is not listening to your ideas or your partner is not paying attention to you. Some of this is because the Year of the Water Tiger is in opposition year for Monkey natives. You must speak up and tell people what you want. Be prepared to say things twice, especially at this time.

November 2022: *November 8 brings the total lunar eclipse. On November 23, there is a new moon, and Jupiter goes direct. Your high-energy days are: 6, 12, 18, 24, and 30.*

November shows you, Monkey native, working a lot behind the scenes. You may have a project you're finishing for your job, or you are perhaps working on your dissertation. This is a perfect time to write a novel or work on your album. This is also a great time to go through paperwork from the past. Maybe you're thinking about going paperless, and this would be a great time to scan all your back records. Then you could shred the paperwork and lighten the load.

November 7 brings the Metal Pig month, and over the next four weeks, there's a lot of emphasis on home and family. There could be a weather event that keeps you at home cooped up for longer than you like. But this gives you an opportunity to playing games with their kids, work on creative projects or declutter the house from top to bottom. You might consider a lifestyle change, like downsizing or making a move across the country. You may be stuck at home, but you are finding things to keep you busy.

The lunar eclipse is on November 8, and there are likely changes in your daily routine. This could mean you have a new job or are exploring a new city. You could meet new people or learn a new computer system. Monkey native, it's also possible that you have made such a significant lifestyle change that now everything is different—such as going vegan, living off-grid in an RV, or you are doing your own business full-time.

The new moon is on November 23, and finally, the spotlight is on you. Now you are noticed for your accomplishments. Over the next two weeks, you may receive a lot of compliments and accolades from friends, family, colleagues, and even your supervisor. Monkey native, this could be when you're launching a business, publishing your novel, or your Tik-Tok posts are going viral.

December 2022: *Neptune goes direct on December 3. The full moon is on December 8. There is a new moon on December 23. Mercury goes retrograde on December 29. Your high-energy days are: 6, 12, 18, 24, and 30.*

In December, there is intense relationship energy for Monkey natives. You and your sweetheart might move in together. You could rent an apartment together or take the big step of buying a house and setting up housekeeping. You may attend a wedding, possibly for a close family member or friend. You may be in the wedding party. Additionally, you may attend several social events or charitable functions over the next two weeks.

On December 7, it's the Water Rat month, and it's also the full moon. If you're single and looking for love, you may feel that it's time to take a risk. Monkey native, you might engage a matchmaker or allow your friends and family to fix you up on dates. Love is close, and you can remove blocks to romance by letting go of the past and fearlessly moving forward. Monkey native, you can do this.

December 23 is the new moon, and over the next two weeks, you can have a financial gain. You may receive a windfall or a surprising amount of money. You could get a bonus from your job or profits from a business venture. Monkey native, your passive income sources could improve, or you may have an investment shoot up in value.

On December 29, Mercury goes retrograde, and you may think a lot about power and control over your life. This is a time to look at your decisions and determine your inner motivations. It's good to reduce influence by outside forces. Monkey native, you are known for your independent thinking, so this is an excellent time to look at your choices and ensure that you're doing what you want to do.

January 2023: *January 6 brings the full moon. Mercury goes direct on January 18. The year of the water rabbit begins on January 22. Your high-energy days are: 5, 11, 17, 23, and 29.*

In January, you have extra luck. You can take more risks with business or romance. You can move forward with big plans, contacting important people, and making connections. This is one of your best times for finding a mentor, someone to collaborate with, or an influencer you can work with. It's okay now to take risks when it comes to love. If you're interested in someone, it's time to make your feelings known.

January 5 begins the Water Ox month, and you may have a renewed interest in taking care of your physical self. Monkey native, you might go back to the gym or a form of exercise you've done in the past. This is a good time to engage a personal trainer or start an ancient practice like yoga or tai chi. You could examine how you are eating and make some tweaks to your diet to improve your well-being.

The full moon is on January 6, and this is a favorable time to assess where you are financially. You have some opportunities to get lower interest rates or to gain funding for a project. This is an auspicious time to launch a GoFundMe campaign or gather with family members to make a significant investment.

On January 18, Mercury goes direct. While the past year was a challenging year, you see how it has strengthened you. You have gained resources and skills. Monkey native, this is the time to assess what you've learned as you move forward into the new energy. Consider doing some journaling to update your goals.

The new moon is on January 22, and this brings the Year of the Water Rabbit. You are now entering your second year of the three-year harvest period. While the Year of the Rabbit is very different energy from the previous year, you'll find the change quite refreshing. It will be easier to gain opportunities and to get attention for your skills and achievements. At the same time, you will have to make some adjustments as the Rabbit energy is not nearly as playful as you are. People will take things more seriously, and you'll need to know when to hold back. That said, this is still a harvest time for you, with many opportunities to bring you what you want. So over the next two weeks, Monkey native, it's a good idea to visualize where you'd like to be a year from now.

Attract New Love

Attracting a new relationship poses a unique puzzle for Monkey natives. In the Year of the Water Tiger, you're not as noticeable as you usually are. This means you have to do a little more to get people's attention. Of course, Monkey natives are known for their cleverness, confidence, and bravado, so this should pose no challenge for you. If you're mindful of the opposition energy Water Tiger brings, and you turn up the volume a bit, you will do just fine. The other thing to remember is that holding on to someone from the past can impede meeting someone new for monogamous-minded Monkey natives.

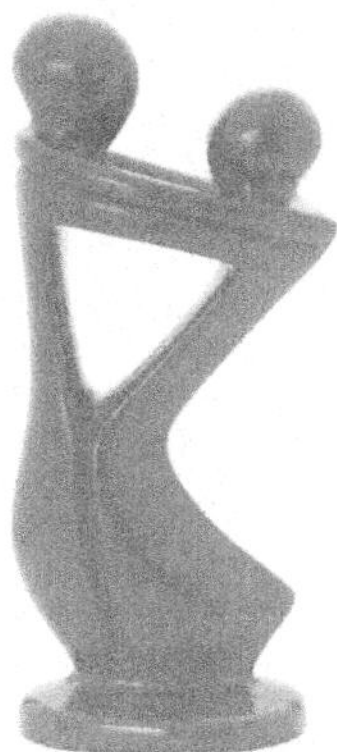

You can enhance relationship energy and bring a bit of art and beauty into your home. Place a figurine or statue of a couple in love in your living room, family room, or bedroom. Place this figurine in a prominent place so it is easily seen. This will help pull the love energy into your space and your life all year long.

One additional tip is to hang a small bag of cardamom seeds from the love figurine. Cardamom has been used in passion/lust potions for centuries. To make a bag, take a small piece of cotton cloth about four inches square and lay it out on the table. In the center, place about a teaspoon of cardamom seeds. Gather the corners of the fabric and tie it together with thread or embroidery floss, leaving a bit of extra string for hanging the bag. Adding this touch of spice will help bring in the romance.

Enhance Existing Love

There's a great deal of focus on your partnership in 2022. For those Monkey natives already in a love relationship, you are more attached to each other than ever. Your sweetheart likely shares your goals (especially the financial ones), and this gives you something to work on together. You are also more comfortable with each other this year as you settle into a routine that might differ from a few years ago but is now at least familiar. Overall, your committed love relationship shows a lot of improvement and gives you both personal satisfaction.

Find some pictures of the two of you in happy situations, like vacations and parties, and have these pictures framed. Place the pictures where your partner can see them. For most people, that means near the television. But if your partner spends all their time in their office, place the pictures there. This will send a subliminal message and increase the happiness energy for the two of you.

Looking to Conceive?

Looking to get pregnant this year? Herd a couple of terracotta elephants into the bedroom. Elephants are considered lucky in many cultures and for a variety of reasons. In India, they are also seen as a fertility symbol—specifically when made from red terracotta clay (said to mimic menstrual blood).

If you can find mama and baby terracotta clay elephants with, perhaps, the little baby holding on to mama's tail with his trunk, you have found the ideal pair. Place them in the bedroom so mama is facing the door and so you can see them from the bed.

(From Donna Stellhorn's book, Fertility Feng Shui)

Family and Kids

In the Year the Water Tiger, you have lots of luck in home and family. This means that when something breaks, you can find a competent repair person who arrives on time and does the work for a reasonable price. If you're moving this year, you find a better place, and the move goes smoothly. When family comes together, there's harmony and enjoyment. Your household may grow throughout 2022. This might mean someone is moving in, a child is born, or you're adopting a pet. All of this makes the house a happier place.

Blue is a power color. It represents the energy of the sky and the ocean. It represents strength, loyalty, and wisdom. This year, to help bring positive protection energy into your home, burn a blue candle about once a month. You can choose a large candle or a little tea light. Find a holder and burn it safely in the house. If you don't enjoy burning candles, then hang a picture of a lit blue candle in your bedroom or the hallway near your bedroom.

Money

There are quite a few money opportunities for Monkey natives in 2022. The Year of the Water Tiger can be challenging, but it's also a harvest year. Therefore, you can capitalize on your skills and experience to bring in financial abundance. You may develop several sources of income this year. You can expand your savings and reduce debt. You're also likely more frugal, using money wisely and keeping track of spending. This is one of your strongest areas this year, and you're probably giving it a lot of your time and attention.

The Jade plant, otherwise known as Crassula ovate, is a succulent with tiny white or pink flowers and round, deep green leaves. The flowers are not prized. It's the leaves that are important. It's called the Jade plant because the leaves resemble jade coins, a symbol of wealth and abundance. It's also called the "money plant." If the plant does happen to bloom in the

Spring, it's said that friendship along with prosperity will visit your home.

Place your Jade plant in a sunny window near the front door or on your front porch. This will help you attract positive financial energy. Don't over water. This plant is a succulent and can withstand drought conditions. This represents money flow, even when the economy is challenging.

Job or Career

While you're likely employed all year, some changes are going on in your job. In 2022, you may find you're learning a new computer system, or you have new tasks at your job. Your shift or hours may change. The challenge for Monkey natives during the Year of the Water Tiger is to be noticed and acknowledged for their accomplishments. If you don't speak up and toot your own horn, you'll likely be passed over for promotion. You may enjoy working behind the scenes, but it doesn't help you move forward in your career this year. You'll need to be bold when stating what you want to colleagues, supervisors, and hiring managers.

To increase your luck and energy in career and business, place a clear quartz crystal in the Wealth Area of your home. The Wealth Area is the far left corner of your home. (See the diagram in "Love Areas of Your House.") The crystal can be large or small, but it should be visible; place it on a shelf or table where you can see it.

Education

There's a lot of positive energy for education in the Year the Water Tiger. Monkey native, it's likely you are a lifetime learner, so you're always taking a class or two. This year, you may teach as well as learn. You may focus on getting prerequisites done or taking more challenging courses than usual. Subjects like programming in a computer language or business accounting are useful for you. You may also do something with time management, habit stacking, or health-related topics.

Legal Matters

There may not be many legal matters for you to attend to in 2022. If you are in a lawsuit, this may drag on through the year and not be resolved in total until the following year. On the other hand, contracts come in quickly and are settled with alacrity. Most of the agreements you're doing are pretty straightforward. You can do some negotiations to get a better interest rate or payment schedule. You may take a test for a professional license or get building permits this year. Things go well when you deal with government agencies in the Year of the Water Tiger.

Health and Well-Being

Monkey native, you're naturally one of the healthier signs. You are generally active, and Water Tiger energy is active, so this can be a very healthy year for you. You may change up your health routines this year, try out a new eating plan, or focus on a different way of exercising. You may incorporate exercise with a sport or pastimes like gardening or biking. Your health and well-being may be the area where you spend money. You could engage alternative health practitioners, find new exercise equipment, or try different vitamins. Overall, 2022 looks to be a healthy year for Monkey natives.

Chamomile is a beneficial herb in Feng Shui. Sprinkle dried chamomile flowers around your property to clear it of negative energy. Place a bowl of chamomile flowers in your bedroom to help you get restful sleep. Make a tea from chamomile, let it cool, and pour it into a spray bottle. Spray it around the house to attract prosperity and peace. (You can store the unused portion in the refrigerator for up to a week.)

Rooster

January 22, 1909–February 9, 1910: Yin Earth Rooster
February 8, 1921–January 27, 1922: Yin Metal Rooster
January 26, 1933–February 13, 1934: Yin Water Rooster
February 13, 1945–February 1, 1946: Yin Wood Rooster
January 31, 1957–February 17, 1958: Yin Fire Rooster
February 17, 1969–February 5, 1970: Yin Earth Rooster
February 5, 1981–January 24, 1982: Yin Metal Rooster
January 23, 1993–February 9, 1994: Yin Water Rooster
February 9, 2005–January 28, 2006: Yin Wood Rooster
January 28, 2017–February 15, 2018: Yin Fire Rooster
February 13, 2029–February 02, 2030, Yin Earth Rooster

Rooster Personality

When considering a Chinese Zodiac animal's qualities, it's a good idea to examine the traits, behaviors, and personality of the mythic creature we are discussing. Most Chinese Zodiac animals do not differentiate between male and female, but the Chinese sign of the Rooster is the male. (No one ever says they're born under the sign of the hen or the chicken.)

When we look at this creature's personality, we think of Rooster as the boss of the hen-house. Roosters are polygamists; they can have many 'hens' under their care. He also will guard and protect all he sees as his from any interlopers. He will oversee from a high perch, keeping a sharp lookout, sounding his distinctive alarm if predators approach.

Rooster always seems to have substantial duties, particularly that of keeping an eye out for others. Rooster personality tends to be perfectionist, someone with a sharp eye for detail and the ability to keep an accounting of everything (and everyone.) In matters of money, Rooster excels. Roosters are adept at handling finances, protecting assets, and making sound investments.

As perfectionists, Roosters are intolerant of even the slightest error. They will aggressively go after what belongs to them, from a small overcharge at the bank to a raise or bonus they believe is owed to them at work. (It's best not to owe a Rooster money unless you can pay them back.)

Roosters like to look good and equate looking good with respect from others. Roosters open their pocketbooks to add things to their lives to make others take notice. Money is well spent on a flashy car, a nice suit, or a piece of sparkling jewelry.

Roosters prefer routine over surprises. Surprises are seen as a danger warning and perceived in a range from merely irritating to stressful. Those born under the sign of the Rooster like to be prepared. They will keep extra things in their home or their handbag just in case—everything from change for the parking meter, to remedies for headaches, to extra pens.

Rooster natives like to be seen as the person who has it all together. Because of this, they can be convinced to take part in projects which prove to be impossible tasks.

Rooster natives are very inquisitive. They end up taking on more and more and still find the energy to do it all. They give parties, volunteer for groups, and make their own bread, possibly all in one day. Overall, they keep a calm demeanor—unless things go very wrong. Then you will witness their extreme distress and hurt erupting from out of nowhere.

If we can find fault with Rooster, it would be their sense of entitlement. It's true, Roosters do a lot, but they also want a lot of praise and compliments for their actions. Roosters can be prone to jealousy when others seem in the limelight, causing the Rooster to take steps that don't benefit him, like being insensitive or vengeful.

When a Rooster falls in love, it's serious business. He follows his practical manner in his approach. This can lead to great disappointments in Rooster's love life, as it's hard to categorize and schedule emotions.

Many Roosters find that being in a relationship is preferable to being alone. It's not that they need the romance, it's more their life, and the house just seems to run better when there's two. Rooster loves an orderly house. To romance a Rooster, share kitchen duties, and he'll pronounce it, "true love."

Rooster: Predictions for 2022

How to use your High-Energy Days: On these days, plan to take action for your most important goals, make vital phone calls, send important emails. Your high-energy days are when your energy and luck are the strongest for the month.

January 2022: *January 2 is the new moon. January 14 has Mercury going retrograde. January 17 is the full moon. On January 18, Uranus goes direct. On January 29, Venus goes direct. Your High-Energy Days are 3, 9, 15, 21, and 27.*

It is January; however, the energy remains under the influence of Metal Ox year the entire month. This is excellent news for Rooster natives, as Metal Ox is harmonious energy for you. The new calendar year has energized you. Others notice you are filled with confidence and can get a lot done. This is a great time to do things at work and to put your name on them!

Don't settle for being a cog in the wheel—take the lead. You may feel some irritation with your financial circumstances. There may be a few delays in receiving money later this month. Plan ahead, so you don't get caught unaware.

On January 2, a new moon brings increased relationship energy for Rooster natives. You and your sweetheart are of one mind. You may finish each other's sentences and are intuitively aware of each other's needs. If this is a new relationship, you may move forward by discussing living together, even getting engaged. If you're interested in meeting someone new, you have an excellent chance of finding a person who is a great match. Enlist the Universe's help with romance by adding (or refreshing) your Feng Shui cures for love and romance.

On January 14, Mercury goes retrograde in your area of finances. You may discover an error in your banking statement, or there might be some suspicious activity on a credit card. It's wise to monitor things closely over the next few weeks. There may be a delay in an expected payment. Be very proactive about this and make calls as soon as you notice. On the plus side, a financial source you had before could come back to give you a little more money.

January 17 brings the full moon and the last two weeks of the Metal Ox energy. Consider completing things that have been in the works during the previous 12 months or so. If you procrastinate over home renovation projects, maybe it's time to give up the project or hire a professional? Now is also the time to declutter, especially your wardrobe. Rooster natives are known for having style, but it's not helpful to keep so many items you no longer wear, ones that don't fit or need repairs.

The energy shifts on January 19, bringing some positive flow to your finances. Although tempered somewhat by Mercury being retrograde, there are indications a new money source will appear. Of course, with Mercury retrograde, you want to be cautious about signing agreements. It's better to be in planning-mode, rather than doing it right now.

February 2022: *February 1 is the new moon and begins the Year of the Water Tiger. February 3, Mercury goes direct. February 16 is the full moon. Your high-energy days are: 4, 10, 16, 23, and 28.*

The Water Tiger year begins on February 1, and Rooster native, you may feel the energy shift right away. You are known for having clear goals and a well-thought-out plan, but in the Year of the Water Tiger, spontaneity and erratic behavior rule the day. This year, there will be many opportunities for you, but you will likely have to pivot or take actions outside your comfort zone. That said, this could be a fantastic year as you take bigger chances and gain large rewards.

The new moon energy on February 1 brings a focus to your finances. There is an opportunity to make more money through your job or profitable side business. You're more frugal in your shopping, and this is paying off. You have more money to put towards debt or to sock away in your savings.

February 3 brings the Water Tiger month, and Mercury moves direct. Your project gets the green light, or you may be told that a new position is opening up and you are amply qualified. Others are seeing your confidence as you stand in the spotlight. Over the next four weeks, there could be some significant changes in your life, putting you on the road to success.

The full moon is on February 16. Over the next two weeks, love and romance energy is exceptionally strong. If you're looking for love, you could find someone with whom you have great chemistry. Rooster native, the physical attraction can be undeniable. If you're already in a committed relationship, you could feel frisky and have a lot of fun behind closed doors.

March 2022: *March 2 is the new moon. The full moon is on March 18. Your high-energy days are: 6, 12, 18, 24, and 30.*

In March, good relationship energy continues. Rooster native, if you're dating, you may see more than one person. Your popularity is soaring, and you could get a lot of responses to your online dating profile. For those Rooster natives in a relationship, now you could introduce your sweetheart to your friends and family or discuss living together. Communication between the two of you is getting better and better.

March 2 brings the new moon, and your personal power is increased for the next two weeks. When you ask for favors or help, people step up to lend a hand. You hear more "yeses" than you have in a while. Consider reaching out to influencers, potential mentors, or people you want to collaborate with and see if you can get a conversation going. Rooster native, the energy right now suggests that you could find someone to help you take your business or creative project to the next level.

March 5 begins the Water Rabbit month, and communication becomes more important. It's time to express honestly what you really want and how you really feel. There is no reason to be around the bush. Don't be subtle. You can make these declarations to the Universe through a goal board or list of things you want to accomplish. You might tell your sweetheart your wish list for your future lifestyle. This is a good time to journal or to record memos of your deepest feelings.

The full moon is on March 17, and it highlights education. This could mean you're in school and taking some tests. Perhaps you have received notification that you have been accepted by a prestigious school. It's also possible that your children are struggling in some classes and need your help and guidance to get them through. If you are a teacher, there could be a new contract to sign or an opportunity for you to do something a little bit different from being in a traditional classroom.

In some parts of the world, there will be a second new moon in March, and for other time zones, it will be April 1. This new moon brings an emphasis on home and family. You may feel a desire to nest at home as you welcome in some out-of-town guests. It's possible that one of your older kids is home from college or that you're helping a relative get settled into a new place. Rooster native, the family is pulling together to make something happen.

April 2022: *April 1 is the new moon. The full moon is on April 16. On April 29, Pluto goes retrograde. There is a partial solar eclipse on April 30. Your high-energy days are: 5, 11, 17, 23, and 29.*

The month of April has you working behind the scenes. You may do lots of projects at home. While you're very productive, it could mean your supervisor doesn't know exactly what you're doing. You may have to speak up to let the boss know all that you have accomplished. But for now, you are focused on your work. This could mean you are getting a lot of things checked off of your to-do list.

On April 4, the Wood Dragon month begins, and for the next four weeks, there are some additional resources you can gather. You may secure a low-interest loan to fund your business or to do some bill consolidation. It's possible to get funding from Small Business Administration. You might do a crowdfunding project. You may now pay a lot of attention to the power of passive income to supplement your future. Rooster native, you may set up your IRA or 401(k) to fund your retirement.

The full moon is on April 16, and Rooster native, you could be handed a job with a lot more responsibility as well as some prestige. This may mean that you get voted to a board position in a group you belong to or that you are taking a management position in your job. This is an excellent time to start a new career. If you're looking for something different to do, consider posting your resume over the next two weeks.

There is a solar eclipse on April 30, and there is some changing energy around creativity and risk-taking. If you're in a creative career, there could be alterations in your job or significant changes in the company itself. Rooster native, this might be the time to go out on your own. Or you may look to close your business to work for somebody else. If you have a product, this is an excellent time to get the patent. If you have a manuscript, it would be helpful to contact agents, publishers or to put it on Amazon yourself.

May 2022: *On May 10, Mercury goes retrograde. There is a total lunar eclipse on May 16. On May 30, there is a new moon. Your high-energy days are:5, 11, 17, 23, and 29.*

During May, there are strong romantic possibilities. Rooster native, if you're looking for love, you can meet someone most unusually. You may chat with them in the line at the post office or sit next to them at the DMV. You may meet someone who's not necessarily your type, but you find very intriguing, and they are quite taken with you. You might meet someone from a foreign land or a different political party, but you find a way to bridge the gap.

May 5 brings the Wood Snake month. For the next four weeks, you have harmonious energy, especially around legal matters and government paperwork. Rooster native, this is an excellent time to get your professional license in order, update certifications or get government permits. You might also get involved in local government to help someone campaign or speak your mind at the City Council meeting.

On May 10, Mercury goes retrograde, and you could be pretty busy at work. Your office may be shorthanded, and they could ask you to fill in. Your hours could expand, or you just have more on your plate than you usually do. Fortunately, Rooster native, you are very organized and highly efficient.

There is a lunar eclipse on May 15, and you may have to say goodbye to a friend who is moving far away. While you will keep in touch by phone or FaceTime, it won't be the same as when they were close by. It's also possible that a friend of yours is getting married or just had a baby, and now they are spending more time with their family and less time doing the fun things you guys used to do.

The new moon is on May 30, and you may be laser-focused on health and wellness. You might engage a personal trainer or fall in love with hiking the local trails. Rooster native, you might get a bicycle and join a biking club. It's also possible you are outfitting a room in your house with exercise equipment so that you can work out every day of the week. This is also a suitable time to make alterations in your eating habits.

June 2022: *Mercury goes direct on June 3. On June 4, Saturn goes retrograde. On June 14, there is a full moon. Neptune goes retrograde on June 28. The new moon is on June 29. Your high-energy days are:4, 10, 16, 23, and 28.*

In June, an opportunity to meet new friends arises. You might do more social events in town or do activities with your kids, such as playing sports or exploring local attractions. You may meet new people through organizations or get-togethers and make some great connections.

June 5 brings the Fire Horse month, and there's an emphasis on your reputation. The things that you are posting on social media could get more coverage. Your YouTube channel might pull in more subscribers. Your posts are likely getting lots and lots of likes. During this time, it's a good idea to stay positive when posting content rather than talking about controversial topics unless you want a lot of mixed feedback.

The full moon is on June 14, and you could use a vacation. Rooster native, you might go away for a little while. A friend of yours may have a place you can stay, such as a cabin in the woods or a beach house. Rooster native, you also might try an Airbnb or the adventure of car camping. Staying close to home is okay, but it would be desirable for you to visit places you haven't been before, even if they're in your hometown.

June 28 is the new moon, and there could be congratulations from friends and family on your relationship. You may announce an engagement, or the two of you have bought a house together, and it's time for a housewarming party. Rooster native, you are feeling closer to your sweetheart than ever. If you're looking for love, you have the opportunity for a brilliant match. It's a good idea to let friends and family help you find your next relationship. You might go on a blind date or two.

July 2022: *July 13 brings the full moon. There is a new moon on July 28. Also, on July 28, Jupiter goes retrograde. Your high-energy days are:4, 10, 16, 23, and 28.*

In July, there's some energy around moving or making some alterations to the house. You might do some redecorating or home repairs. Some Rooster natives may change residences. You might buy a house or change apartments. You may move a long distance though a local move is more likely. It's also possible there are some significant changes in the neighborhood. You may see neighbors move out who have not moved in many years.

July 7 brings the Fire Sheep month, and over the next four weeks, friendships are highlighted. You could meet new people through groups and organizations you belong to. You might do some charitable work, such as a fund drive or help at the local food bank. Rooster native, this is a helpful time to work in the community garden or do a neighborhood beautification project. During these activities, you could meet someone who becomes a new best friend.

The full moon is on July 13, and your charisma and magnetism are powerful. You are drawing impressive people to you. You could collaborate with an influencer or even a celebrity. This is an ideal time to direct message people you admire, as you're more likely to get a response.

The new moon is on July 28, and Rooster native, you have a lot of luck with investments and passive income sources. Rooster native, you might set up a business based on affiliate marketing or network marketing. You may collaborate with family members to buy a rental property. This is a profitable time to look at traditional investments like stocks, bonds, or mutual funds. You might see if your company has a discount stock purchase plan.

August 2022: *August 12 brings the full moon. Uranus goes retrograde on August 24. There is a new moon on August 27. Your high-energy days are: 3, 9, 15, 21, and 27.*

In August, you might be actively seeking a more exciting life. You might look to travel to a foreign country or do an import-export business. With your investments, you might look for leveraged instruments or securities that are considered risky. You might buy a business or franchise. You could take your current business and expand it. All of this requires your due diligence, and this means spreadsheets, accounting, and deep thinking.

August 7 brings the Earth Monkey month, and you show an increase in your intuitive ability. You are tapping into the Universe and the collective consciousness of people. You see trends and opportunities unfold. Over the next four weeks, you may know what people are thinking and know who it is on the phone before you answer. Rooster native, you and your sweetheart are on the same wavelength, as you are more connected than usual.

August 11 is the full moon, and over the next two weeks, you are feeling quite frugal. You might be in a cash flow crunch because you made a large purchase or an outgo for education or a vacation. And while it's not your favorite thing to watch the pennies, you might find it fun to watch videos on frugal living and unique ways to pay off debt.

The new moon is on August 27, and education and travel are highlighted now. You might send an older kid off to college or boarding school. You may travel for education. Rooster native, you might outfit younger kids with what they need for the new school year, including clothing, backpacks, and laptops. And you could jump back into school yourself, getting homework done and looking forward to lectures.

September 2022: *On September 10, there is a full moon, and Mercury goes retrograde. On September 25, there's the new moon. Your high-energy days are: 2, 8, 14, 20, and 26.*

The month of September has you making adjustments to your schedule. You're likely not home much, to the chagrin of family and pets. You could travel for work or spend more time commuting as traffic increases in your area. It's also possible you are with friends after work and on weekends. Rooster native, you may felt restless in general. When you're at home, you want to be out of the house, and when you're out of the house, you want to be back home.

September 7 begins the Earth Rooster month, and for the next four weeks, it highlights your personal energy. You're in the spotlight and readily visible. This is a perfect time to ask for a raise, apply for a new position, or boost your own business through marketing. This is an excellent time to make a push towards your goals. So this might mean you play music in front of an audience, audition for a play, or do karaoke on Friday nights.

The full moon is on September 10, and the same day, Mercury goes retrograde. There's a lot of energy around siblings and neighbors. You may spend more time with a sibling, one who lives far away. Or you might get together with the neighbors to hold a garage sale or do a neighborhood watch. Rooster native, you may also have some difficulty with your vehicle. If you're getting work done on your car, it would be a good idea to get a warranty just in case the shop doesn't do the work correctly.

The new moon is on September 25. Over the next two weeks, you may receive some recognition from a supervisor or written testimonials from clients or customers. Other people are looking up to you, and they may ask you to teach or lead a meeting. If you are on an online dating site, you could get more "winks" and "likes." It's also possible to get some publicity. Your business could expand, or you can gain followers for your social media.

October 2022: *Mercury goes direct on October 2. On October 8, Pluto goes direct. There is a full moon on October 9. On October 23, Saturn goes direct. On October 25, there's a partial solar eclipse. On October 28, Jupiter goes retrograde. Mars goes retrograde on October 30. Your high-energy days are:2, 8, 14, 20, and 26.*

The month of October can bring a new job for Rooster natives. Mercury goes direct on October 2. You may get a call from a headhunter or a former colleague, letting you know of an opening where they work. There also could be an opening within your company, perhaps in a remote office or with a different team. Some Rooster natives will transform their status, possibly going from single to married.

October 8 brings the Metal Dog month, and you're paying a lot more attention to your finances. Now you are looking at spending habits and seeing what subscriptions or monthly costs you can cut. There's an opportunity to do some investing, but you need capital to make this happen. You might save up for holiday gifts you want to get rather than just putting items on a credit card.

The full moon is on October 9, and an issue with a family member clears up (after some lengthy discussions–but it's worth it). Rooster native, the family seems to get along better in general. There is a sense of unity. And some necessary home repairs finally get done.

The solar eclipse is on October 25, and Rooster native, you may examine your future and the path you're on. You may see friends starting businesses or getting married, and you might wonder how you could get on better with your life. It all comes down to what you're doing on a day-to-day basis. Look at your daily activities and maybe implement some mini habits, habit stacking, or a complete shift in your lifestyle.

November 2022: *November 8 brings the total lunar eclipse. On November 23, there is a new moon, and Jupiter goes direct. Your high-energy days are: 1, 7, 13, 19, and 25.*

The month of November shows the community rallying around you. Friends are coming out of the woodwork to help you out. You're getting advice and material support. Someone may have a laptop you can borrow, a sofa that they want to give away, or they may sell you a car at a fantastic price. You are expanding your circle of friends, finding more help, and opportunities to help others. Now you feel part of something.

November 7 brings the Metal Pig month, highlighting communication. You may do some writing, teaching, or just talking on the phone a lot more than usual. It's possible you're attending a conference or recording a podcast. Rooster native, this is a good time to work on your singing voice or stand-up comedy routine.

The lunar eclipse is on November 8, and there could be changes in your love relationship. If you're dating someone, it may start to go south. But this just means a new person, someone who's a better match, is on their way to you. You may find this challenging at first, but it's good to trust in the process. When you let go of something (or someone), you have two hands to take hold of something else. Rooster native, maybe do some Feng Shui cures to attract a better love relationship.

The new moon is on November 23, and your intuition is very strong. You may look at ways to increase your psychic ability through reading tarot cards, mediumship, or having a past life regression. You might take classes in psychic self-defense or celebrate the new moon with people who do natural magic with herbs and crystals.

December 2022: *Neptune goes direct on December 3. The full moon is on December 8. There is a new moon on December 23. Mercury goes retrograde on December 29. Your high-energy days are: 1, 7, 13, 19, and 25.*

In December, you are doing a lot of introspection. You are removing inner blocks by challenging limiting beliefs and shifting your perception of things. You may journal, meditate, or do affirmations. Rooster native, you may study under a master or find information through YouTube videos. You are learning how to eliminate fear and move forward toward your goals.

On December 7, it's the Water Rat month. It's also the full moon. Rooster native, you can have a hectic month. A lot of the inner work that you're doing is paying off. You may get up early, exercise, eat a healthy breakfast, and then you're off to the races. Your productivity could be through the roof as you get things done that have been sitting on your to-do list for months or even years. And all of this happens because you have met your limiting beliefs head-on.

December 23 is the new moon, and over the next two weeks, you're in the spotlight once again. Others compliment your confidence and how you present yourself. You may receive accolades for your style and creative abilities. Rooster native, this could attract an exciting relationship opportunity. And this could blossom into romance or very close friendship.

On December 29, Mercury goes retrograde, and it's a good idea to take care of your physical self. If you work out too hard, you likely have some sore muscles. Watch your knees and avoid jumping onto hard or and even surfaces.

January 2023: *January 6 brings the full moon. Mercury goes direct on January 18. The year of the water rabbit begins on January 22. Your high-energy days are: 6, 12, 18, 24, and 30.*

The month of January brings a fresh start in many areas and a lot of luck to you, Rooster native. Many things now line up in your favor. This could mean you have a great business opportunity or that one of your kids is getting some sort of award. And while these might not come with a monetary prize, it is helping your reputation, and it looks good on the resume.

January 5 begins the Water Ox month, and over the next four weeks, there is abundant creative and fertility energy. If you do creative projects, you can get them out into the marketplace or on display for people to see. If you're looking to add to the family, you have good energy for getting fertility assistance or adopting. Rooster native, you might add a pet to the family home.

The full moon is on January 6, and relationship energy is very strong. You may get quite serious about someone you're dating as the two of you discuss living together or buying property. If you're already in a committed relationship, you're likely having positive discussions about children or pets. You're feeling closer as a family, and you might plan some family adventures together.

On January 18, Mercury goes direct. Now an opportunity you've been waiting for presents itself. If this is a contract, it still may need some work. Allow Mercury a few days to get up to speed before you sign anything.

The new moon is on January 22, and this brings the Year of the Water Rabbit. This means you'll enter the opposition energy as the sign of Rabbit is opposite your own sign of Rooster. This year presents both challenges and opportunities. The challenge is that while the world is focused on the Water Rabbit, people are not paying attention to you. They may ignore your accomplishments and not give you credit where credit is due. You'll have to let others know what you've done and what you're looking for. You'll need to express yourself more loudly than usual. But there is a positive side to this year. You are now entering the first year of your harvest period. This will be the first of 3 years of harvest time. This means far more opportunities are available to you based on your experience and skills. This means there are job opportunities and chances to make money. You can attract new friends and accumulate knowledge. So while there's a lot of work ahead, there is a cornucopia of opportunities for Rooster natives.

Attract New Love

The Year of the Water Tiger brings tantalizing and compelling love opportunities. You could fall head over heels rather suddenly with someone very different from any person you've dated in the past. It's also possible you will come back together with someone you dated previously, but the relationship now seems quite different. Meeting someone new is likely to happen when you're doing new things. You might connect with someone through an online dating website and then realize you've met them before. Or you could meet someone when you're doing a new activity like snowboarding or taking a class in woodworking.

There are many reasons this year that you may want to add the essence of joy to your home to help your current relationship. You can do this by adding floral scents to your home, either by burning floral incense or using a scented floral spray. A lovely floral-scented incense like Nag Champa works very well. Or, pick up a bouquet of floral-scented incense and fill the house with the scent of flowers. Add floral scent to your home once a week or so to keep the energy of love and joy in the home.

Enhance Existing Love

For Rooster natives who are already in a committed relationship, you're feeling closer than ever. You are strongly connected because you value each other. Your personal and financial goals are more in alignment this year. You look like you're on the same page when it comes to taking action. In 2022, you might celebrate a milestone anniversary or sneak off for a second honeymoon. It all boils down to the fact that you are actively taking care of each other. This shows respect and consideration. This helps your love to grow.

Quan Yin (also spelled Kwan Yin) is the embodiment of a goddess representing loving kindness. She is often depicted holding a small vase of healing waters. Place this statue in your bedroom to bring good energy for a happy, loving relationship.

Looking to Conceive?

Find a necklace made of cowrie shells. Cowrie shells have long been associated with pregnancy because the shape of the shell is very like the shape of a uterus. Small cowrie shells, usually white, are made into necklaces and bracelets.

You can also find larger cowrie shells; these may be striped or spotted brown and white. Place one or more of these larger shells on your bedside table. Cowrie shells are not only reputed as fertility cures but also have been used as currency in some cultures, so the shell will attract good money energy, too.

(From Donna Stellhorn's book, Fertility Feng Shui)

Family and Kids

In the Year the Water Tiger, there's a lot of healing energy at home. If there has been a rift between family members, now you can see an olive branch and steps towards understanding each other. There could also be repairs done to the home, which symbolizes the healing within the family. 2022 could also bring an addition to the household. There might be an announcement of a pregnancy, the birth of a child, or the addition of a new pet. It's also possible that the family is getting larger when one of your older children brings home a spouse.

Gain additional protection energy for your home by placing a pair of Foo Dogs (also spelled Fu Dogs) by your front door. These "guard dogs" come in pairs; one male with his paw on the world and one female with her paw gently on the baby. There are some Foo Dog pairs where all four of their paws are on the ground. This is fine. In this case, there may be no visible male or female dog.

Place one dog on either side of the door. This can be inside or outside the house, depending on the size and material the Foo Dogs are made of. Some pairs are so large, they must be outside. Or you can find decorated and painted Foo Dogs of the most delicate porcelain, which should be placed inside.

Display the dogs with their raised foot closest to the door. So the male dog who often has his left paw on the world would have the door to his left. The female dog, who holds the baby with her right paw, would have the door to her right.

Money

There are some great money opportunities in 2022 for Rooster natives, especially when you take time to care for your finances. Sticking to a written budget or actively managing your money is the way to accumulate funds and find additional sources of income. It's likely your investments will do well in your diversified portfolio, even though there are some ups and downs in the market. If you're looking at the long-term, you're not only learning more about handling money, but you're getting better at creating financial opportunities. The Year of the Water Tiger could be one of your most lucrative years in some time.

This year consider displaying an abacus. This device was used for thousands of years to calculate money and do accounting. Displaying a beautiful abacus helps you attract so much money, you'll need help to count it.

Place the abacus in your home office or where you pay bills and work on your finances. You can display it on the wall or place it on a desk or table. You can also learn how to use it. People adept at using an abacus can calculate sums as quickly as a person with a state-of-the-art calculator.

Job or Career

While you have more confidence and a growing set of skills, you need to let others know what you want and what you have accomplished. Rooster native, you are usually quite good at self-promotion, but either you are out of the office (working at home) or not heard this year. But once you present your case, you can receive accolades, promotions, salary increases, etc. So in the Year of the Water Tiger, it's less likely that someone will seek you out to offer you a job or promotion. Still, when you mention you want one, opportunities magically appear.

When considering a new career or new job, you sometimes want to draw the energy in quickly. The traditional cure for this is to take ground cinnamon (the kind in your spice cabinet) and sprinkle a bit on your porch—especially on top of your welcome mat. A single teaspoon of cinnamon should do for the whole porch. This will attract positive career and financial energy. Repeat every couple of days until you have the job you want.

Education

There is a great deal of positive energy around education for Rooster natives in 2022. You may work on a degree or finish up an accelerated program for certification. You're in the flow, and you can maintain a good grade point average and even find more efficient ways to study where it takes less time and brings you better results. There's also positive energy around funding for higher education. You can find loans and possibly grants and scholarships during the Year of the Water Tiger.

Legal Matters

The energy around legal matters is quite prominent for Rooster natives in the Year of the Water Tiger. Water Tiger energy can be combative, and it's known that Rooster natives will never back down from a fight. With legal matters in 2022, you have an edge. But this doesn't mean you should get into frivolous lawsuits. Also, even though you're likely to win, lawsuits are time-consuming, and that's valuable time you can be used for something else. With contracts, you have a lot of luck and can negotiate for what you want. It's also possible that you are testing for a license or certification this year, which can go very well.

Health and Well-Being

There's a lot of attention on your health and well-being in 2022. This is a superb time to take your exercise schedule and eating habits absolutely seriously. You can make enormous improvements in your quality of life by taking responsibility for your well-being—exercising, eating your vegetables, and generally following good health guidelines. As this is a Water Tiger year, you might dance, swim, or cycle as these fluid movements are very much in line with the energy. You also could do well with a full-body workout such as climbing or rowing. Paying attention to your health this year brings you some significant results.

Turquoise, a beautiful blue-green stone, is often made into jewelry. It has long been known for its healing qualities. Find either a piece of turquoise jewelry or a tumbled stone you can carry with you. The turquoise will remind you to stick with positive health changes. Once your new habits are established, you can keep the stone in your kitchen or the bedroom on your bedside table.

Dog

February 10, 1910–January 29, 1911: Yang Metal Dog
January 28, 1922–February 15, 1923: Yang Water Dog
February 14, 1934–February 3, 1935: Yang Wood Dog
February 2, 1946–January 21, 1947: Yang Fire Dog
February 18, 1958–February 7, 1959: Yang Earth Dog
February 6, 1970–January 26, 1971: Yang Metal Dog
January 25, 1982–February 12, 1983: Yang Water Dog
February 10, 1994–January 30, 1995: Yang Wood Dog
January 29, 2006–February 17, 2007: Yang Fire Dog
February 16, 2018–February 4, 2019: Yang Earth Dog

Dog Personality

When looking at a Chinese Zodiac creature's qualities, it's a good idea to consider the animal's traits, behaviors, and personality. When considering the Dog's qualities, many of us have some idea about dog personalities and behavior.

Dogs came to live with humans around 100,000 years ago. Humans found dogs to be valuable—helping to hunt and herd, pull loads, and even protect their people from wild animals.

Sometimes we confuse Dogs' overall personality with the characteristics of specific dog breeds (most of which are only a few hundred years old). We want to consider the energy of a dog as we think about the personality traits of natives born under the Chinese Zodiac sign of the Dog.

The animal dog is known for companionship; similarly, individuals born during the Year of the Dog are usually very well-liked and friendly. They have a deep sense of loyalty and fair play. They are happier around people than on their own. They go with the flow, being less demanding, always meeting others halfway, so everyone gets something of what they want.

Early humans brought dogs into their lives to increase their chances of survival. The dogs would help them find food, keep them warm at night, and protect them from dangers. Those born under the Chinese Zodiac sign of Dog are protective of their friends. They watch over them and will fight for them. Dogs are eager to take up a cause, whether on behalf of an individual, a group, or an organization.

Because they take loyalty so seriously, Dog natives choose their friendships carefully. Accepting a new person into their circle takes time. Even so, many people want to be their friends. Dogs are often in positions of influence and connected with people of power. Dogs are rarely selfish, and when they crave power or money, there is usually a person or cause who will benefit from everything Dog creates.

Dog natives are known to work hard and to play hard. They have to be cautious to avoid overindulgence in food or overspending. They often like competitive sports, and they often love a good hard workout. They don't mind a night out dancing, followed by an early morning yoga session. They like a stylish home, but their home may not be neat—it doesn't matter to them since they're not at home that often.

Dogs make good lawyers, always looking for justice and fairness. These characteristics also make them excellent employees. They're notably good at managing several projects simultaneously. They won't gossip at the water cooler, nor will they speak ill of others. Dog prefers to be a team player, and if you're part of the team, you can count on them.

Dogs alternate between aggressive spending and aggressive saving. Regarding investments, they are better at investing in property, precious metals or stones, or other tangible things, rather than intangible derivatives.

Most in life, Dog wants loyal, honest, intelligent friends who will share a dinner or attend the theater or join them on an impromptu trip to the Bahamas for the weekend. They love to be treated fairly, and honestly don't like to be questioned too deeply about their reasoning and thinking processes. They'd love to have enough money—in fact, so much money they never have to think about what things cost!

Even when Dog seems happy, they are pessimists by nature, capable of worrying a great deal, including the small things. They can count the times when they were overconfident, and it led to disaster, and they use this information as a tool to confirm their need to worry.

They are resourceful and resilient and overcome any difficulty. However, Dog spends a great deal of time visualizing potential problems. They look for the storm clouds and never the silver lining.

Dog: Predictions for 2022

How to use your High-Energy Days: On these days, plan to take action for your most important goals, make vital phone calls, send important emails. Your high-energy days are when your energy and luck are the strongest for the month.

January 2022: *January 2 is the new moon. January 14 has Mercury going retrograde. January 17 is the full moon. On January 18, Uranus goes direct. On January 29, Venus goes direct. Your High-Energy Days are 6, 12, 18, 24, and 30.*

The calendar year begins, but Metal Ox energy lasts for the entire month. This is an excellent time to plan for the future and see what still needs to be cleaned out, filed away, or tossed out. By focusing on completing things, you open up your life to more expansive opportunities. Because Mercury goes retrograde this month, if you find yourself falling behind on your New Year's resolutions, recognize you can start them all over again next month in the New Lunar Year.

There's a new moon on January 2, and your intuition is elevated over the next two weeks. You may receive messages and impressions from the world around you. Unusual thoughts are popping into your head. This is a favorable time to work with tarot cards, Angel cards, or even a pendulum. Allow yourself a few minutes each day to shut off the phone and listen to the Universe. Sit with the cards or the pendulum and ask a single question. Give yourself some time to hear the answer.

On January 14, Mercury goes retrograde. Many things you began in the past two weeks are now interrupted or have to be started over. Mercury retrograde has a purpose besides just disrupting your life—and it is to allow you to go over past decisions to see if you want to rethink your choices. Now you can change your mind. Dog natives are often committed to a course of action, but you must remember you can change, and sometimes change leads you straight to your objective.

The full moon on January 17 highlights relationships. You may have temporarily been separated from your sweetheart because of a work or family matter. But now you come back together, and things are better than ever. For those Dog natives looking for love, someone from your past may return to your present. This may be someone you only met once before and barely remember. But they remember you.

On January 19, the energy shifts, and you come into the spotlight. You have an opportunity to lead a meeting or even be on stage. This is a great time to launch your YouTube channel.

February 2022: *February 1 is the new moon and begins the Year of the Water Tiger. February 3, Mercury goes direct. February 16 is the full moon. Your high-energy days are: 5, 11, 17, and 23.*

The Water Tiger year begins on February 1, and the lucky year for Dog native begins. This is very harmonious energy for you, as a myriad of opportunities could come your way. You're likely to meet more people as this is a very social year. It has some good financial possibilities if you're willing to take a risk here and there. In 2022, it's wise to move fearlessly forward and take significant actions toward your goals. When you do, you will find support from some unexpected sources.

This new moon energy on February 1, and your magnetism is powerful for the next two weeks. You may be pursued for a love relationship. Strangers may compliment you on your deportment, personality, and smile. Someone may move you to the head of the line just because they like your face. This is an excellent time to reach out to influential people you want to connect with.

February 3 brings the Water Tiger month, and Mercury moves direct. And there's good news regarding a creative project for you or one of your kids. An art project could win an award or be in a showing. Dog native, your article, or your child's poem may be featured on a website or even in a magazine. If report cards are coming in, post it on the refrigerator and on social media as well.

The full moon is on February 16, and a problematic relationship may be ending. This could've been a professional connection, and now this person is moving on to another company or position. You don't have to do anything except wish them well as they sail off into the sunset. This won't be the last time you see luck and opportunity come together to benefit you in 2022.

March 2022: *March 2 is the new moon. The full moon is on March 18. Your high-energy days are: 1, 7, 13, 19, 25, and 31.*

In March, you show luck with money. Dog native, to grab hold of this opportunity, you will have to be very aware of your communication. Carefully framing your request and explaining what you need will go a long way to helping you gain this financial windfall. Dog native, you may want to do a little research or even run some different scenarios by a friend. You will grow and learn from this experience.

March 2 brings the new moon, and over the next two weeks, you may have a secret romantic rendezvous. Someone may have a crush on you and ask you out. Or you may surprise your sweetheart with a fantasy dinner date and a night at a local hotel. All this intrigue is making things even more tantalizing than usual.

March 5 begins the Water Rabbit month, and over the next four weeks, there's an emphasis on your habits and routines. You might look at the processes you use to get stuff done both at home and at work. Dog native, consider how "mini habits" could make significant shifts in your behavior. Or you may want to connect with the energy of the Water Tiger and jump into a big lifestyle change all at once.

The full moon is on March 17, and over the next two weeks, you have the option of gaining resources from a financial institution. This could mean getting a credit card at a very low interest rate, a loan to consolidate debt or some funding for your business. This is an excellent time to fill out an application or to talk with a banker about options.

In some parts of the world, there will be a second new moon in March, and for other time zones, it will be on April 1. This new moon brings an emphasis on transportation and how you get around town. Maybe you are standing in line at DMV, or you're at the dealership getting your car repaired. You might sell your vehicle and use public transportation. Dog native, if you're looking to purchase a new vehicle, you could get a terrific deal.

April 2022: *April 1 is the new moon. The full moon is on April 16. On April 29, Pluto goes retrograde. There is a partial solar eclipse on April 30. Your high-energy days are: 6, 12, 18, 24, and 30.*

April brings a lot of energy around neighbors and family members. You may have more interaction with your siblings over the next few weeks. A family member who lives far away may pay a visit. You may help a family member change residences. You may have more interaction with neighbors when you're doing a neighborhood garage sale, or you might invite them to a backyard barbecue.

On April 4, the Wood Dragon month begins and brings some challenging relationship energy. You and your sweetheart may snap at each other as you both feel overworked and underappreciated. This is a suitable time to support each other through patience and understanding. This will help smooth over hurt feelings on both sides. If you're looking for love, you could meet a person with whom you have great chemistry. Dog native, you may find that the relationship is exciting and stimulating.

The full moon is on April 16, and there's an emphasis on school and other education opportunities. You may be asked to teach something to coworkers. You might be encouraged by your friends to do a podcast. It's also possible that you're in school and taking standardized tests or finishing up a term paper. And you could help your kids with their education, especially helping them choose a college or help them study for tests.

There is a solar eclipse on April 30. There are some challenges at home, possibly requiring quick home repairs that put you over budget. You may expect guests and feed a lot of hungry people. You might celebrate more than one event over the next two weeks. The joy you feel will erase all the hard work and expense from your memory. Dog native, you could have a house full of laughter and jubilation.

May 2022: *On May 10, Mercury goes retrograde. There is a total lunar eclipse on May 16. On May 30, there is a new moon. Your high-energy days are:6, 12, 18, 24, and 30.*

During May, you're pretty busy with potentially more than one stream of income. Your side business could become more profitable and require much more of your time. Your primary business may expand, making it necessary for you to hire help. If you work for someone else, your office may be shorthanded, and you're picking up the slack.

May 5 brings the Wood Snake month and activates your house of intimacy. If you're already in a love relationship, you and your sweetheart may spend a little more time behind closed doors. Dog native, you could chase each other around the sofa like you did when you first started going out. If this is a new relationship, you may take it to a more serious level with dinner dates that last so long you end up sharing breakfast.

On May 10, Mercury goes retrograde, and a risky venture may fall through. You have extra luck this year, so if something is blocked, you need to take it as a sign that the Universe is stepping in to protect you. So if you find that an investment you were about to purchase is no longer viable or you are priced out, thank the Universe for watching out for you.

There is a lunar eclipse on May 15, and there could be some significant changes at your job. It's possible that your company is going through a merger or is being bought. There could be some downsizing happening or perhaps changes within your department. Dog native, you may end up with a different job title or different duties. If your company is not going through changes, you should look underneath to see what's happening with its financials. Make sure the company is still fiscally sound and growing.

The new moon is on May 30, and Dog native, if you're looking for love, this is an excellent time to meet someone new. Dog native, you could consider asking friends and family to fix you up. This is a suitable time to engage a matchmaker or to try speed dating. If nothing more, join some groups that you're interested in for hiking, gardening, or charity work, and you could meet some fascinating people.

June 2022: *Mercury goes direct on June 3. On June 4, Saturn goes retrograde. On June 14, there is a full moon. Neptune goes retrograde on June 28. The new moon is on June 29. Your high-energy days are: 5, 11, 17, 23, and 29.*

In June, you are helping the family. Maybe you are pulling resources together to make investments. You may have a family business. Now it's time to expand or even pass the company down to the next generation. Dog native, you may gather with siblings to help older relatives move into a new home. And you may have a wedding to attend for a niece, nephew, or cousin.

June 5 brings the Fire Horse month, and there are some travel opportunities. You might take a vacation or attend a celebration. You could consider taking the trip by car or train so you can see the sights and take your time getting there. This might be when you are looking at different locations where you might live in the future.

The full moon is on June 14, and over the next two weeks, you may do a lot of activities with friends. Dog native, you could camp together, or you might visit them at their new home. You could expand the number of friends you have as you get more involved in a community organization or Meetup group. You could meet like-minded people who share your interest in politics, sports, or the environment.

June 28 is the new moon and is a great deal of emphasis on health and fitness. You may do more exercise with a new bike or exercise equipment. You could engage a personal trainer, or perhaps you're doing tai chi in the park. This is also a great time to shift your eating habits through meal prep or by using a meal prep service where everything comes to your door, preportioned and ready to cook.

July 2022: *July 13 brings the full moon. There is a new moon on July 28. Also, on July 28, Jupiter goes retrograde. Your high-energy days are:5, 11, 17, 23, and 29.*

In July, there are opportunities for love and romance, but you have little free time to engage with others. You could do extra things on the job, so dates and fun activities may have to wait. Or perhaps it's your sweetheart who is very busy right now. That means you are sitting by the phone waiting for them to finish whatever tasks they are working on. Generally, you're a patient person, but during the erratic energy of the Year of the Water Tiger, you may not feel as sedate as usual. But patience will be key.

July 7 brings the Fire Sheep month, and over the next four weeks, you may receive some recognition at your job. This is long overdue, and you may finally move up in the company. It's also possible that someone you used to work with is telling you about an opportunity at their current company. Post your resume for a job that sounds more interesting and lucrative.

The full moon is on July 13, and you may have interesting dreams. Your psychic ability is much stronger right now. You could receive messages as unique number patterns as well as animal signs. Dog native, this is an excellent time to look at different ways of enhancing your intuition, such as using a pendulum, Angel cards, or Nordic runes. Look at various means of tapping into the knowledge of the Universe and in the power of synchronicity.

The new moon is on July 28, and over the next two weeks, there is excellent relationship energy for Dog natives. If you have been dating, you might be ready to make a big announcement to friends and family. Dog native, you might get engaged or buy a house together. If you're looking for love, you could meet someone with whom you have a strong mutual attraction. This relationship could move forward quickly. Now is the time to update your online dating profile to attract several potential love matches.

August 2022: *August 12 brings the full moon. Uranus goes retrograde on August 24. There is a new moon on August 27. Your high-energy days are: 4, 10, 16, 23, and 28.*

In August, it's time to look at your work/life balance and the quality of your life in general. Write out a vision of the lifestyle you want. Or you could create a vision board of the type of house you want to live in, the neighborhood, and the people you interact with within the community. You may become more aware of the questions that you ask yourself. As you shift questions to the positive, new opportunities arrive seemingly out of nowhere. Consider asking yourself questions such as, "how can I make progress on my most important goal today" or "how can I courageously follow my path today."

August 7 brings the Earth Monkey month, and over the next four weeks, there's a lot of emphasis on technology and the future. Dog native, you may upgrade equipment by getting a new phone or laptop. You may do more on social media, gaining followers and subscribers as you put out content. Or you may look for passive sources of income through affiliate marketing or by selling digital products. If technology is not your thing, this is your opportunity to find someone who can help you get up to speed.

August 11 is the full moon, and you may engage in a business partnership or a pivotal collaboration. A person may offer to mentor you in your business. You may follow someone on social media who gives tips about expanding a business or being more productive in daily routines. This is an opportunity for you to reach out to this individual and see if you can have a face-to-face conversation.

The new moon is on August 27, and over the next two weeks, there's a lot of emphasis on investments. During the Year of the Water Tiger, there could be a lot of volatility in the markets, making the more cautious investor a little nervous. It's good to be diversified and clearly understand the investments you are getting into (especially the downside). Now you could meet someone knowledgeable, practically a financial wizard.

September 2022: *On September 10, there is a full moon, and Mercury goes retrograde. On September 25, there's the new moon. Your high-energy days are: 3, 9, 15, 21, and 27.*

September brings a focus on adjusting your actions to improve your life. Not everything goes smoothly, yet one of your talents, Dog native, is your ability to pivot. Once you see that the way you're heading is blocked, you know you can call on friends and colleagues to help you figure out a way forward. A contract you were expecting may fall through, but this could set off a string of events that bring attractive opportunities in another direction. Dog native, it's now time to think of possibilities and make lemonade out of these lemons.

September 7 begins the Earth Rooster month, and over the next four weeks, it would be desirable to have a little more time off. You may have been working extra hours or very focused on school work. It would be helpful for you to take a long weekend to unwind and reset. Dog native, if your business is seasonal and you are about to go into the busy season, it's very important to take time off now before it's too late.

The full moon is on September 10, and the same day, Mercury goes retrograde. There's a robust financial opportunity for Dog natives, but it is outside your comfort zone. A contract (related to the one that fell through earlier) may need to be signed. Or you may need some additional education, certification, or license to move forward. This may be the opportunity you've wished for, and so now it's time to lean in. And with Mercury going retrograde, recognize there will be extra delays in the process.

The new moon is on September 25, and you may be focused on a long-distance connection. You may talk to relatives who live far away. Your sweetheart may travel for work or see family members. This is an excellent time to work on your communication skills. Make sure communication equipment is working. Dog native, you might speak to people via video-conferencing or FaceTime.

October 2022: *Mercury goes direct on October 2. On October 8, Pluto goes direct. There is a full moon on October 9. On October 23, Saturn goes direct. On October 25, there's a partial solar eclipse. On October 28, Jupiter goes retrograde. Mars goes retrograde on October 30. Your high-energy days are:3, 9, 15, 21, and 27.*

October can be a studious month for Dog natives. Mercury goes direct on October 2. You may take a professional test or do paperwork for a government organization. You could fill out forms for student loans or consolidate some other obligations. This is also when you may get a building permit to do some work on the house. You might buy a piece of rental property. There's a lot of paperwork involved, so take things step-by-step.

October 8 brings the Metal Dog month, and over the next four weeks, you are in the spotlight. This means that you have a chance to be seen and acknowledged for your contribution. Your boss is now more open to hearing your request for a raise or promotion. Dog native, this is a good time to market your own business or to look to others for collaborative advertising.

The full moon is on October 9, and over the next two weeks, you may look for pieces of paper. You may get your filing in order, shred unnecessary paper and perhaps even go paperless entirely. This is a useful time to automate your bill-paying and create systems for other tasks so that you don't have to monitor things closely. Dog native, this will free up your brainpower for more important tasks.

The solar eclipse is on October 25, and Dog native, you may get a new job. You may receive a call from a headhunter or an offer letter for a job you interviewed for previously. There could be an opening at your current job that gives you more responsibility, a better title, and more money. You're climbing the corporate ladder of success. This is an excellent time to take a leap forward. If you want to stay in your current position, the solar eclipse could make things less stable. It's better to make a move now than to stand on shaky ground.

November 2022: *November 8 brings the total lunar eclipse. On November 23, there is a new moon, and Jupiter goes direct. Your high-energy days are: 2, 8, 14, 20, and 26.*

November shows you in the limelight. You may be on stage announcing awards, leading a meeting, or showing off your talents. If you're in a choir or dance troupe, you could perform in front of a live audience. The same goes for Dog natives who are in a play, improv group, or want to do stand-up comedy. This is your chance to show people what you can do. And you will probably receive applause and encouragement.

November 7 brings the Metal Pig month, and there's a great deal of emphasis on your finances over the next four weeks. You can do some Feng Shui cures to increase money flow. This could include clearing out the front entryway and finding other places for boots, hats, and gloves. Dog native, you may want to get a new welcome mat. Consider placing a bowl of coins on your entryway table to activate the "like attracts like" energy to bring money into the household.

The lunar eclipse is on November 8, and a family member needs your help. They may need some advice, a place to stay, or an infusion of cash. You may pull together with other family members to help this individual. This is probably not the first time they have been in some hot water, but you have to take everything on a case-by-case basis. Dog native, you're devoted to the family, and so it's likely you're going to help.

The new moon is on November 23, and Dog native, you share your gifts with the community. You may do some charity fundraising or support a good cause. You may be part of a community group distributing toys, food, or warm clothing to the less fortunate. This is also a time to visit people in the hospital or a nursing home.

December 2022: *Neptune goes direct on December 3. The full moon is on December 8. There is a new moon on December 23. Mercury goes retrograde on December 29. Your high-energy days are:2, 8, 14, 20, and 26.*

In December, it's time to rein in your spending. If you have been going over budget for the last few months, it may be time to get back on a written plan or even use the cash envelope system for a while. Dog native, when other people need help, you forget your own budget. But this is a time to set up a system that helps you pay down debt and save money. You can use your leftover money (and your time and energy) to continue being a valuable member of the community. In this way, you can cover your rent or even save up to buy your own house.

On December 7, it's the Water Rat month. It's also the full moon. You may be ready to sign an employment contract or a purchase agreement for a vehicle. Dog native, you want to read this contract exceptionally carefully, as it's not all it seems to be. If you agreed ahead of time, the written version might not reflect what you talked about. You may need a professional to review this agreement before you move forward.

December 23 is the new moon, and Dog native, you need some time off. This is a great time to upgrade your bedroom so you can get more restful sleep. You might get a new comforter or finally replace your old mattress. Dog native, you may feel thrifty and make your blackout drapes yourself. You can ask friends and family to chip in to help you redo the bedroom entirely.

On December 29, Mercury goes retrograde, and your intuitive ability is quite strong. Look into healing modalities such as reiki or touch healing. Get a massage or have someone do reflexology on your feet. If you want to move forward on a new path, you might rub some lavender oil on the soles of your feet.

January 2023: *January 6 brings the full moon. Mercury goes direct on January 18. The year of the water rabbit begins on January 22. Your high-energy days are. 1, 7, 13, 19, 25, and 31.*

In January, there's a lot of harmony at home. Even those family members who are usually contentious and cantankerous now seem to be all smiles and agreeable. This is a proper time to introduce your sweetheart to your extended family or welcome the partner of one of your kids. If an agreement needs to be reached regarding a family business or estate, this is the time to gather siblings to discuss it.

January 5 begins the Water Ox month, and you might declutter, distributing family heirlooms, or just getting rid of stuff you don't need anymore. Dog native, you might do a big run to a charity shop with loads of all the clothes, kitchen stuff, and old holiday decorations. This is a perfect time to set up an eBay store to sell off more valuable items. Perhaps put furniture up for sale on Facebook marketplace. With each drawer and closet that you clear, lightness and better energy circulate throughout the house.

The full moon is on January 6, and Dog native, you may want a clean slate. This could mean that you're doing a water fast or juicing to clear out your system. You might forgo sugar or stay away from processed foods. This can markedly benefit your health overall as it starts the calendar year off right.

On January 18, Mercury goes direct. You may be attracted to reengage with a psychic modality you have done before, such as tarot cards, pendulum, or past life regression. The Universe will send you messages about the route to take. Dog native, you will see the signs everywhere.

The new moon is on January 22, and this brings the Year of the Water Rabbit. You are now entering your last year of "seed tending." The seed tending period lasts for three years, and during this time, it's vital to focus on what's working in your life. Dog native, you have many activities that are bringing profits and satisfaction, but weeds have cropped up. There are things you're doing regularly that are not bringing growth, profit, or joy. These "weeds" need to be pulled up and discarded to give you more space for the things that are working in your life. In

2023, you want to make sure your time, energy, and resources are going toward your important goals and not busywork.

Attract New Love

In the Year of the Water Tiger, love comes unexpectedly and from surprising circumstances. Dog native, you could meet someone when you least expect it and suddenly have an amazing connection. In 2022, go out and do things you enjoy. Be social and involved in the community. Do things in nature or where you get some exercise. This year, love comes to find you. Also, consider visualizing a great relationship and doing Feng Shui cures to attract love energy.

Burn a red candle in your bedroom about once a month to stimulate the energy for bringing a love relationship into being. You can use a tea light or votive candle for this purpose, or you can choose a large pillar candle to burn over a series of days.

Burn the candle an hour or two each night until the candle burns out. A large pillar candle or a jar candle could take all month to finish, but that's okay. The act of burning the candle over many days strengthens the energy. As you light the candle, visualize happy times together for the two of you in your new relationship.

If you don't feel comfortable burning candles in your home, you can use a battery-operated or electric candle. Choose one that has a red base. Because this type of candle is not as powerful a cure as a real candle, it's helpful to "light" this candle each day. You don't need it on at night, as that might disturb sleep, instead keep it on during the day.

Enhance Existing Love

In 2022, Dog native, your committed relationship goes along smoothly. You are valuing each other. But you are also very busy. When it comes to handling the kids, paying the bills, or getting stuff done, you're a champion. But if you want romance, you need to make an effort. If you want to sit in front of the fireplace sipping wine with your sweetheart, you may have to put it into the schedule. Overall, your relationship is good, but the fun parts are going to need some planning.

The mighty Dog needs an equal, someone they can respect. So when you are looking for new love, you need to attract someone you consider worthy. A good Feng Shui cure for you this year is the Yin/Yang symbol.

The Yin/Yang symbolism depicts a balance of energies—the talents of one partner support the lack in the other. To successfully attract a new love, wear the Yin/Yang symbol (as jewelry, printed on a T-shirt, a patch on a jacket, etc.) or place the symbol in the bedroom.

Looking to Conceive?

If you're looking to get pregnant this year, place gemstone eggs in the bedroom. You will find gemstone eggs at rock and mineral shops, or check online, where you'll be able to find a variety of stones carved in the shape of eggs. The egg shape represents a baby. Reasonably priced eggs carved from Agate, Jasper, and sometimes Rose Quartz are easy to find.

(From Donna Stellhorn's book, Fertility Feng Shui)

Family and Kids

You are experiencing changes at home during the Year of the Water Tiger. You might get a roommate, one of your kids moves in or moves out, or perhaps you rent out a room through Airbnb. It's also possible that relatives will come to stay with you as they travel through your area. There could be issues around mechanical items in the house, or you could do some electrical work. There is a possibility that you're moving. Also, the family seems to be moving in different directions. You may come together occasionally, but mostly you are like ships passing in the night. You're getting along but hardly seeing each other.

The Peace Lily is a favorite, easy-to-grow house plant. This plant is quite adaptable and can even grow in rooms where there are no windows at all. Of course, the Peace Lily symbolizes peace in the home and promotes calm and balance. This plant helps clean the air, and its pretty white flowers are a joy to see.

Find a good, healthy Peace Lily to have in your dining room, family room, or living room. This will bring positive energy to the home and family.

Money

Dog native, you have luck with money in 2022. You have an opportunity to increase revenue or to get a second source of income. You may bring in money through a passive income source. But you're almost too lucky and may not be paying a lot of attention to your money. If you keep track of your spending and emphasize income-producing opportunities, you can have an outstanding financial year. But if you ignore your money, you can still have a good year, just not a great one.

This year hang chili peppers to stimulate the flow of money. You can use pictures of chili peppers, chili pepper lights, chili peppers made of fabric, or actual dried chiles strung together. Hang them in your entryway to bring luck with money. If you use dried chilies, however, hang them outside; otherwise, the smell can be overwhelming.

Job or Career

With your career in 2022, things are humming along nicely. If you wish, you can keep a low profile and still gain salary increases or be in line for a bonus. When you want to step forward to take on more responsibility, the door of opportunity opens for you. The only caveat here is to make sure you keep your social life private, especially on social media.

Controversial posts or pictures could put you into some hot water with your boss or your customers. If you're looking for a new job in 2022, it will be necessary to knock on several doors before you get one to open.

When we think of gold in the West, we think of a gold bar, but in the East, a gold ingot is shaped like a little boat. This is called the yuan bao. These ingots were used as a form of currency. Now you can find replica gold ingots in painted metal to be used as a symbol of wealth. They often have embossed Chinese characters of "wealth" and "fortune." Place your ingot on your desk or in your family room on a shelf near a picture of your family to attract a great job opportunity or a raise from your current employer.

Education

There can be some challenges for Dog natives in 2022 around education. If you are in school, you may be bored, or perhaps you can't get the classes that you want and need for your degree. You have a lot of luck in the Year of the Water Tiger, but in the area of education, you have more difficulty. If you want to excel in this area, make contacts, tell people what you want, and find the right people to help you.

Legal Matters

In the Year of the Water Tiger, people can be more contentious and argumentative, leading to lawsuits. 2022 is a lucky year for you, but it's still a good idea to avoid legal entanglements. If you are already dealing with a legal matter, you may get a sudden resolution to the situation. Your best bet is to settle out of court. If you're looking for professional certification, make sure that you study for the test; otherwise, you may need to retake it. If you're looking for building permits or licenses, you may have to ask more than once or deliver paperwork several times.

Health and Well-Being

Dog native, this could be quite an active year for you. You might do more exercise and get good results with a personal trainer or accountability buddy. In 2022, you may focus a great deal on healing past injuries or health issues. You can make significant headway in this area. You may look at a combination of traditional treatments as well as alternative medicine. Also, consider adding activities like meditation, positive thinking, or other more spiritual methods for healing. You could finish the year feeling much better than you have in some time.

The fragrant herb, rosemary, does more than just flavor your dinner. Rosemary is a powerful herb for protecting health. It's been used for centuries for medicinal and spiritual purposes. It's been used for guarding people and activating the energy of longevity.

When possible, grow a rosemary plant on your front porch when it's the right season. Otherwise, place a small rosemary plant in your kitchen window. Whenever you need a boost, you can snip off a small leaf or two to add to your meal.

Pig/Boar

January 30, 1911–February 17, 1912: Yin Metal Pig/Boar
February 16, 1923–February 4, 1924: Yin Water Pig/Boar
February 4, 1935–January 23, 1936: Yin Wood Pig/Boar
January 22, 1947–February 9, 1948: Yin Fire Pig/Boar
February 8, 1959–January 27, 1960: Yin Earth Pig/Boar
January 27, 1971–January 15, 1972: Yin Metal Pig/Boar
February 13, 1983–February 1, 1984: Yin Water Pig/Boar
January 31, 1995–February 18, 1996: Yin Wood Pig/Boar
February 18, 2007–February 6, 2008: Yin Fire Pig/Boar
February 5, 2019–January 24, 2020: Yin Earth Pig/Boar

Pig Personality

There are two signs of the Chinese Zodiac that nobody ever wants to be, and one of them is Pig (or Boar) (in case you haven't guessed it already, the other is Rat). You should understand Pig is one of the best signs to be! Pig is the symbol of the prosperity and good fortune of the family.

When considering a Chinese Zodiac creature's qualities, it's a good idea to examine the animal's traits, behaviors, and personality and associate our traditional knowledge about the animal with the metaphorical zodiac creature. Throughout history and in many cultures, there are traditions and stories about the pig.

The ancestor of the domesticated pig is the wild boar. While the male wild boar is solitary, the females and piglets live in groups and welcome the males at breeding season. Therefore, the Chinese zodiac sign of Pig (or Boar) represents one of the most sociable signs, known for being community-minded and gregarious.

The animal pig is an omnivore, consuming both plants and animals. Pig/Boar natives are known for their culinary abilities (or at least their love of great food). They are delightful hosts who provide their guests with lots of comforts and splendid meals.

The animal pig is renowned for its acute sense of smell. People born under this sign are very discerning and able to suss out what's going on. Scientists tell us that in social situations when we are connecting with others whom we may not know (or not know well), we often use our sense of smell to determine friend or foe. People born in the Year of the Pig (or Boar) can better access this ability in their daily lives.

At home, Pig loves a social gathering. The kitchen is always filled with ingredients should they be needed for an impromptu party. At the sound of the doorbell, Pig is ready to greet guests. The people who come to the party are lucky; Pig does whatever they can to make their guests feel welcome and comfortable. This doesn't necessarily mean that the house is spotless. Some Pig natives keep a very messy house, but they still welcome guests with open arms.

In the business world, Pig is often underestimated. On the outside, they seem "sweet," gullible, and rarely able to say "No!" However, Pig is rather smart and ready to take on a leadership role whenever called upon to do so.

Pigs dislike confrontation and are always looking for a win-win situation; they dismiss insults and easily shrug off negativity. Should you hire a Pig to work for you in your struggling business, they will devote their time and energy to building your success.

Pigs are generous. They like to see a smile on someone else's face. They love the good things in life: gourmet food, designer clothing, the upscale exotic car. They are looking for a life of luxury, comfort, and ease, and they are willing to put effort into your being comfortable, too.

Pigs can trip themselves up, though, with excessive rules and limitations they put upon themselves. When others cross them, they can respond aggressively, which can shock the person on the receiving end.

Pig natives are susceptible to lawsuits and can become entangled for years. Because they want to see the best in people, they can be swindled and need to watch out for con-men. Pig has a warm heart, and when things don't go well in their lives, they can be subject to depression. Their desire for perfection can overwhelm them, resulting in increased stress.

Pig: Predictions for 2022

How to use your High-Energy Days: On these days, plan to take action for your most important goals, make vital phone calls, send important emails. Your high-energy days are when your energy and luck are the strongest for the month.

January 2022: *January 2 is the new moon. January 14 has Mercury going retrograde. January 17 is the full moon. On January 18, Uranus goes direct. On January 29, Venus goes direct. Your High-Energy Days are 6, 12, 18, 24, and 30.*

The new calendar year begins, but an entire month remains of the harmonious Metal Ox energy. As others rush around trying to start new things, intuitive Pig native realizes beginnings only come after an ending. This is a great month for looking at what you have, paring down to only those things that genuinely bring you joy. It's possible you love everything in your house and about your house. But if there are items stuffed in a closet that haven't seen the light of day in some time, perhaps they need to be with someone else. What's essential is to plow through the paperwork of the previous year (or years). Scan what's necessary, shred where you need to protect your privacy, and discard the rest. Your home will feel lighter, and energy will circulate throughout your entire life.

There's a new moon on January 2, and for the next two weeks, there's an emphasis on courageously following your dreams. In the morning, start with spiritually centering yourself. Perhaps the tool you use is yoga or meditation, or perhaps you recite affirmations or your goals. As you go through the day, you'll see the Universe's generous hand in your life. Over the next two weeks, an acquaintance may offer you something entirely out of this world.

On January 14, Mercury goes retrograde. Over the next few weeks, you may return to studying a subject you have left in the past. You can be drawn to reread a novel or series. Mercury retrograde allows you to go back and collect some information from your past and bring it forward now because it is needed. Let your intuition guide you. Trust when the feeling pushes you in one direction or the other. You'll notice if any of your friends are moving toward something, and you may be attracted to join in as well.

On January 17, there's a full moon and intense love and romance energy, especially if you're willing to take a few risks. Recognize any blocks you've put on yourself which hold you back from love. You're stronger now and able to handle the ups and downs in life. So why not let a special someone know you are interested? It could be the beginning of a whole new adventure.

On January 19, there's a shift in the energy. You may work behind the scenes on a project at the office. The amount of work ahead may be daunting. Break things down into manageable parts and put them into your schedule. Knock one thing off the list whenever possible. Soon you will celebrate success.

February 2022: *February 1 is the new moon and begins the Year of the Water Tiger. February 3, Mercury goes direct. February 16 is the full moon. Your high-energy days are: 6, 12, 18, and 24.*

The Water Tiger year begins on February 1 and brings positive energy (and a few challenges) for Pig natives. Each Chinese zodiac sign has a secret friend, and yours is the Tiger. This means that while some signs will struggle with the erratic energy in the Year of the Water Tiger, circumstances can come together to benefit you. You'll need a watchful eye so you can move on to opportunities as they appear. But overall, you're poised to have a good year in 2022.

This new moon energy is on February 1, and Pig native, you're likely lying low for the first few weeks. This allows you to sense to find the rhythm of this new energy. You may work behind the scenes or work from home or on vacation during this time. Consider checking in with friends and family to see how they are dealing with the shift of energies. This will give you indications of what's ahead.

February 3 brings the Water Tiger month, and Mercury moves direct. You may attend a wedding or other special event. Friends who live some distance away may fly in for a visit. You may play host to a sleepover for your kids and their friends.

The full moon is on February 16, and now there's attention on you. Pig native, you may be singled out for recognition or a high-profile project that could be pivotal to your career. This may be when you finish a large project, putting the final touches on the presentation that you'll be doing for your supervisor or the entire company. You will probably receive more praise than you're generally comfortable with.

March 2022: *March 2 is the new moon. The full moon is on March 18. Your high-energy days are: 2, 8, 14, 20 and 26.*

In March, attention is on you, and people recognize you are more confident than in previous years. You gain skills as you face challenges in your life. Now you are aware that it takes a lot to ruffle you. You can do well during interviews and other instances when the spotlight is on you during the month.

March 2 brings the new moon, and over the next two weeks, your charisma is high, and you may attract many admiring looks. Others are coming to you, bringing compliments and perhaps offers to get together and collaborate. Much of this is for business and friendship, but there can be some romantic interest as well.

March 5 begins the Water Rabbit month, and this brings a very harmonious period for Pig natives. You have a desire for adventure and may want to take more chances. This is the perfect combination for bringing in a new love interest. Pig native, you may be pursued by a person who has a crush on you. If you're already in a committed relationship, you may take your sweetheart by the hand and do a few things from your bucket list.

The full moon is on March 17, and for the next two weeks, there's a great deal of emphasis on your personal appearance and physical well-being. Pig native, you might change your wardrobe, hairstyle, or perhaps get a new tattoo. You may look at different exercise systems. This is an advantageous time to get exercise equipment or engage a personal trainer. All of this could lead to some long-term benefits.

In some parts of the world, there will be a second new moon in March, and for other time zones, it will be April 1. This new moon brings an emphasis on your money and available financial opportunities. You may gain an additional source of income that becomes a regular occurrence. A side business may become more profitable, or you may be laying the groundwork for a future source of passive income. This is a good time to refresh the Feng Shui cures you have placed for attracting wealth energy.

April 2022: *April 1 is the new moon. The full moon is on April 16. On April 29, Pluto goes retrograde. There is a partial solar eclipse on April 30. Your high-energy days are: 1, 7, 13, 19 and 25.*

April puts the spotlight on your possessions, debt, and income. You may realize you have more stuff than you need or that you are shopping for emotional reasons rather than being prudent with your funds. Pig native, it's time to look at different ways of keeping track of spending. Do a written budget each month. You may bring in extra cash by selling off household items or clothing you no longer need.

On April 4, the Wood Dragon month begins, and you may be pretty busy for the next four weeks. You may fill in for someone out on leave, all the while doing some projects at home. You may cram a lot into a few days. Everything will get done, but there could be several days where you feel you're scrambling from one task to the next. And the whole time, you may wish for time off.

The full moon is on April 16, and over the next two weeks, there's intense intimacy energy for Pig natives. You and your sweetheart may feel frisky. You could spend some quality time together. You may have some time away from the kids when you can indulge in some adult activities. If you're looking for love, you can find someone with whom you have great physical chemistry. You can engage in a passionate connection, even if it's short-lived.

There is a solar eclipse on April 30. There can be a miscommunication between you and a family member or roommate. No matter how carefully you outline your plans and state your position, others may not understand or willfully misrepresent your words. Eclipses are difficult energy. But you have the opportunity now to grow spiritually as you explore different communication styles.

May 2022: *On May 10, Mercury goes retrograde. There is a total lunar eclipse on May 16. On May 30, there is a new moon. Your high-energy days are: 1, 7, 13, 19 and 25.*

During May, you may sign a contract for employment or a large purchase, such as buying a vehicle or piece of rental property. Your intuition is amplified this month, and it will guide you to the correct decision. If an agreement falls through, it's likely the Universe is stepping in to protect you. This month, trust in the process and know that things work out in the end as they are supposed to.

May 5 brings the Wood Snake month, and Pig native, you are pulled in multiple directions. Many people need something from you or want to see you. You already have a busy work/home schedule and what you really need is a break. Pig native, you need some time to pamper yourself, perhaps with a spa day, time at the beach, or an afternoon to sit in your backyard and watch the hummingbirds play among the flowers. You are very social, but every once in a while, you need some alone time.

On May 10, Mercury goes retrograde, and something at home that you thought was fixed or finished now needs your attention again. You may decide whether to renew your lease. You may think of selling a piece of rental property rather than renting it out again. You're looking over decisions you've made about home, family, and real estate in general. Put your thoughts on paper, including a pros and cons list, as you make these difficult decisions.

There is a lunar eclipse on May 15, bringing issues around education or government paperwork. One of your kids may bring home a disappointing report card, or there may be a foul-up in paperwork stopping you from getting a stamp of approval that you need. Much of this energy requires you to be patient, as other people seem too busy to help you (even if it's their job).

The new moon is on May 30, and there could be challenges with transportation. Your car may be in the shop, or you may receive a recall notice. Someone might forget to pick you up at the airport, or you are hitting more traffic than usual, causing you to be late for a crucial appointment. The Universe is suggesting you rethink your schedule and reconsider how you get from one place to another.

June 2022: *Mercury goes direct on June 3. On June 4, Saturn goes retrograde. On June 14, there is a full moon. Neptune goes retrograde on June 28. The new moon is on June 29. Your high-energy days are: 6, 12, 18, 24, and 30.*

In June, you can find good financial opportunities. You might start a business with a family member, possibly a sibling or cousin. A friend's business may inspire you, and you might work with them. As you move forward, consider getting agreements in writing so all parties know their obligations and the benefits of being in the partnership.

June 5 brings the Fire Horse month, and there's romance in the air. Pig native, you and your sweetheart may spend more time enjoying each other's company. You could be outdoors, biking or swimming. All this togetherness leads to more romance in the evenings. If you're looking for love, this is an excellent time to meet someone by attending sporting events or participating in outdoor activities.

The full moon is on June 14. Pig native, you could gain a new job, promotion, or some overdue recognition from your supervisor. If you are negotiating for extra perks like working at home or additional vacation time, you can now set up a meeting with the boss to get your request approved. Additional money is possible now, especially a one-time payment such as a bonus.

June 28 is the new moon, and there's excellent energy for meeting someone new, especially for a very close friendship or love relationship. Pig native, you may be introduced to this person by a friend or family member. And now you are two peas in a pod. You can't believe how many interests you have in common. Once you start talking, you can talk with this person for hours.

July 2022: *July 13 brings the full moon. There is a new moon on July 28. Also, on July 28, Jupiter goes retrograde. Your high-energy days are: 6, 12, 18, 24, and 30.*

In July, you're in a spending mood. You may put money towards college or private school for your kids. If you do something creative, you could buy equipment like a new guitar or keyboard or upgrade your computer so you can edit videos. This month the money is flowing out faster than it is flowing in.

July 7 brings the Fire Sheep month, and there is energy around travel. Pig native, you might have a family vacation or make arrangements for someone to fly to you. This is a great time to take a trip by car or train (though flying is fine). You may explore a national park or local museums.

The full moon is on July 13, and you may be pursued for a relationship. This might be someone from your past returning to give things another go. You may be less enthusiastic about this idea or take a wait-and-see stance. You may poll friends and family to see what they think about your chances for a relationship with this person. It's wise to slow down and take your time making this decision.

The new moon is on July 28, and now work heats up. Pig native, you could put in some overtime, work on Saturdays, or scramble to finish a project. It's also possible that you're working on a side gig that takes more hours than you thought (and it's bringing in extra money). You may get some help, so you don't have to do everything alone. Ask a friend or coworker if they can lend you a hand.

August 2022: *August 12 brings the full moon. Uranus goes retrograde on August 24. There is a new moon on August 27. Your high-energy days are: 5, 11, 17, 23, and 29.*

August brings an interest in health and fitness. You may get excited about a piece of exercise equipment, or you have found a great personal trainer. You might do more cooking for yourself or give up sugar, processed foods, or meat. You may have regular health checkups, annual exams, or check in with your Chinese medicine doctor or chiropractor. All this helps your health and well-being now and in the future.

August 7 brings the Earth Monkey month. Pig native, if you're looking for a new job, you may have an interview or get an offer letter over the next four weeks. There's also a possibility of a position opening up where you work now. You may look at remote or satellite offices that your company has. Or maybe you're looking into programs where you can teach English in another country.

August 11 is the full moon, and over the next two weeks, you're looking at your habits and processes for doing things. Pig native, you might find a new way to clean the house or decide to go minimalist and get rid of much of your staff (which will make housecleaning much easier). This is an excellent time to get rid of bad habits and replace them with new, healthy routines.

The new moon is on August 27, and you and your sweetheart feel more connected than ever. If you're dating, you may announce that you're getting engaged. You may set a wedding date or date for moving in together. This is an excellent time to introduce your dating partner to your friends and family. And if you're looking to meet someone, you are attracting fascinating people to you every time you step out the door.

September 2022: *On September 10, there is a full moon, and Mercury goes retrograde. On September 25, there's the new moon. Your high-energy days are: 4, 10, 16, 23, and 28.*

September brings a focus on partnerships, friendships, and collaborations. Now you can reach out to others and form connections. These may start out as tenuous but could become long-lasting bonds. You can do this through community meetings, clubs, or your work with charities. If your business, you can find mentors or influencers to help you out.

September 7 begins the Earth Rooster month, and you may look at the future. You could plan out the next year or even the next five years. Pig native, you might update your vision board or your goal list. You might write a bucket list of all the things you want to do for the rest of your life. It's helpful to have direction, and a list like this helps the Universe know what opportunities to bring to you.

The full moon is on September 10, and the same day, Mercury goes retrograde. Pig native, all eyes are on you. You may be tapped to lead the group or to speak for your department. You might be more voted to a board position for your networking group or professional organization. This is a big deal. And even though you may feel a little uncertain, you are amply qualified for the position.

The new moon is on September 25 and lights up your area of resources. You may get excellent advice about investments or passive income opportunities. Pig native, you can get help with loans or refinancing your house. Now is the time to connect with bankers and brokers. Then again, Mercury is still retrograde, so it's not a great idea to change institutions now (although you might be quite tempted.)

October 2022: *Mercury goes direct on October 2. On October 8, Pluto goes direct. There is a full moon on October 9. On October 23, Saturn goes direct. On October 25, there's a partial solar eclipse. On October 28, Jupiter goes retrograde. Mars goes retrograde on October 30. Your high-energy days are:4, 10, 16, 23, and 28.*

October brings Pig natives a realization of your worthiness. Mercury goes direct on October 2, and now you can move forward on your plans. You now realize you may limit yourself. The obstacle in your way has been you. Now you see you have the skills and deserve success. This month, you're freeing yourself to welcome in more opportunities.

October 8 brings the Metal Dog month, and Pig native, you show a marked increase in your psychic ability (which is saying something as you are one of the most psychic signs of the Chinese zodiac). You may have dreams that give you a lot of information. You could work with tarot cards or a pendulum to get detailed answers not just for yourself but for others as well. You may explore these modalities through classes or even think about getting a professional certification.

The full moon is on October 9, and you may receive a windfall. An unexpected amount of money may come into your account. Someone you thought would not repay you suddenly sends you a check. Or you may have sold an item for more money than you expected to get. It's also possible you have won a prize that has a cash value.

The solar eclipse is on October 25 and could bring difficulties with a contract or legal matter. You need to be careful if you're involved in a lawsuit. Make sure you have all the required paperwork submitted on time. Pig native, check in often with your legal counsel to stay updated on what's happening. If you need a government permit or some other official certification, move slowly and deliberately to ensure that you have everything you need before leaving their office.

November 2022: *November 8 brings the total lunar eclipse. On November 23, there is a new moon, and Jupiter goes direct. Your high-energy days are: 3, 9, 15, 21, and 27.*

November shows the possibility of travel. You might be off to visit relatives who live some distance away. You could visit a sunny location to sit on a beach. While you are traveling, you may consider whether this could be a permanent home someday. You may do some house-hunting in the area. That you visit

November 7 brings the Metal Pig month, and you're pretty noticeable. Plus, you have extra luck energy because you're the secret friend of the Tiger. Someone may come from out of the blue and offer you just what you were looking for. Pig native, you may get an opportunity to meet a new friend or find a romantic relationship. As you put yourself out there and meet new people, your magnetism and smile will draw the right people to you.

The lunar eclipse is on November 8, and there's now a lot of emphasis on communication. You're very good at making people feel comfortable and empathizing with their situation. However, sometimes you're not so great at making requests of others. When you want something, you either whisper it, or it comes out like an order. Practice asking for favors from everyone you meet.

The new moon is on November 23, and your career is highlighted. You are probably working during one or more of the upcoming holidays. Your supervisor sees you as someone they can count on. Of course, this is helpful in the long run with your next review, but at the moment, it may not feel so fun. Despite that, you're dedicated and responsible. When asked, you're often ready, willing, and able.

December 2022: *Neptune goes direct on December 3. The full moon is on December 8. There is a new moon on December 23. Mercury goes retrograde on December 29. Your high-energy days are: 3, 9, 15, 21, and 27.*

In December, there's energy around your reputation. You might send out a newsletter, or perhaps you've written a book. More people recognize you or know your name. You could rise to a leadership position within your social group. But as you gather more followers and subscribers, remember that reputation is a delicate thing. Guard it by staying positive when you're on social media.

December 7 begins the Water Rat month, and it's also the full moon. This can be a valuable time for Pig natives regarding your finances. As you pay attention to your money, you gain more financial opportunities. You can also heal a money issue. Pig native, you could let go of negative messages you received as a child or the guilt you may have from poor money decisions you made in the past. It's a tabula rasa. You now have a clean slate.

December 23 is the new moon, and you may be itching to upgrade your technology. You may want to new phone or laptop. Pig native, you might use technology to do art and so you could get a drawing tablet. Or you might look for a keyboard to reduce your music. This is a great time to check in with friends, neighbors, and family members to see if somebody has a piece of equipment that you could borrow or buy.

On December 29, Mercury goes retrograde, and a friend from long ago comes back into your life. This could be someone that you went to grammar school with or knew in your early years. They may find you on social media. You may get to see them face-to-face.

January 2023: *January 6 brings the full moon. Mercury goes direct on January 18. The year of the water rabbit begins on January 22. Your high-energy days are. 2, 8, 14, 20 and 26.*

January can be quite a happy month for Pig natives. You are connected to your community, possibly through networking or some charity work. Pig native, you feel a sense of contribution and togetherness from what you've been doing with this group.

January 5 begins the Water Ox month, and there's a lot of interaction with siblings, cousins, and younger relatives. You may be the peacemaker between two warring siblings. You may consider taking a trip with a niece or nephew to show them some of the world. If you have a sibling you haven't spoken to in a while, this is an excellent time to send an olive branch.

The full moon is on January 6, and there's a lot of emphasis on creativity and fertility. Pig native, you may do art or play music with friends. If you're looking to add to the family, check in with your doctor, find a fertility expert, or look into adoption. You may also adopt a pet.

On January 18, Mercury goes direct. Some miscommunication with your sweetheart suddenly clears up. Now you're back together, enjoying each other's company and supporting each other. In fact, this is an excellent time to clear up misunderstandings with other people in your life as well.

The new moon is on January 22, and this brings the Year of the Water Rabbit. You are now entering your second seed tending year. During this time, it's imperative to focus on what's working in your life and give it your time, resources, and support. If you have been working on a side business, and you're seeing a profit. You might want to lean in to give it more attention. You have friendships that are getting closer. It's time to schedule more opportunities to get together. Also, during a seed tending year, you want to pull the weeds. This means looking at what is not working in your life and getting rid of it. This can include objects, people, or obligations. Overall, 2023 can be a promising year for Pig natives because Rabbit energy is harmonious with your own. It's going to be a good year.

Attract New Love

In the Year of the Water Tiger, you may be pursued for a love relationship. Others are going out of their way to tell you they admire you or are attracted to you. These individuals may not be your "type," and perhaps you would feel more comfortable just being friends. But you will also meet some intriguing possibilities, including an individual who differs from anyone you've dated before. Pig native, you will probably meet people when you're out in the community doing activities with friends or allowing your friends and family to fix you up on dates.

To create more harmonious feelings and happier times, spray orange scent in the bedroom. You can also put out potpourri made with dried orange peels. If you prefer not to have the scent in the house, have pictures of orange blossoms in the bedroom. Orange blossoms not only help relationships but can also attract prosperity energy, which certainly doesn't hurt.

Enhance Existing Love

In 2022, you and your sweetheart are getting along rather well. You likely see your partner as your best friend. You're helping each other when and where it's needed. When you do have disagreements, they're not long-lasting, and makeup activities are rather pleasant. Pig native, you may do more things as a couple. You might dine with other couples, go on cruises, or travel in groups. You may team up to help organizations within the community, bringing the two of you closer together.

Not all Feng Shui cures have to be traditionally Chinese in origin. There are many symbols broadly used in many cultures. The wedding ring quilt is such a symbol, in this case, of love and fidelity. To enhance your existing love relationship, place a wedding ring quilt on your bed. You can also hang a small lap quilt or quilted wall hanging in the same design on your bedroom wall to help enhance the energy of your partnership.

Looking to Conceive?

Pomegranates have a long history as a symbol of fertility. In addition to the seeds of the pomegranate being eaten for bringing in conception energy, the skin of the fruit can also be dried and carried (not eaten) to encourage a pregnancy to happen.

Also, tradition says that the first day you eat a pomegranate each year, you're entitled to make one wish–and your wish has extra power to come true. The pomegranate tree is a late-blooming tree making this a very good symbol for an older woman who wants to conceive.

(From Donna Stellhorn's book, Fertility Feng Shui)

Family and Kids

Pig native, as usual, there is a lot of emphasis for you on home, family, and your kids. Meanwhile, everyone seems to be going in their own direction. Getting everyone to agree on a date for a family dinner or vacation could be challenging. In the Year of the Water Tiger, you may work more at home. You are available to see family members who are coming and going on their own schedules. There is some moving energy this year. You might change residences, or you may help a family member move. There also could be changes within the neighborhood involving construction or extensive roadwork.

An excellent Feng Shui cure to add some additional positive energy to the home is to place houseplants in clay pots in or around your home. Clay pots that commonly hold the houseplants are made from the Earth element and have a grounding energy. The plants themselves symbolize growth, health, and prosperity.

The brick red, terra-cotta color is the most grounding of the colors you can choose, but ceramic pots in various colors will work as well. Place several in the living room or home office. Also, place a couple of small ones in the kitchen.

Money

This can be a good money year for Pig natives. In 2022, not only are you making more money, but you are healing money issues from your past. You might clear out blocks to accumulating money by doing inner work, hypnosis, or placing feng shui cures. During the Year of the Water Tiger, you may find good passive income sources either through investments or by selling digital products. You are multiplying your money-making potential this year.

A good Feng Shui cure for attracting new prosperity energy (and attracting more money in general) is to get yourself a golden piggy bank. Choose a style that appeals to you, perhaps a classic western-style piggy bank in metallic gold or the traditional Feng Shui piggy bank decorated with the Chinese characters for wealth and good fortune.

Place your bank near your front door or in the home office and feed it coins at least once a week (no pennies, please). Place a list of your money wishes inside the bank along with the coins to bring in opportunities and positive career energy.

Job or Career

The Year of the Water Tiger brings good career opportunities for Pig natives. You show a probable increase in salary (as well as more responsibilities) in your current job. You could change jobs to parlay your experience into a better position with perks such as working at home or more vacation time. You are aware of trends. If you have a sudden desire to change jobs, maybe your company's financial health is not so strong, or the industry will go through a major shift. Overall, you can do well in 2022 with your career.

The traditional red envelopes are used each year to give presents of money to people, mostly children. These envelopes are glossy red with colorful pictures and prosperity sayings printed on the front. You can use this energy to help you attract a new career.

Take a traditional red envelope and write down a description of your desired new career. You may name the profession, or you may describe some aspect of the work ("I get to use my creative abilities." "I work with enthusiastic people." "I leave each day with a sense of accomplishment.", etc.) Place a small amount of money in the envelope and place it near your front door, either on a table or in a drawer.

Education

The area of education shows quite a few changes for you in 2022. If you're not in school, you may start going to school. If you are in school, you may suddenly decide to take a gap year. It's also possible you are changing majors this year or changing schools entirely. In the Year of the Water Tiger, you may find new ways of learning, such as accelerated programs online or private tutors. Financial help for education is possible, but it will take some digging.

Legal Matters

You could finish up an old legal matter during 2022. A lawsuit could be resolved in your favor (however, the time and energy it has taken may mean the results are less beneficial than you hoped.) There is elevated energy around professional certification and licensing. You may be dealing with a government body to take a test, get a background check, or complete paperwork so you can do a particular job. Pig native, when it comes to signing contracts, there is some wiggle room for negotiation. And you likely have a friend who can help you figure out the wording you're looking for.

Health and Well-Being

In the Year of the Water Tiger, you are paying more attention to your health. Pig native, it's beneficial to review how you live your life and adjust to healthy living. This might mean getting regular exercise into your schedule. You might look at a meal prep service or have healthy food delivered from a farm co-op. You show significant improvement in your quantity and quality of sleep this year. You may redo your bedroom or do a sleep study to find what you need for restful sleep. This alone goes a long way to helping you in 2022. This year, you have a lot of luck, and you can find the professional help you're looking for.

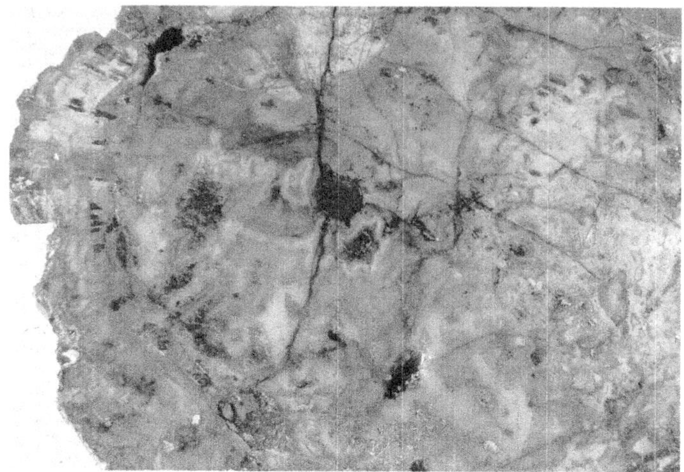

To protect your health this year, consider getting a piece of petrified wood. It can be part of jewelry you wear or a piece of polished stone displayed in the home. Petrified wood is from ancient trees and represents a long life filled with joy and peace. It's been used for centuries as a barrier to protect against negative energy.

If you find a piece of petrified wood, you can display it in your kitchen or family room. If it's a small, smooth stone, you can keep it in the dirt of a houseplant. If it's large and flat, you can use it as a coaster. Or you can display it near family photos to protect everyone in the house.

Compatibility Between Signs

In this section, I will explain a little about the compatibility between the Chinese Zodiac signs concerning love and friendship. Sometimes there is a lot of harmony, but at other times a pairing of two signs isn't the most promising. We can often improve the energy by placing a Feng Shui Crystal cure to support the relationship energy.

Feng Shui Crystals are round, cut glass crystals which have a prismatic effect. When light hits the crystal, a rainbow of glittering, shiny light prisms twinkle around the ceiling, walls, or floor. Shiny things attract energy, so the sparkling crystal attracts energy to balance the relationship.

Cut glass crystals come in many shapes, but round is the most balanced and harmonious shape, so it's used to balance relationship energy. Whenever a Feng Shui Crystal is called for, you can use a clear one (clear crystals are the easiest to find). Or you can use colored crystals to bring in the energy of one of the five elements.

Use green to represent the Wood element if you want to increase growth and prosperity.

Use blue to represent the Water element to activate excellent communication, flow, and harmony.

Use amber or yellow to represent the Earth element, to bring stability and longevity.

Use red to represent the Fire element to stimulate energy and passion.

Use clear to represent the Metal element to attract resources and business success.

Along with the compatibility listings below, you will find suggestions about where to place the crystal if your relationship needs some help. Choose a green crystal if troubles in the relationship are because of finances. Choose a blue crystal if the problems in the relationship center on communication.

Choose an amber or yellow crystal if there has been infidelity, and you want to heal the relationship. Choose a red crystal if there's been a lack of passion, romance, and sex. Choose a clear crystal to come closer together, and to receive help and support from your partner.

To find the correct direction for placing the crystal, think of your home and the rising sun. The sun always rises in the east. The sun sets in the west. If you know where the sun rises and sets in relation to your home, you can easily identify the other cardinal directions, north and south. (Hint: Google Maps aerial view can make this task very easy, as it always shows north as up, south is down, to the left is west and to the right is east.).

To find the inner directions such as North-by-Northwest, find north and find west. Halfway between these two is Northwest. North by Northwest is halfway between north and Northwest.

Place the diagram on the floor, east pointing towards the rising sun. The diagram will help you find the right direction for placing the appropriate crystal.

If you can place the crystal in a window, it will catch the most light. If there is no window in that direction, hang the crystal on a lamp, a plant, a drawer pull, or from a wall hook.

To see all the different ways to use Feng Shui Crystals and how to hang them, go to www.fengshuiform.com.

We can divide the 12 animals of the Chinese Zodiac into four groups. Each group has some key personality traits:

Rat, Dragon, Monkey are the action-oriented ones. The Rat takes care of the details; the Dragon has the big ideas, and the Monkey can improve the skills of others.

Ox, Snake, and Rooster are the deep thinkers. The Ox is methodical, thinking things through. The Snake is wise and sees things from various perspectives. The Rooster is alert and aware of everything going on around him.

Tiger, Horse, and Dog are the freedom lovers. The Tiger is impulsive: he sees what he wants and pounces. The Horse runs across the prairies and lands with power and grace. The Dog can work alone or within a group and still keep his independence.

Rabbit, Sheep/Goat, and Pig/Boar are the peace lovers. The Rabbit is diplomatic and can bring opposing forces together. The Sheep/Goat is the humanitarian, wanting to bring peace to the world. The Pig/Boar is the homebody, wishing to create comfort and peace for the family.

Chinese Zodiac Signs and Compatibility

Rat Compatibility

Rat with Rat: Well suited and lots of fun. Always busy, doing things, making deals, and making money. You'll need to respect each others' time and secrets. Occasionally you'll need time apart as much as you need to be together. If you find one of you is too bossy, or you both need to focus a little more on the big picture and the future, hang a Feng Shui Crystal in the North side of the house.

Rat with Ox: A happy and long-lasting relationship. You will benefit from Ox's stability and strength. You are both optimistic and enjoy the little things in life. You can start the job and know that Ox will be there to help you finish it. If you find your partner is stubborn and not open to your ideas, hang a Feng Shui Crystal in the North by Northeast part of the house.

Rat with Tiger: Hot and cold, with lots of energy and excitement in this relationship. Sometimes the Tiger will ignore the little Rat, and sometimes the Tiger will be surprised at how loud a Rat can squeak. If Tiger's unpredictable ways get on your nerves, you can steady this relationship by hanging a Feng Shui Crystal in the East by Northeast part of the house.

Rat with Rabbit: Arguments after the fling is what we have here. You are both clever, but a little too clever. One wants commitment, and the other wants freedom, and neither wants the same thing at the same time. If you find Rabbit too passive and you're looking for more dedication to this relationship, hang a Feng Shui Crystal in the East side of the house.

Rat with Dragon: Happiness abounds when the Rat joins with the powerful Dragon. The relationship can be very intense. But use caution (and flattery) because if you break the spell, there is no putting the broken relationship back together again. If you find Dragon's head in the clouds and need a more grounded partner to help you with the day to day parts of the relationship, hang a Feng Shui Crystal in the East by Southeast side of the house.

Rat with Snake: Volatile pair that sometimes can be a good relationship… at least until the Snake gets hungry. Avoid being on the menu. This is more of a learning experience than a love match. If you find Snake too secretive and a little on the manipulative side, hang a Feng Shui Crystal in the South by Southeast part of the house.

Rat with Horse: Unhappy pair that can't see eye to eye. You find Horse's needs exhausting. If you get into this relationship, keep a life raft handy. You'll be paddling to shore in no time. If you insist that this is the relationship of your dreams and you want Horse to settle down and be not so restless, hang a Feng Shui Crystal in the South part of the house.

Rat with Sheep: Poor match because the sensitivity of the Sheep is no match for your quick tongue. Communication starts well, but there will be problems with words, and that will be the end of the relationship. You would think with horns; he wouldn't have such thin skin. If you only see eye to eye when pampering your Sheep partner and want to have things be a little more equal, hang a Feng Shui Crystal in the South by Southwest part of the house.

Rat with Monkey: Very lively meeting of people from different worlds. Monkey can take Rat on the trip of a lifetime and open new worlds. It's the unlikely pair in love. You will give each other new perspectives on life and living. But if all the excitement and Monkey's high energy starts to wear on you, hang a Feng Shui Crystal in the West by Southwest part of the house.

Rat with Rooster: Need to work hard at this to make it work at all. You are natural barnyard enemies, both hunting for the same big prize—and not just chicken feed. So you're better off avoiding this cage-match. If you find yourself with an overly critical Rooster on your hands, hang a Feng Shui Crystal in the West part of the house.

Rat with Dog: Lots of energy and togetherness; this is good for you, you both enjoy being out and about, enjoying others and each other. However, you may find you have trouble finding personal space. Dog will tag along wherever you go, and keep trying to pull you back home. If you feel your life restricted by Dog's constant bark, hang a Feng Shui Crystal in the West by Northwest part of the house.

Rat with Pig: Picture this charming pair of homebodies, both taking care of the other. There is optimum togetherness when you want it, and alone time when you need it. Pig keeps the house cozy and warm. If you find all this happiness and optimism is maxing out your credit cards, hang a Feng Shui Crystal in the North by Northwest part of the house.

Ox Compatibility

Ox with Rat: You are a happy, practical pair that compliment each other. You have the potential here for a very stable relationship with benefits for both partners. Rat sees the details, and your tireless energy can envision what will become of them. If you find Rat is too picky about the small things and can't get the big picture, hang a Feng Shui Crystal in the North part of the house.

Ox with Ox: A caring pair where each is interested in the comfort and security of the other. Not exciting to others, perhaps, but you can be quite content. You can enjoy decades of holding hands and feeling safe, as the cold winters blow outside. While you can remain content for long periods, should you want to add some fun (or at least a break from the constant work), hang a Feng Shui Crystal in the North by Northeast part of the house.

Ox with Tiger: Your goals in life are entirely different, as are your methods of pursuing outcome. This cat doesn't come when he's called (what cat does). There are quarrels that lead to nowhere. Build a stable home, and Tiger looks for the door. If you want this temperamental kitty with claws to be your lifelong partner, you have some work ahead. Hang a Feng Shui Crystal in the East by Northeast part of the house.

Ox with Rabbit: A so-so match. You want stability and clear rules, and Rabbit wants some pampering and kindness. It takes a while to get this one to work, but when it does, it lasts. He can be your lucky Rabbit in the end. But if you honey-bunny spends his or her time sulking in the corner and being overly sensitive, hang a Feng Shui Crystal in the East part of the house.

Ox with Dragon: Tricky pair; expect battles to start from day one. These are two powerful forces with two different ideas of what a relationship is and should be. Ding goes the bell, and the fight begins. If you can see the strong qualities in each of you, there's hope. Hang a Feng Shui Crystal in the East by Southeast part of the house.

Ox with Snake: Supportive, though there can be some conflicts. This is the strong Yin and Yang: together, opposite sides of the same coin. You need each other, and over time with Snake's clever thinking and your perseverance, you both can prosper. While Snake can make an attractive partner, if they are draining your bank account on clothes and toys, hang a Feng Shui Crystal in the South by Southeast part of the house.

Ox with Horse: Difficult match for you. The Horse is fast and careless, compared to your slow and thoughtful ways. There is little Horse can give you that you really want, and so you're more likely to send him on his way. If you want to stable this pony and try to make this restless soul settle down, hang a Feng Shui Crystal in the South part of the house.

Ox with Sheep: Steer clear, this one is trouble from beginning to end. You will have to be exceptionally patient to ride this one out. After butting heads for a while, heartbreak is the most likely ending. You can make this work if you have deep pockets, but it's more likely he/she will spend the money when they're feeling hurt or insecure. To balance the energy, hang a Feng Shui Crystal in the South by Southwest part of the house.

Ox with Monkey: Love and joy can abound with this combo. Monkey will bring you fun times and surprises every day. That will make your steady life more interesting. Once the Monkey settles down, the match can be good for both. If you find Monkey is only interested in him or herself, and too independent for your peaceful dream of a relationship, hang a Feng Shui Crystal in the West by Southwest part of the house.

Ox with Rooster: Good match for these barnyard pals. You both understand the need for hard work, and Rooster appreciates your patience and understanding. You like having someone around who can mind the details. Together you're the soul of productivity, if you would like to have a bit more romance or at least the occasional cuddle, hang a Feng Shui Crystal in the West part of the house.

Ox with Dog: Possibly good, but too many compromises will be required. This is too much Yin energy together; communication will suffer. Both of you are hesitant to lead. Let the Dog go and see if he comes back of his own accord. If you are tired of coming home and always finding a house full of people, or your partner is always on the phone, you can hang a Feng Shui Crystal in the West by Northwest part of the house.

Ox with Pig: This needs effort and adjustments on both sides. If there is chemistry (and good cooking), the relationship may last. But most likely, the Pig won't respect your goals and effort. You get frustrated with his/her play-all-the-time attitude. There can be harmony if there is an understanding of the work and sacrifice it takes to create a financially stable home. If overspending is a problem, hang a Feng Shui Crystal in the North by Northwest part of the house.

Tiger Compatibility

Tiger with Rat: Hot during the chase, and cold when caught, Rat is not a great match for you. Rat is too cynical to see your splendid qualities, and it will need to be taught how to behave. This is more work than you want to do. If you think this is a mouse you want to keep, but the pettiness and demands are hurting the relationship, hang a Feng Shui Crystal in the North part of the house.

Tiger with Ox: Needs effort to keep from being a boring relationship. You might think that Ox will help you settle down and get serious, but in the end, you are just bitter from having all the fun taken out of your life. But if you long for an established relationship that will withstand a bitter winter or a wild party, hang a Feng Shui Crystal in the North by Northeast part of the house.

Tiger with Tiger: Happiness… with claws. As long as you both retain your thick skins, this will be a happy, fun relationship. But arguments can get nasty, so be ready to forgive each other later—and keep bandages on hand. Of course, making up can be the most fun, and what's life about but having fun? So hang a Feng Shui Crystal in the East by Northeast part of the house.

Tiger with Rabbit: Can be good, but Rabbits are not known for their decisive action. You'll have to be patient with this one and prepared to leap into the fray of this relationship without waiting for the careful Rabbit to make the first move. If this Rabbit keeps sprinting away and you want to lure him/her back, hang a Feng Shui Crystal in the East part of the house.

Tiger with Dragon: The explosive power of you and the Dragon is legendary, making for either the most exciting relationship ever, or you'll both knock the world off its axis. If you want to be looked up to, this is not your match, but if you can work things out and share the leadership roles, giving credit where credit's due, this can work. Hang a Feng Shui Crystal in the East by Southeast part of the house.

Tiger with Snake: Steer clear no matter how attracted you are! You are not going to get the Snake's attention easily, and as soon as your back is turned, he's moved on. You can chase again, but after a while, it just gets tiresome. When you leave, Snake chases you; and when you are available, Snake is off without a care. To get this match together, hang a Feng Shui Crystal in the South by Southeast part of the house.

Tiger with Horse: Good ally out in the world, but there may be a conflict about who has to stay home and do the dishes. If you can accept and be happy with an unstable relationship, then grab an apron and give this one a try. Or, better still, pool your creative minds and social nature and make enough money to hire a maid. Stimulate this energy by hanging a Feng Shui Crystal in the South part of the house.

Tiger with Sheep: Can work it out over time, but the Sheep will be cautious. You will have to follow the rules given to you by the Sheep, and this can bring conflicts into the relationship. Mr./Ms Planner will not appreciate your impetuous nature. If you find Sheep too clingy (which surprises you, you thought you were the one with claws), and you wish he or she had more confidence, hang a Feng Shui Crystal in the South by Southwest part of the house.

Tiger with Monkey: It's very difficult to catch a Monkey who's swinging from tree to tree. You might be attracted to one playing hard to get, but after a while, it's no fun always being the one who has to chase… even for a Tiger. If you want to make this work, but Monkey's loud, know-it-all behavior is grating on your nerves, hang a Feng Shui Crystal in the West by Southwest part of the house.

Tiger with Rooster: You come from different worlds, so once at home, there's not much to talk about. You feel bossed around by the nagging Rooster who's frustrated that you don't seem to fall in line like the other chickens. If you find he or she is always on you about your spending and your inability to do the laundry right, smooth things over by hanging a Feng Shui Crystal in the West part of the house.

Tiger with Dog: Strong ally and a good match for you. The Dog can keep the home fires burning while you prowl the world for wealth to acquire. There are a few differences of opinion, but the good definitely outweighs the bad. Sometimes it's hard to get Dog to agree to a quick vacation or a last-minute party, but you can bring some energy to this partnership by hanging a Feng Shui Crystal in the West by Northwest part of the house.

Tiger with Pig: Good match if you take it slow. Pigs can be a little nervous facing Tiger's mandibles of death (actually that's just your smile). But if you approach Pig with gentle understanding, Pig will comfort and take care of you. You both have a tendency to help others before yourselves. If you find you're giving away too many resources to hapless friends, hang a Feng Shui Crystal in the North by Northwest part of the house.

Rabbit Compatibility

Rabbit with Rat: You may argue and fight, and this doesn't make your peace-loving nature euphoric. Rat will have too many demands on you, so a long-term relationship will be very challenging. You may seem similar, but your differences are huge. If your Rat partner is running you ragged with work and social plans, temper the energy by hanging a Feng Shui Crystal in the North part of the house.

Rabbit with Ox: If you want a long term relationship, this one can work—after you get past the boredom of the stable Ox. However, if you are looking for a fling, look elsewhere. Be in this one for the long haul, or not at all. If you find your Ox partner is not the one to sit down and have a good discussion about feelings and the relationship, hang a Feng Shui Crystal in the North by Northeast part of the house.

Rabbit with Tiger: Can be good if you like being pursued and what Rabbit doesn't? If the Tiger catches you, you can have a happy relationship… after you teach him to behave. Tip: Play hard to get even after you've been got. If you find this energetic Tiger keeps you up all hours discussing life and relationships and you just want a peaceful time to hold hands, hang a Feng Shui Crystal in the East by Northeast part of the house.

Rabbit with Rabbit: The pair of you are truly loving and having endless fun. You will play and laugh and bring each other tokens of your affection. You can cuddle in front of a fire or talk until you fall asleep in each other's arms. If you find, however, your bunny-buddy is not doing his or her share of the home duties, hang a Feng Shui Crystal in the East part of the house.

Rabbit with Dragon: Hard going at first, but things get easier over time. The Dragon is a bit of a show-off and hogs your stage. He may think you're small, but you're packed with power and easily a match for any Dragon. Your Dragon has big ideas for both home and business, and if you want to bring him or her back down to earth, hang a Feng Shui Crystal in the East by Southeast part of the house.

Rabbit with Snake: It'll take hard work to get this to be a happy match. The Snake may want you for a relationship, or just for dinner. Once you're in this relationship, you will be looking for a way out of it. You both have good taste and a desire for a good life, but if you're keeping secrets from each other, trouble is ahead. Hang a Feng Shui Crystal in the South by Southeast part of the house.

Rabbit with Horse: Can work it out as friends, even if it doesn't work out as lovers. There are a few conflicts here and there, but in the long run, there are many possibilities with this match. Just don't try to possess this one. Horse may want to run free, but he'll keep coming back. Trouble can arise when your Horse partner does everything by intuition rather than as a result of a discussion between the two of you. If more sharing is needed, hang a Feng Shui Crystal in the South part of the house.

Rabbit with Sheep: Great fun at times, because you'll always win against a Sheep. The Sheep will love you and keep trying. If you give a little to this relationship, the Sheep will give a lot. This could be the peace and happiness you've been waiting for. Your Sheep partner will be quick to depend on you, and this can make you feel great, but if the dependence becomes a burden, hang a Feng Shui Crystal in the South by Southwest part of the house.

Rabbit with Monkey: You'll need effort to understand the changeable and tricky Monkey. This is not a match that happens easily. You could be in danger of getting your heart broken by bad Monkey if you're not careful. If he or she is not understanding your feelings and is glossing over your anxieties, you may feel this Monkey's mocking you. Balance this relationship by hanging a Feng Shui Crystal in the West by Southwest part of the house.

Rabbit with Rooster: Many conflicts with this noisy bird who's constantly pecking and prodding you. Rabbits are the silent ones, and these Roosters are constantly making noises at you—too much so to make you happy. If your Rooster partner is telling all the friends and neighbors the intimate details of what works and doesn't work in your relationship, you can create a tighter bond between you by hanging a Feng Shui Crystal in the West part of the house.

Rabbit with Dog: More chasing than actually having fun. The Dog will make lots of demands on you, and you may find this relationship quite tiring in the beginning. If it lasts, it can grow into a real loving relationship, but it will take quite a bit of work. The loyalty of this partner can make this match worth it, but if you find the communication just not flowing, hang a Feng Shui Crystal in the West by Northwest part of the house.

Rabbit with Pig: Superb match; both of you can have a lot of fun. But if you get bored, you may try to create a little drama in the relationship just to stir things up. That could backfire big time! Once Pig's feelings are hurt, it will hard to tempt him back. Count your blessings, as your Pig partner can be devoted to you. If you find his or her attention on you is not strong enough, hang a Feng Shui Crystal in the North by Northwest part of the house.

Dragon Compatibility

Dragon with Rat: Suitable match where both feel compatibility and interested in one another. You can explore the world together. You will have secrets, and so will Rat, but the secrets won't hurt the relationship. Learn to trust, and Rat will take your grand ideas and turn them into reality. There is much the two of you can accomplish, although sometimes Rat will keep a tight hold on the purse strings. If you need to balance this energy, hang a Feng Shui Crystal in the North part of the house.

Dragon with Ox: Tricky times with the stubborn Ox will make the relationship rather exhausting. If you hold on, you can smooth things out and have a good long term relationship. This can happen because Dragons are said to live a thousand years. You love to dream up new ideas, but your Ox partner could be unsympathetic if he or she doesn't see immediate results. To temper this energy, hang a Feng Shui Crystal in the North by Northeast part of the house.

Dragon with Tiger: Requires patience and understanding, as together you represent two powerful Yang forces. Those around you might not believe the relationship will work out, but if you don't make too many demands on each other, you have a chance at a happy time with the Tiger. With two leaders and no followers, there can be some fights, even out the "eventful" energy by hanging a Feng Shui Crystal in the East by Northeast part of the house.

Dragon with Rabbit: Hard going at first, but you will soon find the Rabbit admires your good qualities. Rabbit also helps you strengthen some areas where you are weak: like being calm and quiet. You can help Rabbit be more detached and able to deal with the world. If you can let Rabbit have a soft place to land, you two will get along just fine, in the meantime, hang a Feng Shui Crystal in the East part of the house.

Dragon with Dragon: The best or the worst relationship for you. You love to be the center of attention, and so does your partner. This [airing will work if the two of you can share the stage. It can be glorious, or it can be a battle. You could make an enviable couple and rule the social scene. Agree now that you, together, will hang a Feng Shui in the East by Southeast part of the house to make this happen.

Dragon with Snake: Can be good as friends, but as lovers, things tend to break down. Snake wants you to try harder in the relationship, but your attitude is, "It will work if it's meant to be." This causes the Snake to slither away eventually. If you feel that holding on to this relationship is going to benefit you both, you can hang a Feng Shui Crystal in the South by Southeast part of the house.

Dragon with Horse: Lively pair; this combination can bring both fun and fights. You may become irritated that the Horse always thinks you're up to something. There will be more physical compatibility than intellectual or emotional. You both have a lot of energy but no patience for mundane tasks; create enough income to hire help by hanging a Feng Shui Crystal in the South part of the house.

Dragon with Sheep: Sheep thought he was on top of the world until he saw you flying overhead. You may want this relationship to work, but Sheep may get frightened by your power and energy. Coax him in slowly before you reveal all your greatness to him. If you feel strongly about this relationship, you can put in the effort to help temper your Sheep partner's moods by hanging a Feng Shui Crystal in the South by Southwest part of the house.

Dragon with Monkey: Good pair because you admire Monkey's cleverness. You have the inner strength to get Monkey to behave; this can be a good match. Monkey will amuse you every day! Take this act on the road, and you can be stars, or keep it close to home and be the toast of the neighborhood. Adding a Feng Shui Crystal to the West by Southwest part of the house will bring you some exciting opportunities.

Dragon with Rooster: The legendary Dragon and Rooster (okay, Phoenix). This pair feels a lot of attraction to one another. You can have a long term happy relationship as long as the Rooster doesn't look for reasons to be suspicious of all the happiness. If your Rooster partner starts snapping at you, hang a Feng Shui Crystal in the West part of the house.

Dragon with Dog: Not suitable, unless you like putting oil and fire together. This is a battle waiting to happen! Dog doesn't care how powerful you are; he's willing to take you down a notch. If your Dog partner wants to curtail your freedom and put you on a leash, hang a Feng Shui Crystal in the West by Northwest part of the house.

Dragon with Pig: It's hard not to like being at home with your Pig partner, nothing but comfort and good food abounds. But to keep Pig happy, you'll have to pitch in and do your share of the chores. Ever the peacemaker, your Pig partner will support you on your goals. Attract what you both want by hanging a Feng Shui Crystal in the North by Northwest area of the home.

Snake Compatibility

Snake with Rat: Is it love you're feeling? Or, is it just casual amusement? You may feel common interests at first, but unless you want to commit, Rat will flee the first chance he gets. You can have a very profitable relationship if you set the right tone from the beginning. Keep things moving upward by hanging a Feng Shui Crystal in the North part of the house.

Snake with Ox: Can be so supportive of each other, but someone has to make the first move. If you two get together, you are likely to enjoy a long and happy relationship. Set your boundaries and then take a chance. You both have the drive and interest in making this work. To keep the lines of communication open, hang a Feng Shui Crystal in the North by Northeast part of the house.

Snake with Tiger: Steer clear, this is a battle waiting to happen. The Tiger is seductive, and you might be tempted, but it's you who should be doing the tempting. This is a match destined for a breakup. If you're determined to stay together, and yet you're both suspicious of the other's actions and intentions, hang a Feng Shui Crystal in the East by Northeast part of the house.

Snake with Rabbit: It's hard work to find the balance here. Rabbit will bring out your deeper qualities, but his thin skin won't stand up to your assessments. There could be pain on both sides. On the other hand, if you can see the best in the other, you will both benefit from your refined sense and mental acuity. Hang a Feng Shui Crystal in the East part of the house to stimulate this positive energy.

Snake with Dragon: Can make a good couple—from dating to a long term relationship. There is fun to be had by both. Keep your demands light, and you and the Dragon will fare very well. Keep in mind how much you admire the qualities of the other and communicate this often. To bring more harmony, hang a Feng Shui Crystal in the East by Southeast part of the house.

Snake with Snake: Wonderful pair that can balance each other. If you share leadership with your partner, you can expect a long and happy relationship. You can work together to bring yourselves power and success. Hang a Feng Shui Crystal in the South by Southeast part of the house to increase success energy.

Snake with Horse: This combo is difficult. You might be afraid of being stepped on, but you should be more worried about being forgotten or left behind by the popular Horse. Keep your eyes open because Horse may not be all that faithful. If Horse's impulsive nature starts to drive you around the bend, hang a Feng Shui Crystal in the South part of the house to calm that energy.

Snake with Sheep: Needs concentrated effort, but by taking a thoughtful approach, you can find happiness together. Be considerate of the Sheep's feelings, and you will have to tread lightly at times, but you can work this out. This relationship may start out with you both in a constant embrace, but after a while, Sheep's clingy behavior may put you off. To ease this energy, hang a Feng Shui Crystal in the South by Southwest part of the house.

Snake with Monkey: Long-lasting match, once you get past the game-playing. You are both very clever, and you can learn much from each other. There is fun and romance for both here. But if this relationship is punctuated with fights and competition, temper that energy by hanging a Feng Shui Crystal in the West by Southwest part of the house.

Snake with Rooster: What seems impossible at first turns into a wonderful pair. Rooster may be lots of talk and fussy behavior, but deep down, he truly cares for you. Try not to get irritated, don't take things too seriously, and things will work out. Turn your attention to business, and you two will be the dynamic duo. For wealth energy, hang a Feng Shui Crystal in the West part of the house.

Snake with Dog: Quite charming match with you being both friends and lovers. But try not to be too possessive—Dogs need to run and play sometimes. (Know that Dog always comes home afterward.) On the other hand, when Dog is out of sight, you can do some of the things you may not be able to do under Dog's keen nose. Hang a Feng Shui Crystal in the West by Northwest part of the house for harmony in this relationship.

Snake with Pig: Not a good match, as your temperaments are entirely different. You are a deep thinker, and the Pig is looking for a comfortable, non-drama home. You might appreciate all that Pig can do for you, but the conflicts will be challenging.

If you find your Pig partner being loving and supportive, not just to you, but the whole neighborhood and every charity they can find, you can bring Pig's attention back to you by hanging a Feng Shui Crystal in the North by Northwest part of the house.

Horse Compatibility

Horse with Rat: Poor match, because neither wants to compromise. Things may start out fun, but they will, for the most part, end badly as you exert your desire for freedom, and Rat extends his desire for control. Your Rat partner may be a big help to you at home, but often you will find you're not on the same level. Balance the energy by hanging a Feng Shui Crystal in the North part of the house.

Horse with Ox: Difficult to balance this relationship. You are impressed with Ox's stability, yet also bored by it. You wish Ox would not be so demanding, and pretty soon, you break out of the paddock to run free. If you're trying to get your Ox partner to drop the workload and live a little, you can try hanging a Feng Shui Crystal in the North by Northwest part of the house.

Horse with Tiger: Both enjoy good times! You and Tiger are the life of the party; you are always where the action is. As long as neither of you thinks the other should sit at home, you will have a great time. Instead of fighting about who does the housework, attract more money to pay for the help by hanging a Feng Shui Crystal in the East by Northeast part of the house.

Horse with Rabbit: Given time, this can be a good relationship. At first, you will enjoy a lot of passionate fun with Rabbit; this can easily grow into trust and companionship. But keeping up the romance will take some planning. If Rabbit feels lonely at your wanderings and starts to kick up a fuss, you can balance the energy by hanging a Feng Shui Crystal in the East part of the house.

Horse with Dragon: Lively discussions and dates for these two. You are likely to be involved in the best fun together, or the biggest fights. Both of you are powerful and energetic beings, and together you are unstoppable. Try to base your relationship on what you have in common. Look for the partnership to extend to business as well as personal, and you can attract much success. Hang a Feng Shui Crystal in the East by Southeast part of the house to attract opportunities.

Horse with Snake: This is a tough match. There's a lot of finger-pointing (at each other), yet both are guilty of something. Too much complaining leads to more fights. You might win, but that just results in a squished Snake. If you're Snake partner just seems like a stick in the mud, you can loosen up the energy by hanging a Feng Shui Crystal in the South by Southeast part of the house.

Horse with Horse: Caring and sharing and having a great time, frolicking through the pastures without a care in the world. You are beautiful together, and the world is your happy playground. Sometimes you're so alike it's uncanny… and a little boring. Spice things up by hanging a Feng Shui Crystal in the South part of the house.

Horse with Sheep: If you get past the first couple of months, this can work out just fine, but Sheep's sensitive nature may take offense when you try to be honest and straightforward. Give him time to cool off, then try again. If you find your Sheep partner glum and lifeless at times, you can stimulate the positive energy by hanging a Feng Shui Crystal in the South by Southwest part of the house.

Horse with Monkey: Quite a painful duel can result from your mixing with the tricky Monkey. But if the Monkey cares about you, he will make an effort, and things may work out over the long run. You're both smart enough to understand each other. Sometimes that makes things better, but sometimes it breeds contempt. Bring in the positive energy by hanging a Feng Shui Crystal in the West by Southwest part of the house.

Horse with Rooster: There are some pluses and minuses to this pair. You may feel that Rooster is leading you around by the nose, then dropping you without a moment's notice. Guard your heart if you're interested in this chicken. If you're feeling a little hen-pecked, hang a Feng Shui Crystal in the West part of the house.

Horse with Dog: Running and playing, two hearts beating fast, this is a great match. Dog is faithful and forgiving and looks up to your power and grace. You feel gratitude and dedication in this positive puppy. But if you feel your Dog partner snapping critically at your heels, you can hang a Feng Shui Crystal in the West by Northwest part of the house.

Horse with Pig: You can't help kicking up a fuss with the fussy Pig. Pig doesn't want to do battle, but an argument usually ensues. This can be a long term relationship if you don't mind a knock-down-drag-out every few months. If your Pig partner's clingy-ness is starting to bore you, spice things up by hanging a Feng Shui Crystal in the North by Northwest part of the house.

Sheep/Goat Compatibility

Sheep with Rat: Always starts well and ends badly, as both are under the impression they have a lot in common. But it doesn't take long to figure out that Rat is not a Sheep, and you just don't see eye to eye. If Rat seems nicer over time, you might take a chance—but don't put too much money on the bet. If you are determined to make a go at this, hang a Feng Shui Crystal in the North part of the house.

Sheep with Ox: Steer clear of this steer. You're both too stubborn to compromise, and butting heads with this giant will only give you a headache. Ox is too clingy, and you want balance; this just won't work. On the other hand, Ox will get a lot of the work done before you have even stirred, so if you want to smooth out the bumps in this relationship, hang a Feng Shui Crystal in the North by Northeast part of the house.

Sheep with Tiger: Can work it out—if you can house-train this kitty. Tiger wants worship, and you usually have more sense than that. But if you can stomach giving out all that flattery, this relationship will work just fine. If you need a little something to balance out the Tiger temper, hang a Feng Shui Crystal in the East by Northeast part of the house.

Sheep with Rabbit: Hot romance is possible with this pair. Rabbit wants to go have fun, and you are more than willing. It may be a hot date night after night. If you're a Sheep who likes to stay home, you may have a little trouble convincing this bunny, but everything will work out if you exercise some patience. To ensure this positive energy, hang a Feng Shui Crystal in the East part of the house.

Sheep with Dragon: Be prepared to be completely overwhelmed by Dragon's power and enthusiasm. Later, you may feel claustrophobic in this relationship. You will have to reach a compromise to make this work, and it will have to start with you. If you want to have Dragon share in some of the relationship responsibilities, hang a Feng Shui Crystal in the East by Southeast part of the house.

Sheep with Snake: Requires a good grip to hold onto slippery Snake. You might be a little shocked at the verbal matches you are drawn into with this forked-tongued lover. If Snake cares about you, he will tone it down, and you'll work it out in the end. The solution here will be a joint effort and a real understanding of the other's position. To facilitate compromise, hang a Feng Shui Crystal in the South by Southeast part of the house.

Sheep with Horse: A fabulous time filled with banter and playful kicks at each other. This can be a wild ride if you don't take things said too personally. You both want to run; try not to run in different directions. To have the thrill of running off into the sunset together, hang a Feng Shui Crystal in the South part of the house.

Sheep with Sheep: Your friends might think this is the dullest match ever, but you feel delight as both of you do kind and thoughtful things for the other. You're happy, dancing on cloud nine. Combine your strengths and learn you can rely on each other by hanging a Feng Shui Crystal in the South by Southwest part of the house.

Sheep with Monkey: You can work anything out if you can forgive some of Monkey's antics in the beginning. Let the past be the past, and you will find that you have a lot in common. Love will bloom after a time. To encourage the love and romance, hang a Feng Shui Crystal in the West by Southwest part of the house.

Sheep with Rooster: No one is as confusing as a Rooster. You seem to have similar beliefs, and yet you go about doing things so differently. You can become a depressed little lamb if you think that Rooster will ever see your point of view. If you find the energy of your Rooster mate a bit too dizzying, hang a Feng Shui Crystal in the West part of the house.

Sheep with Dog: It's a tough life with a Dog nipping at your heels. You're not sure you want to be herded. Dog is trying to show you loyalty and love, but sometimes it feels like you are penned in at the farm just when you want to climb mountains and be free. Soon you'll be looking to unlatch the gate. If you want to stay in this energetic match, hang a Feng Shui Crystal in the West by Southwest part of the house.

Sheep with Pig: What a pretty couple you make, and you're both so nice. Sometimes Pig is too casual, and you have to do all the heavy lifting in the relationship. But if you can let it slide, this could be a very nice romance. However, if you're finding that Pig has overbooked your social calendar and you just want a break, then hang a Feng Shui Crystal in the North by Northwest part of the house.

Monkey Compatibility

Monkey with Rat: If you've got your eye on a Rat it's because you're intrigued by his clever, money-making skills. Rat is easily flattered and impressed by your ability to take chances and fly through the trees. You can find yourself in a happy relationship with no effort at all. Boost your financial prospects by hanging a Feng Shui Crystal in the North part of the house.

Monkey with Ox: This can be a great match as long as you understand that an Ox can't climb trees. Come down to share Ox's domain every once in a while, and things will be just fine between you. Ox will give you the stability you crave while not curtailing any of the fun. But if this ends up being a contest of wills, you can balance the energy by hanging a Feng Shui Crystal in the North by Northeast part of the house.

Monkey with Tiger: Very rocky, so stay out of Tiger's reach. Tiger's impulsive nature and desire to be respected above all else rubs your fur the wrong way. Consider swinging past this potential disaster. If you've already been snared by this fellow jungle creature, you can bring more love to the relationship by hanging a Feng Shui Crystal in the East by Northeast part of the house.

Monkey with Rabbit: You can have a good time if you hold back on the tricks and teasing until Rabbit is in a happy mood. An unhappy bunny will take out their pain on you, so don't push. This can be a good combination, so save your witty remarks for someone else. If you're trying to coax this Rabbit out of the house for social occasions, you can hang a Feng Shui Crystal in the East part of the house to increase the energy of fun.

Monkey with Dragon: The perfect balance between power and intelligence, even your fights are fun. Dragon will show you the big ideas, and you will show him how it can all be done. There is so much potential for this relationship. There is also the potential to extend this partnership into money-making activities. Attract wealth energy by hanging a Feng Shui Crystal in the East by Southeast part of the house.

Monkey with Snake: A long-lasting match filled with intimacy and strong feelings. Emotionally, as time goes on, you bond more and more with the wise Snake. Anytime you want, he will wrap himself around you and gently squeeze. But although there are tumultuous times due to jealousy on either side, you can temper this energy by hanging a Feng Shui Crystal in the South by Southeast part of the house.

Monkey with Horse: Is this a relationship or a competition? Sometimes you're supportive of each other, but the inflexibility of Horse means that you have to do all the compromising and understanding. After a while, this rodeo is less and less fun. If you feel like you're always coming in second place, you can hang a Feng Shui Crystal in the South part of the house to brighten up the energy.

Monkey with Sheep: This may be fun in the beginning, but Sheep has a whole bunch of rules and regulations for you to follow to stay in this relationship—rules that are sure to drain the fun right out of it. But if you can stay, it could become a happy, loving, long-lasting relationship. Balance this uncertain energy by hanging a Feng Shui Crystal in the South by Southwest part of the house.

Monkey with Monkey: Full of fun and play; this is an easy, happy relationship. There may be times when you don't see eye to eye, but keep those times brief, or one of you may find someone else to chase. Work out some boundaries, and you will be laughing together for a long time. To bond you two into a strong partnership, hang a Feng Shui Crystal in the West by Southwest part of the house.

Monkey with Rooster: Like magnets, you feel pulled magically together, but at any moment, the poles can shift, and you will find yourself repelled by each other. This is a pair born to fight, and yet should the two of you have a long relationship, it will at least be interesting. More prosperity would help you both be happy in this match, so hang a Feng Shui Crystal in the West part of the house to attract more money.

Monkey with Dog: At first, it just doesn't seem to work. You swinging in the trees, and the Dog barking and dancing around on the ground—but if you both persist, suddenly, one day everything falls into place. If you get to that point, this can be an excellent match. Remember, it's a partnership, not a competition. To blend the skills of you both, hang a Feng Shui Crystal in the West by Northwest part of the house.

Monkey with Pig: This may be the easiest relationship you'll ever find: no hassles, no commitments, just comfort, and joy. Pig would love a commitment, but he's too much in love to ask, afraid you'll run for the hills. Consider settling down with this one; this could be one you cherish. To balance and harmonize this energy, hang a Feng Shui Crystal in the North by Northwest part of the house.

Rooster Compatibility

Rooster with Rat: You might work well together with Rat, but avoid getting into a relationship with this little mouse. He discovers all your weak spots, and he'll take you down a peg or three. If you're serious about your future happiness, kiss the Rat goodbye. But if you're committed to staying, temper the little mouse's petty complaints by hanging a Feng Shui Crystal in the North part of the house.

Rooster with Ox: Potentially a very good match, because even though you're both stubborn by nature, you are stubborn about different things. There's strength in unity, and as a united front, you can have a very happy relationship. Even your fights turn out okay. Strengthen this relationship further by hanging a Feng Shui Crystal in the North by Northeast part of the house.

Rooster with Tiger: This relationship will take a lot of effort because you both have different values. You have strength, but so does Tiger—and there will be communication issues. Your friends will try to help you stay together until they get tired of trying, and then they'll suggest you part. If you want to stay together and have fun instead of fights, hang a Feng Shui Crystal in the East by Northeast part of the house.

Rooster with Rabbit: A relationship between you and Rabbit just makes for one angry bunny. You try to use logic and reason, but you just make him madder. Even though initially you felt a kinship, you're just too different to have any harmony. To get your Rabbit partner to pitch in and pull half the weight of this relationship, hang a Feng Shui Crystal in the East part of the house.

Rooster with Dragon: The perfect pair, representing the Dragon and the Phoenix, this relationship is liberating and strengthening for both. With this winged creature, you revel in feeling on top of the world. Dragon feels like he's finally got his feet on the ground. Great times ahead. Hang a Feng Shui Crystal in the East by Southeast part of the house to capitalize on this successful union.

Rooster with Snake: You may have some differences in your daily routines, but that can be to your benefit as you will enjoy the times you are together all the more. Snake may like to argue with you, but you can hold your own. In the long run, this could work. Balance the extremes in this relationship, and you can make some serious money. Hang a Feng Shui Crystal in the South by Southeast part of the house to help.

Rooster with Horse: You are probably more interested in making this work than Horse is. When you fight, it will be you who has to say, "Sorry," first. This may be fine in the beginning, but after a while of eating crow, you may just give this one up. If you insist that this is the one for you, hang a Feng Shui Crystal in the South part of the house to soothe your differences and create harmony.

Rooster with Sheep: You are probably the more impatient one, so Sheep can outlast you anytime. This will cause conflicts at home and with raising children. Sometimes you're both playing a game to see if you can get what you want, but neither of you shares your rules with the other. If you find that Goat/Sheep has a hard head and way too soft feelings, you can hang a Feng Shui Crystal in the South by Southwest part of the house to balance the energies.

Rooster with Monkey: Hard going at first, but things can be smoothed over. You may be fascinated with Monkey's clever antics, and so you keep working on it. Over time there can be progress; it depends on how much you want to sacrifice to get this to work. If you start to think that Monkey is just in it for what he or she can get, you can hang a Feng Shui Crystal in the West by Southwest part of the house to bring the scales into balance.

Rooster with Rooster: Intense passion and intense fights will typify this relationship. Feathers will fly, and lots of words will be exchanged—but what you dish out you can receive. In the end, you will stick it out because you have put so much effort into it. If you both are too focused on being right rather than being happy, hang a Feng Shui Crystal in the West area of the house to remedy this.

Rooster with Dog: A Dog around the barnyard chases the chickens rather than being guided by one, so this relationship may be about who gets to be in charge. This power struggle will continue, and getting out may be your best bet. This is not an easy time for either of you. If all this relationship has become is two people snapping at each other, hang a Feng Shui Crystal in the West by Northwest part of the house to bring in loving, harmonious energy.

Rooster with Pig: You have a true admirer in this relationship, yet you doubt, thinking this is too easy. Pig wants to make you feel comfortable and happy, and yet your eye is ever wandering. Learn to respect the Pig, and this could be a dream match. Or, toss it all away and get chicken-scratch in return. Things can be good here if you can welcome in the positive energy. Hang a Feng Shui Crystal in the North by Northwest part of the house and be prepared to be happy.

Dog Compatibility

Dog with Rat: It will take cool nerves to make this match work. There's a lot of nervous energy between the two of you, and you may find Rat running for the door. Keep the lines of communication open to make progress long term. You may find you only fight over little things. Ease the disruptive energy by hanging a Feng Shui Crystal in the North part of the house.

Dog with Ox: You two can be great together because you're both stable and want to protect your partner. But power struggles can ensue. Your best bet is to lean back and allow Ox to drag the relationship forward. Ox can hold on to hurts from past fights for a long time. Heal the energy by hanging a Feng Shui Crystal in the North by Northeast part of the house.

Dog with Tiger: After a rough beginning, a relationship of mutual respect and admiration blossoms. The attraction to each other runs deep, and both can feel great happiness here. There are good times ahead for this cat and Dog. Together you can do a lot a good out in the world. Hang a Feng Shui Crystal in the East by Northeast part of the house and bring in the opportunities you desire.

Dog with Rabbit: After an exhilarating chase, you could end up with a perfect match between you and the happy Rabbit. You both bring something to the relationship that the other lacks, and together you make a good team. It's the tiny things, like how he or she squeezes the toothpaste, that irritates you about your partner. Hang a Feng Shui Crystal in the East part of the house and find some peace.

Dog with Dragon: This is a star-crossed pair, intense love followed by severe pain. Dragon's power may tempt you, but he'll just fly away at some point. At some level, you know this, and so you may try to leave first. Save yourself the pain and avoid this match. If you insist on staying together, you must alternate with each other on who will lead. Hang a Feng Shui Crystal in the East by Southeast part of the house to find a truce.

Dog with Snake: If you do get together—which is not easy—you will need to work on your communication with each other. You are both smart but in different ways. You are much more loyal than Snake; don't give all your loyalty until you know it will be returned. If you stay realistic, this can work, so hang a Feng Shui Crystal in the South by Southeast to improve communication.

Dog with Horse: Dating will be an exciting chase, and if you do rope this Horse, you may end up with a very happy relationship. But Horse won't be caught easily. Be prepared for some work. Once you break this Horse of running, the romance will blossom. Hang a Feng Shui Crystal in the South part of the house to encourage cooperation.

Dog with Sheep: There is such strong attraction at first, but Sheep doesn't like being herded, and you are having trouble putting up with his not agreeing with anything you say. After quarreling constantly, you may not find anything to save in this relationship. If you find you're more irritated than in love, hang a Feng Shui Crystal in the South by Southwest part of the house and smooth over the differences.

Dog with Monkey: At first sight, you didn't think this was going to be a match... and you were right! Monkey's antics and different ideas can hurt your feelings deeply. Even when it seems to be working, the timing will be off, and the gestures you offer each other are misunderstood. But if you want to make a go of it, hang a Feng Shui Crystal in the West by Southwest part of the house to attract money, which will, in turn, attract a Monkey.

Dog with Rooster: Lots of chasing can make the beginning of this relationship a little rocky. Be patient, because there is more to this than meets the eye. There is a genuine compatibility here if you can get past some of the surface irritants. If you want to do more than just coexist, hang a Feng Shui Crystal in the West part of the house to bring out the best qualities in both of you.

Dog with Dog: You can run and play together, and you'll always be competing. You may even compete to show how much you'll sacrifice for the other. If you don't mind the constant quarreling, bickering, and barking, this will work out just fine. Hang a Feng Shui Crystal in the West by Northwest part of the house to promote mutual respect and material success.

Dog with Pig: You find that Pig is a blissful partner, and have never felt so happy. This makes you nervous, which in turn makes Pig nervous—and that could bring a breaking point. But in general this is a great match, just lie down and enjoy it. Celebrate and hang a Feng Shui Crystal in the North by Northwest part of the house to attract the resources for a comfortable and happy home.

Pig/Boar Compatibility

Pig with Rat: This is an interesting match, you share many interests. You see the world in a similar way and value similar things. The little mouse may need some puffing up sometimes, but flatter him, and together you will build a comfortable house, with lots of money in the cookie jar. Hang a Feng Shui Crystal in the North part of the house to bring abundance and happiness to the relationship.

Pig with Ox: This works at first, but if you think you will get your way, you're wrong here. You may be obstinate, but nothing beats an Ox for sheer stubbornness. The more you push, the more he will not budge. Save yourself the effort and pass on this match. If you plan to stay in this relationship, hang a

Feng Shui Crystal in the North by Northeast part of the house to relieve some of the friction.

Pig with Tiger: You may think the hungry Tiger will have you for dinner on your first date, but after the initial nerves of a new relationship, you two can settle down and make a good match. Tiger's possessiveness will feel comforting and protective. Hang a Feng Shui Crystal in the East by Northeast part of the house to bring joy, laughter, and good times.

Pig with Rabbit: Once you get past the well-meaning criticism by this little bunny, you have a thoughtful, interested partner with whom you can share much. Rabbit may be slower to realize how good a match this is, so be patient. Rabbit will happily receive the outpouring of your affection, so to get some in return, hang a Feng Shui Crystal in the East part of the house.

Pig with Dragon: You are dazzled by the power and vision of your Dragon partner. He loves coming down to earth to be with you. While your friends may not understand this match, you are in heaven. You are sailing on the back of a Dragon. At times one or both of you will get carried away; balance out the energy by hanging a Feng Shui Crystal in the East by Southeast part of the house.

Pig with Snake: You have so many differences that you can't even begin to communicate. You are naturally nervous around the clever Snake, and so you become rigid and critical. It's not you; it's just a bad match. If you're staying in the partnership but can't stand all the secrets, hang a Feng Shui Crystal in the South by Southeast part of the house and let what's been hidden come out.

Pig with Horse: Horse feels this is a great relationship and that nothing needs to change. You, on the other hand, have a list of what needs to happen to start making this a happy relationship. But none of your subtle signals or overt signs will be a clue to over-confident Horse. To get your pony partner to pay attention, hang a Feng Shui Crystal in the South part of the house.

Pig with Sheep: Can work, but certainly not the most exciting relationship you'll ever have. This feels like the backup date for New Year's—maybe someone who might be a friend, but the passion's not there. If you want commitment, demand it; otherwise, let this one go. Stir up the romance here by hanging a Feng Shui Crystal in the South by Southwest part of the house and watch the magic happen.

Pig with Monkey: You and Monkey are so different, but somehow it works. This relationship is like a fine wine; it needs to age—and you both will occasionally need some time to breathe. Some irritations on both sides can make this relationship feel sour. Hang a Feng Shui Crystal in the West by Southwest part of the house to sweeten up your love life.

Pig with Rooster: As barnyard buddies, this is tough in the beginning as Rooster wants to be in charge. You will find it hard to get respect from this bossy boss as he is sure he rules the roost. But deep down, there is more love here than you may think. Give this a try before saying goodbye. Between the two of you, there is a solution to every problem. Hang a Feng Shui Crystal in the West part of the house to attract the solutions easily.

Pig with Dog: You feel secure and safe with Dog (and nipped at, and barked at, too). There are some strong positives in this relationship and a big helping of irritants. Give nervous Dog some time to settle into the relationship, and you will feel safe and loved in no time. If you find your lively pup too quick with the criticism, hang a Feng Shui Crystal in the West by Northwest part of the house to soften his or her words.

Pig with Pig: Hand in hand, here's a perfect match. You both share great depth of feeling and compassion for the other. Communication is fun and easy, and you spend many nights just staying up and talking. This may get to be a little routine after a while, but the deep feeling of happiness will last. Together you both give too much and may find others taking advantage of your kindness. Hang a Feng Shui Crystal in the North by Northwest part of the house to protect your finances.

What Is Feng Shui and How to Use Cures

This book differs from most Chinese Astrology books. It contains information on usable Feng Shui cures to turn bad luck into good and make stuck, negative energy flow and be positive.

Feng Shui is the ancient Chinese art of placement. Feng Shui is based on the concept that everything present in our environment affects us: the colors, shapes, symbols, building layout, furniture, and décor affect our energy, mood, and decision-making process.

Consider for a moment two buildings which both represent how we connect with money: a casino, and a bank. When you walk into a casino, your head spins with all there is to see. There are flashing lights in every direction, ringing bells signaling a win, the sounds of coins falling. You can feel the abundance of good fortune and money, money, money.

Looking down at your feet, you'll see the floor carpeted in a busy, colorful pattern. Look up, and you will see moving lights, curved ceiling soffits guiding us in different directions, and huge rooms filled with aisles of machines, tables, and open chairs inviting us to be seated. There is an overwhelming feeling originating from this décor; it tantalizes: "You'd be a fool not to sit down and try your luck," it tempts us.

Contrast this feeling with the one you have in a bank. The environment here is also a large room, but this room is nearly silent. People speak in lowered voices. A velvet rope guides us to a waiting teller who sits (or stands) behind a marble counter (perhaps even behind a plexiglass shield).

Behind her is a large round door made of shiny metal, a foot and half thick, standing open to reveal a few safe deposit boxes. Even though we know there are no stacks of money in the vault and it's mostly a prop, the image created by all of it still gives us the impression that our money is safe.

We're all affected by the décor of a place. We may not think so per se, but run-down areas in need of repairs cause us to feel less hopeful. We are more apt to believe it's not worth the effort to try something new.

When we see a neighborhood with flowers and manicured yards, we become more optimistic. We feel a sense of possibility, the desire and willingness to take on new things. When we face a desk topped with disorganized clutter, we'll likely avoid working on our finances, and instead, check out what's on the television (or on Facebook).

Thousands of years ago, it was found that if you set up a temple or a palace in a certain way, the people in these environments would make better decisions. They would become more prosperous and happy. Scholars of the time collected this information and created a system they called Feng Shui. In the West, we know this system as Environmental Psychology.

Feng Shui is much more complex than merely cleaning up the clutter in your home or office—this is what many Westerners think about when they hear the term. Clearing away clutter is almost always a beneficial activity to carry out when we want to improve our environment. But it's important to understand that to achieve the best effect from our Feng Shui efforts, we must learn to place certain objects in specific places, with intention, creating harmonious change in our lives.

There are many schools of Feng Shui. Different schools emerged at different times and in different areas of China and the Far East. Some schools were formed in mountainous regions and were based on the topography of mountains, rivers, and lakes. Some schools were more focused on Astrology and timing, and these practitioners would predict the future and change things around as the seasons changed. Some schools used a compass to measure the quality and quantity of energy from each direction.

All the schools of Feng Shui are valid. They all work. For our purposes, we're going to focus on a school called Form School, which has straightforward principles we can readily apply to a western way of thinking about traditional and environmental practices.

Your Front Door: The front door is where all new energy will enter the home, and therefore your life. Even if you never use your front door, this is the traditional area of a home where all new energy is welcomed into the lives of the people who reside in the home. (If you found a stranger coming through your back door, you'd call the police). If you invited the CEO of your company to dinner, you wouldn't say, "Just go through the garage, squeeze past my car, past my boxes of Christmas decorations, and old ski equipment, until you find the door into the kitchen."

Important people are greeted at the front door and invited to enter a home or place of business. Many deliveries are made to the front door of a home or apartment residence. Using this principle, when we want something new, such as a new job, new love, money from a new source, etc., we will concentrate on the area around the front door (inside and out).

Your Bedroom: Your bedroom is where love happens. If you want to attract a new relationship or you want to improve your existing relationship, your bedroom is the area of the home we are going to focus on. We also look at the bedroom when you want to conceive a child, to rest, or to recover from illness. So, if you have trouble sleeping, or if you are recovering from something, we want to focus our attention on your bedroom.

The Kitchen: Your kitchen is your source of health and weight loss. Kitchens are often the most powerful rooms in the house. You can confirm this by observing when you have a party, your guests often want to congregate in the kitchen. Kitchens are where we cook and prepare our food; food is the key to our health and well-being.

The Living Room: If you want to attract new friends, but not necessarily an intimate partner, focus on your living room. The living room represents a public area of the home where we can welcome and entertain people without revealing the private areas of the home (like a bedroom). Thus, when we entertain people in our living room, we can enjoy people, yet safeguard the private things in our lives.

The Family Room: If you have a separate Family Room, focus on this area to enhance family relations overall—both between members of the family who live with you and those who live elsewhere. So if your family fights (or is dysfunctional in some other way), or the teenagers are sullen and uncooperative, this is the area your Feng Shui practitioner will focus on. (If you only have a Living Room, then we would focus on that area for family relations.)

The Home Office: If you have a separate room where you take care of bills and investments, or a room from which you run your home business, focus on this room when we seek to increase prosperity. If you don't have a separate office, consider the area where you pay your bills—whether at the kitchen table, in your bedroom, or in the dining room. (Or we can focus on enhancing the area around your front door for bringing in money.)

The Dining Room: If you have a separate dining room, it affects not only family relations but also your weight and the weight of all who live in the home. If you are trying to lose (or to gain) weight, we will consider this area, even if meals are seldom served in this room.

The Bathroom: There are a lot of Feng Shui rules and misinterpretations around the bathroom. The bathroom is an area for health, but it can also be an area that affects the prosperity of everyone in the home. When things are not going well in your life, this is the first area we consider.

Other rooms like garages, media rooms, craft rooms, guest bedrooms, and more, all have energy linked to their use.

In general, they are not as significant as the rooms previously mentioned.

There are, however, some exceptions. If you run a classic car business out of your garage, then the state of your garage will affect your success in your business. If you have a guest who is driving you crazy and won't leave your home, the state of your guest room will affect how your guest is treating you—even how long they'll stay. For tips on these and other more specific situations, contact me for a personal consultation, or see my book, Feng Shui Form.

Now that we have examined the energy of the various spaces in a home, let's define the concept of a Feng Shui cure. If you've ever experienced acupuncture, you know the doctor uses tiny needles, placed in specific areas of the body to stimulate your body's energy and natural healing ability.

Feng Shui cures are similar to these acupuncture needles—they are intended to stimulate your home's energy and help create benefit, good fortune, and natural harmony by working within the environment of your home, instead of your physical body. Cures are objects which represent a specific energy: such as love or money. For example, a heart-shaped pillow would be a representation—a cure—of love energy. (The heart shape is a universal symbol of love.)

Universal and cultural symbols make the most powerful cures in Feng Shui. This may all sound a little strange, But Feng Shui cures do work, just as the acupuncture needles stimulate specific body energy and facilitate our natural healing ability. If you want to know more about the science behind Feng Shui energy, keep reading; otherwise, you can skip to the next section.

Why Feng Shui Works

It may sound strange to you that placing a gold cat bank in the far left corner of your home would attract money, but it does. The Feng Shui cure is based on two principles. The first is the idea of collective consciousness.

Collective consciousness is a shared idea which creates a unifying force in the world.

One example might be the number of people who are afraid of spiders. Spiders shouldn't be scary; they're tiny, and they tend to mind their own business. But some people are so afraid of them they are classified arachnophobic, even when they have not had personal, life-threatening encounters with spiders. In humankind's past, spiders have been perceived to be dangerous in many cultures. So today, many, many people have this innate fear.

Likewise, most people in the world for centuries have considered round metal discs to be money. Even currency from a foreign country is still seen as valuable, even when it cannot be spent at the neighborhood store. Many objects not only have a universal meaning but also evoke an emotion. They are potent symbols in our collective consciousness.

Besides universal symbols, there are also cultural symbols—particular to one culture, but not another. They also can be used effectively (in fact, I have found using symbols from a different culture is particularly effective).

A symbol, such as a gold cat bank (a.k.a. Lucky Money Cat), is a popular symbol in Asia and works very well here in the U.S. If you have enjoyed a meal at a Chinese restaurant recently, you have probably seen one of these symbols next to the cash register, Lucky Money Cat waving his little golden arm, calling in money.

The reason cultural symbols work is there are enough people in the world who understand the symbol and connect to it emotionally; a mini "collective consciousness" is formed.

Our Reticular Activating System

The second reason Feng Shui cures work is our Reticular Activating System. This is a system within each of us, which allows us to filter the information reaching us through our five senses. If we were actually aware of all the information bombarding us all the time, we would go mad.

For instance, just sitting here at my computer, if I were also listening to the computer hum, and the traffic outside, and the ticking clock, while watching the sun go down, observing the computer screen, not to mention all the things I'm touching, smelling, and tasting simultaneously, I would be completely overwhelmed. But fortunately, my Reticular Activating System allows me to focus only on the task at hand.

Your own Reticular Activating System activates when you place a Lucky Money Cat somewhere in your space. When you place your Lucky Money Cat in the far left corner of your home, also known as "the wealth corner," your subconscious awakens and begins looking for money opportunities.

When the money opportunity is detected, your ERAS-system alerts your brain. These opportunities were around you already, but you were unable to identify them specifically. Therefore, it was impossible for you to grasp them or focus on taking necessary action. But when your Reticular Activating System uncovered the opportunities around you, they became clear to your conscious mind, and now it is easy to welcome in the new money.

Because of these two reasons, Feng Shui cures work. It is essential to understand why we use universal or cultural symbols, rather than just any old item/personal symbol. For example, you might tell me that for you, the vulture is a symbol of love because your beloved had a vulture tattoo on his right shoulder.

But this symbol is only a love symbol for you (and this particular relationship). So all the energy behind this symbol must be generated by you alone. If you're interested in focusing on vulture-tattoo-guy, you can fill your house with vultures, and it might attract his energy to your door.

But let's say you want to attract a new man—maybe one who is vulture-free. In that case, it will be much easier to attract the new love energy if you choose to use a universal or cultural symbol of love. Many other people recognize these symbols. When you choose to use one of them, the combined energy of all these others who acknowledge this symbol as a sign of love combines with your energy to attract what you want.

The peony flower is a cultural symbol of love. In Chinese art, this symbol is used to represent love and beauty. So if you choose to use this symbol, your energy combines with a couple of billion other people who also use this symbol to attract love. By using the collective consciousness, and your Reticular Activating System, you can use specific objects to attract wealth, love, and other things you want into your life.

As we talk about the individual predictions for each sign, I will suggest specific Feng Shui cures for creating the most positive energy for your year. You can substitute these cultural symbols for universal symbols if you choose. If you have questions about these concepts or substituting cures, you can write to me at donnastellhorn@gmail.com

2022 Flying Star

6—Northwest Luck Star: lucky To increase success in career, military, science, or technology, add large crystals like citrine, amethyst, or smoky quartz. To balance energy of health and wealth, add brass vases or bowls.	1—North White Star: very lucky To increase wealth and fame and improve career, add earth by adding granite, marble, or citrine. To balance spirituality and thinking, add metal in the form of a music box or iPod dock.	8—Northeast Prosperity Star: very lucky To increase happiness, wealth, and family unity, add fire by burning white or gold candles. To balance career energy and have good relations with kids, add earth by placing a clear quartz crystal.
7—West Violent Star: unlucky To decrease bad luck, add water. To protect from robbery, legal problems, injury, or health issues, burn off excess negative energy by burning black or dark blue candles. Add exterior lighting or keep porch light on.	5—Center Misfortune Star: very unlucky To protect from accidents, illness, or lawsuits, remove stone and heavy objects. To balance mental energy and have happier children, place coins.	3—East Conflict Star: unlucky If having problems with career, lawsuits, or arguments, burn off excess negative energy by burning a blue or yellow candle. If needing a job or lots of change, add a string or pile of coins.
2—Southwest Illness Star: unlucky To protect from illness and loneliness, reduce negative energy by adding plants, dried medicinal herbs, or pictures of flowers. To balance health, pregnancy, or communications, add a six-rod metal wind chime.	9—South Future Prosperity Star: lucky To increase achievement and growth, add wood, such as a green healthy plant. To have good luck, add fire by burning gold or purple candles.	4—Southeast Romance Star: lucky To have romance, better education, and career choices, add the color red and pairs of ducks. To protect against bad investments, divorce, or family pressure, add silver or Chinese coins.

2022 Flying Star

Each year, the energy changes, and "stars" fly into new locations. Some directions, which may have indicated positive, lucky energy last year, become weaker and unlucky this year.

Some, which vibrated with weak, unlucky energy in the past, have found strength and become more favorable.

In other forms of Feng Shui, we are concerned with the directions of our home, based on the position of the front door, but not with Flying Star. With Flying Star, we are concerned with compass directions.

The general principle of Flying Star is to increase energy in the direction of good stars and reduce energy in the direction of bad stars. If you live in a giant mansion and your bedroom is now on a negative star, you can choose a new bedroom to sleep in. But for the rest of us, we use "cures" to mitigate the negative energy and increase the positive energy. Here's the forecast for 2022:

Flying Star 1—The White Star: Luck finds its way to the North of the house with the 1-Star. This is a star whose energy has changed over the last few thousand years. It has become luckier, although it's a good idea to keep its history in mind as you increase the energy of this star.

If, after placing the cures, you find things are not going as well as you hoped, switch from increasing the energy (by adding water or metal cures) to reducing the energy (by adding wood cures).

That being said, to increase wealth and fame and improve career, increase the earth energy by adding granite, marble, or citrine (a gemstone) to your space. To balance spirituality and clear thinking, add metal in the form of a music box or an iPod/radio.

Flying Star 2—The Illness Star: A somewhat unlucky star, the 2-Star, flies to the Southwest. I say this star is somewhat unlucky because years ago in China, this was a lucky star for those working in government. Therefore, if you have a government job, you can receive some benefit from this star.

For the rest of us, this Star can cause health problems, especially digestive and intestinal problems. To protect from illness and loneliness, reduce the negative energy effects by adding live plants, bundles of dried medicinal herbs, or pictures of flowers to the Southwest part of your home.

If you are pregnant, you can support and protect pregnancy energy by adding a six-rod metal wind chime outside of the Southwest part of the house.

Flying Star 3—The Conflict Star: The somewhat unlucky 3-Star flies to the East this year. This is the star of quarreling and disputes, but you can direct its energy positively to help you keep a job and pay your bills. Balancing the energy of the 3-Star is essential.

If you have problems with career, lawsuits, or arguments, burn off the excess negative energy by burning a blue or yellow candle in this area once a month on the full moon. If you are searching for a job, need more work, or wish to preserve a source of income, set some coins on a windowsill facing the East of the space.

Flying Star 4—The Romance Star: The 4-Star lands in the Southeast this year bringing mixed luck. This star is associated with both positive romance and career opportunities, but it is also known as "The Six Curses." Like the 1-Star in the North, as you enhance the energy in the Southeast, notice how your luck changes.

If you find that your experiences in romance are not as positive as you would like, add fire (by burning candles or wood in a fireplace) to reduce the 4-Star energy. Also, be cautious about participating in games of speculation or signing off on risky investments.

To enjoy more romance, add the color red and pairs of Mandarin ducks as cures. To protect against unwise investments, add silver or Chinese coins. For better education and career choices, add green plants with round-shaped leaves.

Flying Star 5—The Misfortune Star: Trouble comes as the 5-Star flies to the Center this year. This star represents illness, potential disaster, and lack of knowledge. Remove the stone and heavy objects from the house's Center area to protect from accidents, illness, and lawsuits.

If heavy objects are attached to the house (such as a stone fireplace), channel some of that energy away from the Center of the house by adding objects made of wood, like a wood bowl, wood furniture, or a picture of trees. To balance stressful energy and to have happier children, place photos of them in metal frames in this area.

Flying Star 6—The Heaven Luck Star: The 6-Star flies to the Northwest this year, and luck comes with it. To increase success in career, military service, science, or technology, add large crystals (over 2 inches in size) such as citrine, amethyst, and smoky quartz to the Northwest part of the home.

To balance the energy of health and wealth, add brass vases or bowls. You can place messages and wishes for your family's health and prosperity in the bowls each New Moon.

Flying Star 7—The Violent Star: The unlucky 7-Star flies to the West this year, bringing the very unlucky energy of robbery, legal troubles, fire, injury, and arguments. To decrease bad luck, add the Water element. Good Water element representations are fountains, fish tanks, pictures of moving water, or decorative objects made of glass.

It is best to 'burn off' excess negative energy by burning black or dark blue candles once a month to protect yourself from robbery, legal problems, injury, and health issues. Because this is the Violent Star, adding protective symbols to the West of your home is wise. These can be things from your ancestors, your religion, or your country.

Flying Star 8—The Prosperity Star: Luck moves to the Northeast as the 8-Star finds its home there for the year. This is your home or space area to enhance and experience increased happiness, wealth, and family unity. Do so by adding representations of fire. For instance, you can place red pillows or art that depicts a distinct triangular shape; or burn white or gold candles in this part of the home.

To balance career energy and enhance good relations with children and young people, add earth to the 8-Star area by placing clear quartz crystals on a table in the Northeast of the house.

Flying Star 9—The Future Prosperity Star: This star brings us more lucky energy. The very lucky 9-Star flies to the South this year. This is your success area for the year. Try to do things like goal setting, meditating, beginning new projects, or making essential contacts by phone from this area of your home or office.

To increase achievement and growth, add wood energy to the space with things like green, healthy plants, pictures of forests and greenery, or a new wood floor. To increase good luck and good fortune, add fire cures by burning purple or gold candles once a month.

For more information on the cures mentioned in this book, refer to the Feng Shui cure guide at the back of my book, "Feng Shui Form." In it, you will find an 80-page guide to how to use Feng Shui cures.

This year, the Grand Duke (or Tai Sui) lives in the Northeast area between 52.6 and 67.5 degrees. You can use a compass to locate this exact location.

The Grand Duke doesn't enjoy being disturbed. The Grand Duke is like the King of all the Kings. It's said that you cannot confront him, only show him deference and respect. This year, those born in the Year of the Monkey should keep a protective

Feng Shui cure by their bed. This could be a Pi Yao (winged lion) statue or a Tai Sui plaque.

This year you can plant a tree in the Grand Duke's section of your property to show your respect. But beware, you cannot cut down a tree in this direction, or there will be misfortune. Also, be cautious about construction or renovation in this area of your home or property this year. The process can be plagued with problems and bring trouble to the household.

The Five Elements

The natural element of Tiger is Yang Wood. With the excited, energetic Tiger energy this year, we feel this element's creative and destructive nature. In 2022 we are in a Yang Water year. With this combination, the desire to communicate and connect will be great. Being alert, flexible, and able to pivot will bring success. Prosperity comes through innovation this year. At the same time, we need to be aware that others may try to dig in their heels and stop the process out of fear that things are moving too quickly or moving in a direction they don't want to go. In a Tiger year, it's okay to follow your path, leaping over those who are in your way. This year, don't wait for permission but take courage and follow the path ahead.

Wood and Water are just two of the elements. The ancient Chinese philosophers looked at the world and categorized all they could see into five elements, five building blocks, which are the basis of all things. The five elements and their representations are:

Wood—represents growth and all things that grow.

Fire—represents energy itself and all the things energy creates or produces.

Earth—represents stability and things in a state of rest.

Metal—represents resources and things that make up the material of tools.

Water—symbolizes connectivity, things that help connect one thing to another.

As mentioned, each of the five elements can be Yin or Yang. Yin represents the more subtle and flowing energy, and Yang represents the more "in-your-face," direct energy. The Yin/Yang symbol is probably familiar to you. The black part represents Yin, and the white part is Yang.

The dot in the opposing color in the Yin/Yang symbol represents the concept: "One cannot exist without the other." To understand the concept of larger, we must be familiar with smaller. For us to understand the essence of weaker, we must know stronger.

Each of the five elements exists in a state of Yin or Yang.

Yang Wood is like a forest of the tallest trees, growing in the wild. Or, energetically, expressed in the life of a student who studies all the time. It is like the way you feel starting a new job, when you have to learn everything as quickly as possible (and you love every moment of it.)

Yin Wood is like a seedling, just popping out of the dirt to see the sun for the first time. It's the realization that you've grown as a person and don't need as much help as you did when you were younger. It's the act of tweaking a favorite recipe with just one new ingredient to see how it will taste.

Yang Fire is a forest fire burning out of control. It's like celebrating a college spring break at a beachside resort, daddy's credit card in hand. Or, it's like driving in a NASCAR race, exhilarating, demanding your entire focus and all your attention, purely to keep from crashing.

Yin Fire is represented by the image of a match or a single candle. Imagine the energy of taking a stroll down a beautiful path and having the time to enjoy nature. Or, think of the amount of energy our body uses to digest food: it happens automatically, without effort or thought.

Yang Earth is a tall mountain, majestic and still. It's like a lazy retirement, one where you enjoy your time sitting on the porch, day after day, in a comfortable chair. There are no worries about finances. There are no obligations to create stress in your life.

Yin Earth is like a sandy beach, flat and smooth. It's like a Sunday afternoon in summer, nothing pulling at you, your list of chores complete. You take a restful, peaceful nap.

Yang Metal is like the power of collecting gold bars, having them stacked, and representing greater abundance than you will ever need. It's a world filled with unlimited resources. You can present a Black Visa card and purchase anything you wish. Or, it's like becoming CEO and receiving or having access to all the perks.

Yin Metal is like possessing a stack of coins or receiving a regular paycheck. You have just enough to feel secure; you can count on support to arrive as expected, week after week. It's like having just the right amount of cash in your pocket to buy what you need.

Yang Water is a springtime waterfall, rushing downhill and churning up the body of water below. It's water bursting from a dam and rushing towards the town. Or, it's like melted snow pouring down the mountainside to flood the fields below.

Yin Water is like a still pond on a summer's day; with no movement on the surface, it appears to be as still as a sheet of glass in the sunlight. Or, it's like a peaceful lake in the quiet of a moonlit night, the moon's reflection glimmering on the surface. It's a glass of water, the exact perfect amount you need to drink to quench your thirst.

When the ancient people who brought us Feng Shui looked at the world, they divided every existing thing into these Five Elements. They also observed how one element could interact with another. This interaction is expressed in a Creative Cycle or a Destructive Cycle.

The Creative Cycle is: Wood creates Fire, Fire creates Earth (by producing ash), Earth produces Metal (because when we dig into the earth, we find metal), Metal produces Water (when metal becomes cold, it pulls water from the air in the form of condensation) and Water produces Wood (when water pours on the ground, things grow).

The Destructive Cycle is: Wood depletes Earth (Trees and plants take nutrients from the earth), Earth blocks Water (dams can be made of earth), Water puts out Fire, Fire melts Metal, and Metal chops Wood (when metal is formed into an ax or other sharp tool, it can cut wood).

In Feng Shui, we are always looking for the larger to support the smaller. For example, if you, as a single individual, need to feed and clothe your entire community, you would soon become depleted of energy and resources. But if the community helps feed and clothe you, food and clothing would be abundant for you.

This year is a Water Year. Your individual element may be in harmony with this year's element being part of the Creative Cycle. Your individual element may be in disharmony with this year's element by being part of the Destructive Cycle. Check the list at the beginning of the book and find your element.

If your element is Wood: Your element is Wood, and the element this year is Water. You are on the creative cycle as Water creates Wood. This year the whole world is available to offer support and help with your ventures. This doesn't mean everyone will line up in perfect order. There will be many who come to you with an agenda. But there will be many opportunities, and in what they are offering, it's possible to find some benefit for both of you.

Water is in great abundance this year, and it's what you need to grow. This could take the form of the right information or the right connections to get you where you want. You may reach out to a single person who then sets up a chain of responses from their friends and others they know. One bit of information could lead you to the next and the next, like finding a gold nugget and then a larger one and then the entire gold mine. But there can also be an overwhelming amount of information and connections this year. And this can have you growing in all sorts of directions. Occasionally take the shears out and prune away what's unnecessary. And this will help you focus on your goals.

If your element is Fire: Your element is Fire, and the element of this year is Water. This is on the destructive cycle as Water destroys Fire. It is like an endless line of people with buckets of water to pour on your enthusiasm and your action plans. It's not that they mean to be unsupportive, but the energy is just incompatible with your own. As you point to a mountain you want to climb or outline a project you want to do, many are going to tell you it cannot work, or you need permission, or it's not the right time. So this year, focus on doing and tell people about it later.

It's also a challenge when you need help with your projects as you find people are all talk and no action. You are ready to jump in and start work while they are doing spreadsheets, taking surveys, and forming committees. It's crucial to stay true to your action plan this year and take action, whether people are supportive or not. As you do, others will join in. You need to be the leader. Otherwise, you will have to wait for a quorum.

If your element is Metal: Your element is Metal, and this year's element is Water. You are on the creative cycle as Metal creates Water. However, you as an individual are the smaller trying to create the larger—the whole Earth. This means that nearly everyone you meet will believe you are vital to their success. You get pulled in every direction. Many projects and opportunities will come to you, but many of these will be more work than you are looking for, and indeed, not all of them will be along the path you want to take.

This year you must consider what you want to accomplish and be picky about where and when you get involved in other people's plans. As you gather the resources and people you need for a project, others will want to discuss endlessly what is needed and who should do each task. Since you're on the creative cycle, you can still get many opportunities and get things done as this Water energy will help you create new connections and find collaborators. But it's easy to overextend yourself or waste resources on projects that are not in line with your goals. Sometimes, in the joy of being asked to be part of the group, you can forget what it is you're trying to accomplish.

If your element is Water: Your element is Water, and this is a Water year. So you are in harmony with the energy. You have an innate understanding of the energy of Water and its desire to connect and communicate with others. You are admired for your ability to bring different people together and to collaborate. Focus on helping people see eye to eye or to empathize with each other. Cultivate your ability to take the things other people do and incorporate the best parts into your process.

Allow yourself to flow from one project to another and not get stuck and stagnant out of stubbornness or an external block.

Your challenge this year is not to get overwhelmed by information. Avoid endless scrolling and allowing the algorithm to pick what you're going to watch next, as this means you are not directing your energies. It's okay to allow serendipity to bring some new information to you, but if you are not directing the energy, you'll just run into the same information repeatedly. Look for divergent views to bring knowledge that can synergize what you're working on.

If your element is Earth: Your element is Earth, and this year the element is Water. This is on the destructive cycle as Earth blocks Water. You, the individual, are trying to hold back the tide so that the things you want to accomplish are not swept away. You will have a seemingly endless supply of information and connections you can make. But sometimes, people get carried away and expect you to do much more than your share. They may rely on you to give them boundaries or to build the structure of whatever it is you're trying to accomplish. Others will think they're helping you when they're actually drowning you in questions, suppositions, and ideas.

Many people will come to you with offers and opportunities, but you have limited time and energy. It will be necessary for you to have patience in an impatient world. Take the time you need to meditate on what it is you want. Also, if what others are offering is not to your liking, just wait, as another will come along soon with a new opportunity. If you can get a clear picture of what you want to achieve, this will be an exceptional year because an abundance of choices is available to you.

Using and Clearing Feng Shui Cures

"Okay, I did what you said, and it worked for a little while, but now it's not working."

When we place an object to attract new energy—and we place it correctly—we will get results within the first week. But after that, the energy will start to dissipate. There are several reasons for this.

Mainly, we rapidly adapt to the new energy, and so even though new energy is flowing in; we cease to notice it. Also, when we first place the Feng Shui cure, we see it every day, but after a time it becomes part of the background and therefore is no longer activating our subconscious.

Often, the solution is to move the cure, or if that's not possible, to take the cure down and dust it off and then replace it where it was. I had a client who was using my "double lucky money fish" cure to attract money. She placed a pair of fish by her front door, and business started to flow in effortlessly. However, after a week or two, she would become overwhelmed by so many new clients.

So she would take the "double lucky money fish" cure away from her front door, and place the cure in her home office instead. The result of this was she would receive quick and easy payment from her clients.

Then, after a couple of weeks, she would find she needed new clients again. So she would take the "double lucky money fish" cure and once again hang them by her front door. By moving the fish over and over, she was always attracting positive money energy.

How to Clear Gemstones and Crystals

After a few weeks, gemstones and crystals have been absorbing energy, and it can seem they are not as effective as they were when you first placed them. Here is an easy solution. The gemstone or crystal needs clearing. There are several methods you can use. Each is very effective, choose the method that is most convenient for you.

Clearing with Sage: You can smudge the gemstone or crystal using Sage. Take your smudge stick and light it, then pass the crystal through the smoke several times. Turn the crystal so the smoke touches all sides. The crystal is now clear, and you can hang it back up where it was. You should see a bump up in the energy levels during the next few days.

Clearing with Salt: you can clear gemstones and crystals using salt. Some gemstones and crystals are sensitive to salt, When clearing these with salt, place the crystal on a dish and draw a ring of salt around the crystal. (The salt should not touch the crystal.) Then place the dish where it will not be disturbed for 24 hours.

Once the 24-hour period is completed, remove the crystal from the plate and dispose of the salt in a trash can outside of your home. (Tossing the salt in the kitchen garbage will just release the energy back into the house.) Replace the crystal where it was. You'll see an increase in energy within the next few days.

Clearing with Sunlight: you can also clear gemstones and crystals in sunlight. Take the crystal down and wash it thoroughly in clear water and a gentle soap. Dry the crystal with a soft cloth. Place the crystal on a dish outside in the sunlight for a full day. In the evening, bring the crystal back into the house and allow it to cool. Then re-hang the crystal where it was. If you don't see an increase in energy in the first week, use one of the other two methods to clear the crystal.

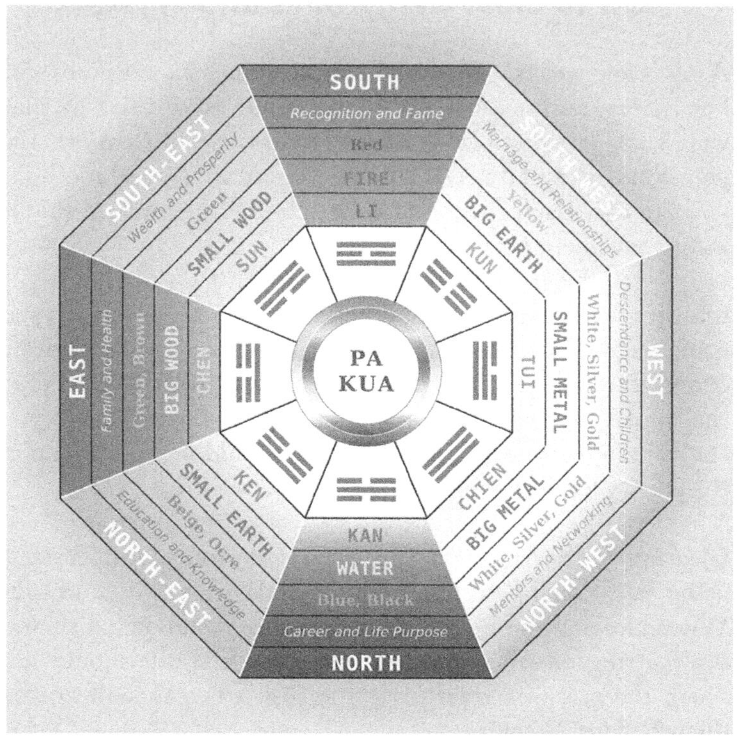

How to Identify the Wealth and Love Areas of Your House

To identify the Wealth areas of your home, stand inside the front door entrance to the house, take the above diagram, and place the side that says "career" up against your closed front door. The diagram will show you the location of the Wealth area.

In fact, you will quickly identify two Wealth areas: one is the far left corner of the entrance area (or the far left corner of the room where the front door opens into the home). The other important Wealth area in your home is the far left corner of the whole house.

To identify your "love" areas, stand inside your home by your front door. Using the above diagram, place the side that says "career" against your front door.

Now the diagram shows you the location of the Love area in the far right corner of the entrance area (or the far right corner of the room where the front door opens into the home). The other significant Love area in your home is the far right corner of the house.

Bibliography and Recommended Reading

Bartholomew, Sarah, "Feng Shui: It's Good for Business," ETC Publishing, Carlsbad, CA, 2005

Brown, Simon, "Practical Feng Shui," Wardlock, London, 1997

Carus, Paul, "Chinese Astrology," Open Court, LaSalle, IL, 1974

Chuen, Master Lam Kam, "Personal Feng Shui Manual: How to Develop a Healthy and Harmonious Lifestyle," Henry Holt & Co, New York, 1998

Craze, Richard, "Teach Yourself Chinese Astrology," Arbingdon, England, Bookpoint, 1997

Cunningham, Scott, "Cunningham's Encyclopedia of Crystal, Gem and Metal Magic,."Llewellyn Publications, St. Paul, MN 1988

Cunningham, Scott, "Cunningham's Encyclopedia of Magical Herbs,." Llewellyn Publications, St. Paul, MN 1997

Cunningham, Scott, "The Magic of Food," Llewellyn Publications, St. Paul, MN 1996

Eberhard, Wolfram, "A Dictionary of Chinese Symbols," Routledge, London, 1983

Gong, Rosemary, "Good Luck Life," New York, Harper Collins, 2005

Kwok, Man-Ho, "The Elements of Feng Shui," Elements Books Limited, Dorset, England, 1991

Lau, Kwan, ."Secrets of Chinese Astrology: Handbook for Self-Discovery,." Tengu Books, Trumbull, CT, 1994

Lau, Theodora, "The Handbook of Chinese Horoscopes," New York, Harper & Row, 1979

Lip, Evelyn, "Chinese Numbers," Heian International, Union City, California 1992

Lip, Evelyn, "Chinese Practices and Beliefs," Torrance, Heian International, 2000

Ronngren, Diane, "Color: A Secret Language Revealed," ETC Publishing, Carlsbad, CA, 1997

Ronngren, Diane, "Eclipses," ETC Publishing, Carlsbad, CA, 2001

Ronngren, Diane, "Mercury Retrograde," ETC Publishing, Carlsbad, CA, 2000

Ronngren, Diane, "Sage & Smudge: The Ultimate Guide," ETC Publishing, Carlsbad, CA, 2003

Ronngren, Diane, "Simple Feng Shui Secrets," ETC Publishing, Carlsbad, CA, 2005

Ronngren, Diane and Stellhorn, Donna, "Money and Prosperity Workbook," ETC Publishing, Carlsbad, CA, 1999

Rossbach, Sarah, "Interior Design with Feng Shui," Arkana, London, 1987

Skinner, Stephen, "Flying Star Feng Shui," Tuttle, Boston, MA, 2003

Stellhorn, Donna, "Feng Shui Form," ETC Publishing, Carlsbad, CA, 2006

Stellhorn, Donna, "How to Use Magical Oils," ETC Publishing, Carlsbad, CA, 2002

Stellhorn, Donna, "Sage & Smudge: Secrets to Clearing Your Personal Space," ETC Publishing, Carlsbad, CA, 1999

Sun, Ruth Q., "The Asian Animal Zodiac," Castle Books, Boston, MA, 1974

Tai, Sherman, "Principles of Feng Shui: An Illustrated Guide to Chinese Geomancy," Asiapac Books, Singapore, 1998

Too, Lillian, "Easy-To-Use Feng Shui: 168 Ways to Success," Collins & Brown, London, 1999

Too, Lillian, "Unlocking the Secrets of Chinese Fortune Telling," Metro Books, New York, 2006

Twicken, David, "Classical Five Element Chinese Astrology Made Easy," Writers Club Press, New York, 2000

Twicken, David, "Flying Star Feng Shui Made Easy," Writers Club Press, New York, 2002

Walters, Derek, "Chinese Astrology," Watkins Publishing London, 2002

Walters, Derek, "The Feng Shui Handbook," Aquarian Press, San Francisco, CA 1991

Williams, C.A.S., "Outlines of Chinese Symbolism & Art Motifs," Dover Publications, New York, 1976

Wydra, Nancilee, "Feng Shui: The Book of Cures," Contemporary Books, Lincolnwood, IL 1993

Acknowledgments

I want to thank Diane, Gary and Kelly at ETC Publishing for their support, patience and hard work on these books each year. I couldn't have done it without their help. All their names should be on the cover too.

About Donna Stellhorn

Author, Astrology, and Feng Shui expert, Donna Stellhorn, is a speaker, a supportive personal coach, and a practical business consultant with over 25 years of experience. In addition to building three successful businesses of her own and logging over 20,000 hours of consultations with clients, she teaches a variety of classes, offers apprenticeship programs, leads workshops, and continues to write on various topics. She believes in encouraging others to achieve success in their careers and their personal lives.

Donna has written 18 books. According to Amazon, her Chinese Astrology series, of which 2022 Chinese Astrology Year of the Water Tiger is the latest, is the most popular Chinese Astrology book series.

One of her earliest books is Feng Shui Form. First published in Germany, it is a collection of the best and most popular concepts to help her readers create a supportive and comfortable living and working environment.

For over 20 years, her best-selling booklet, Sage and Smudge: Secrets of Clearing Your Personal Space, shares the concept of how to cleanse and clear space, objects, or environments.

A recent book is a Feng Shui expert's look at the fertility puzzle, entitled "Fertility Feng Shui".

Donna has video courses on Udemy.com, including Plate Size Matters, a Feng Shui expert's guide to losing weight by changing how you eat, where you eat, and how best to store your food in the home.

Donna lectures on both Chinese Astrology and Western Astrology, as well as Feng Shui. Recently, Donna has lectured at Western Digital, Warner Records, Room & Board, the Rancho Santa Fe Water District, Brion Jeannette Architecture, and the San Diego Airport Authority. She's been on Coast to Coast AM with George Noory. She spoke at the 2018 United Astrology Conference in Chicago and the 2019 NCGR conference in Baltimore. Donna writes for Horoscope.com, Astrology.com, SunSigns.com, and Conscious Community magazine. She is on the Boards of the International Feng Shui Guild and the National Council for Geocosmic Research—San Diego.

For fun, Donna does improv comedy with ImprovCity, and when she wants to be terrified, she does standup comedy. She lives in Oceanside, California with the magical cat, LaRue.

YouTube Channel: https://www.youtube.com/c/DonnaStellhorn

Website: http://www.fengshuiform.com/
or email her at donnastellhorn@gmail.com

One last thing…

Thank you so much for purchasing this book. I hope you found the information helpful, and if you did, please let your friends know about it. If you can take a moment to give it a review at your favorite retailer, I would be very grateful.

Made in the USA
Coppell, TX
03 January 2022